D0583455

GUILTY KNOWLEDGE, GUILTY PLEASURE

Also by William Logan

Guilty Knowledge, Guilty Pleasure

THE DIRTY ART OF POETRY

WILLIAM LOGAN

COLUMBIA UNIVERSITY PRESS   *New York*

COLUMBIA UNIVERSITY PRESS
Publishers Since 1893
NEW YORK   CHICHESTER, WEST SUSSEX
cup.columbia.edu
Copyright © 2014 William Logan
All rights reserved

Library of Congress Cataloging-in-Publication Data
Logan, William, 1950–
Guilty knowledge, guilty pleasure : the dirty art of poetry / William Logan.
pages cm
Includes bibliographical references and index.
ISBN 978-0-231-16686-7 (cloth : alk. paper) — ISBN 978-0-231-53723-0 (e-book)
1. American poetry—20th century—History and criticism—Theory, etc.
2. Criticism—United States—History—20th century.   3. American poetry—
20th century—History and criticism.   4. Poetry—Authorship.   5. Poetics.   I. Title.

PS323.5.L6435   2014
811'.509—dc23
2013030071

Columbia University Press books are printed on permanent and durable acid-free paper.
This book is printed on paper with recycled content.
Printed in the United States of America

c 10 9 8 7 6 5 4 3 2 1

JACKET IMAGE: COLLAGE BY DEBORA GREGER

Library
University of Texas
at San Antonio

For Dorothy Drew Damon and Young Buffalo

He is charged with the **guilty knowledge** of this concealment. He must *show*, not *say*, how he came by this knowledge. If a man be found with stolen goods, he must prove how he came by them.

—Daniel Webster, *Speeches and Forensic Arguments*, vol. 1 (1835)

Thus, in the midst of riot, imagined spectres have been known to haunt the man of **guilty pleasure**. He sees hands coming forth to write on the wall against him. The very portraits of his ancestors, which hang in his hall, appear to him to look with frowning aspect.

—Hugh Blair, "On a Life of Dissipation and Pleasure," *Sermons*, vol. 2 (1822)

The fourth witness as to the **guilty knowledge** was the coachman, for though the press removed was not such a one as would print the paper, it at least showed an anxiety to get rid of a suspicious article.

—*The Asiatic Journal and Monthly Register*, September 1831

If he is dwelling with delight upon a stratagem of successful fraud, a night of licentious riot, or an intrigue of **guilty pleasure**, let him summon off his imagination as from an unlawful pursuit.

—Samuel Johnson, *The Rambler*, no. 8, April 14, 1750

Contents

Acknowledgments

Critics are like Blanche DuBois in this way, that they depend on the kindness of strangers. It doesn't make much difference if the strangers happen to be literary editors. I must express my thanks once more to the editors of the *New Criterion*, the *New York Times Book Review*, *Poetry*, *Southwest Review*, and the *Virginia Quarterly Review*, who commissioned these pieces or let me commission myself—though a critic is an army of one.

"A Critic's Notebook" was proposed by one magazine, accepted by another, and in the end never published. I include it in part for the informality of its obsessions, and because only a rare piece of prose earns two kill fees.

Thanks are due to Frank Bidart, executor of the Elizabeth Bishop Estate, for permission to quote excerpts from the correspondence of Elizabeth Bishop and Louise Bradley, now held at Indiana University, as well as early poems by Elizabeth Bishop from the *Camp Chequesset Log* and from the Louise Bradley correspondence. Thanks are also due to the Wellfleet Historical Society; the Wylie House Museum, a department of the Indiana University Libraries; and the Archives and Special Collections Library of Vassar College for permission to include photographs of Elizabeth Bishop and Louise Bradley.

GUILTY KNOWLEDGE, GUILTY PLEASURE

Against Aesthetics

"Good sir, how many angels may jig upon the point of a needle?"
"The answer, friend, would be metaphysical, and you must inquire of
Aquinas."
"But what of the dance itself?"
"That would lie within the physics, and you must ask Aristotle."
"And whether the jig be good or bad?"
"That must be aesthetical, and of aesthetics 'twere best not to speak."
— *The Papers of Methodius*, book III

A stranger asks me to write an Aesthetic Statement. He demands my notion of the ideal poem, so he'll know the secret of my love of some poems and my distaste for others. I feel his pain. Perhaps he wants to prosecute me should I praise a poet who deviates from my Platonic ideal. An aesthetic statement is of little use to a critic unless he's a lover of manifestos, a maker of quarrels, or a host who treats his guests like Procrustes. Aesthetics is a rational profession for the philosopher, but for the working critic it's a mug's game. To write about your aesthetics is no better than revealing your secrets, if you're a magician, or returning a mark's stolen wallet, if you're a pickpocket.

Most aesthetic statements are of value only if they're vague enough not to offend a fly—and most sound like a Mozart sonata written by committee. Even the plain aesthetics concealed in a definition of poetry, when the definition is not merely clowning (Newton called poetry a "kind of ingenious nonsense," quoting his teacher Isaac Barrow), would look shaky under a Philadelphia lawyer's cross-examination.

Coleridge considered poetry "the best words in the best order," a perfectly reasonable thing to say—yet doesn't good prose require the best words in the best order? (Coleridge would go only so far as "words in the best order.") Doesn't even his own definition satisfy those terms? Pound claimed that literature was "news that STAYS news," and he therefore badgered poets to "make it new." I'm sure the Georgians felt their poems were making it new, as did most of the minor Imagists in the twenties—yet we don't read either, and with good reason.

There are problems even with Wordsworth's compelling suggestion, in the second edition of *Lyrical Ballads*, that "poetry is the spontaneous overflow of powerful feelings: it takes its origin from emotion recollected in tranquillity." That describes only a limited part of Wordsworth's poetry, and there have since been many good poems neither spontaneous, nor a flood of rugged feeling, nor emotion recalled in quiet solitude. (Hardy's "emotion put into measure" suffers similar problems.) Trying to define poetry makes me sympathetic to A. E. Housman, who remarked, "I could no more define poetry than a terrier can define a rat." However detailed or slippery the aesthetic justification, a good poem works like God—in mysterious ways.

A critic can make himself useful by describing those ways, and how they turn words available to anyone into something that might stir the language (or even other languages) a hundred or a thousand years hence. Homer can move us as Callimachus never could, yet Callimachus was one of the best poets of his day, highly regarded centuries later, at least by rhetoricians. Had the knights of the Fourth Crusade not burned the Imperial Library of Constantinople, we might have shelves of Callimachus still—but it's unlikely that anything found there would be much better than the fragments we have inherited.

A critic should have principles rather than aesthetics. He should have tastes, though never at the cost of praising the bad book seductive to his taste rather than the good one that offends it. He should also have prejudices, but not ones that blind him to merit, not ones that have him shouting, every three books or so, "A miracle! A miracle!" Prejudices are often inverse principles, but a critic should hold his principles unless they contradict his reading, just as he should accept his prejudices until a poem forces him to war against them. By principles I mean that, for example, a poem should repay the labor of reading, that the content of a line should bear relation to its length (short lines bear a lesser burden of meaning than a long one), that diction and syntax should be natural except when artifice is more artful, that when a poet accepts the contract of form he should fulfill it—if he begins with exact rhymes, exact rhymes should follow unless he has better reason than a stutter of imagination.

Why not simply list your prejudices, then, in a pamphlet published in eighteen-point bold? But is a critic really the best judge of his prejudices? The most crucial prejudices may be subconscious, well beyond the critic's knowledge. Think of all the ink spilled over poetry's nature and name. I'm about as interested in what poetry is *for* as a plumber in what plumbing's for. You have to understand the mechanics, but you don't need to go on about it. Still, some readers think it the reviewer's job to announce his prejudices in every review. That way madness lies. Pinning your aesthetics to your sleeve makes you seem prejudiced in a way that concealing your prejudices, and perhaps revolting against them, does not. Beyond the obvious—declaring that the author happens to be his mother or that he despises poems in couplets—the critic should save his breath for his job of work. Even if you are reviewing the bard of Schenectady, it shouldn't matter that you've just been elected mayor of Schenectady, as long as you're really a critic.

We should not trust critics always true to their natures. If you claim the day for proportion, let proportion rule—but, when readers tire of your see-saw antitheses, your lead-crystal phrases, your well-tempered rhymes, then the aesthetics of Pope will be thrown on the dung heap while the private emotion, the roughened phrase, and the organic stanza of the Romantics bloom. There's no poetry that, taken to perfection, does not provoke a reaction. (Think how ugly Shakespeare seemed to the age of Dryden—and how, even to the Victorians, Bowdler's Georgian defacing had a point.)

If I admit that I take little interest in contemporary experimental poetry, it's not a prejudice born of ignorance. I have read the anthologies as well as too many of the revered names—much have I traveled in the realms of tin. I admire avant-garde ingenuity, with the cantankerousness, self-confidence, and outrageousness attached—but I rarely, rarely like the poems. This may be the prejudice of a prejudice, one that later generations may profitably put on display to confirm just how blinkered twenty-first-century critics were. For my taste, however, and to my prejudice, avant-garde poems have advanced very little from language experiments first tried when Ruth was hitting sixty home runs. Indeed, reading many experimental poets now is like listening to some bar band's cover of "Satisfaction"—it's not a patch on the original, even if you're under the influence of a quart of gin. I don't expect lesser things of avant-garde poetry; I expect things much greater.

Perhaps avant-garde poetry is what poets will holler from the barricades, the harbinger of a better poetry tomorrow (that tomorrow ever delayed, like the date of the Second Coming). Perhaps avant-garde poems will finally overthrow the *elitist patriarchy of syntax* or the *hegemony of the lefthand margin* (I've heard both things damned). Perhaps the avant-garde of today really is the mainstream of tomorrow—a lot of academic careers have backed that horse and thrived, but the laws of academia are not those of physics, or taste. Consider the dispossession of the Augustans by the Romantics, or the Victorians and Georgians by the Moderns—such radical changes offer neither a strategy nor a tactics to the avant-garde. The congealed sentiment of so much experimental poetry, the sermonizing forms and soapbox politics, the meaning frittered away in visual and lexical disjunction—these seem marks of despair (as do the high-flown and often impenetrable aesthetic justifications). Poetry overthrows its predecessors usually by some new intensity of feeling cast in the vivid language of the present. Imagine what Pope would have done with the subjects in *Lyrical Ballads*, and you shudder.

Our avant-garde, which learned much from Pound, Williams, and Stevens (and too little from Eliot and Auden), has become increasingly static, the way that in certain subcultures ceremonies or manners of dress have fossilized—you need a costume museum to understand the Burgess-shale history of Catholic vestments, and a body of acolytes to explain the work of a J. H. Prynne. There are poets who dabble in the experimental, who borrow its radical means to conservative ends (Jorie Graham is perhaps the most important but impotent example), yet they would hardly keep Charles Olson awake at night. It's curious how often avant-garde poetry, that supposedly outsider art, is kept alive by universities, requiring a hermeneutics in advance of any necessary for Revelation or the Apocrypha.

We have not two but many poetic cultures, and all a critic can do is follow his taste where it leads, opening new books by old favorites and sometimes being disappointed, condemning poets who have made a loud noise with small gifts, perhaps praising a poet whose memorable whisper has come with talent unnoticed, but always, always reading the unknown hopefuls whose works pour over the transom like a cataract. I begin reading every book with hope, even books by poets I have long criticized. Without hope, a critic is nothing but a bundle of prejudices.

A critic must follow his taste or his whim, whimsically, tastefully, moving where he is moved, often wrongheaded, no doubt, but true to his instincts—and on occasion he must throw caution out with the bathwater. He should never dismiss the past as merely old fashioned, or believe with a sense of revealed religion that something brand spanking new must be the real thing. Nor should he think the old ways sacrosanct and new ones just upstart pretenders. He should be, in other words, ready to raise his hand against all, yet happy and untroubled at being surprised into joy. A critic requires a genealogy rather than a set of laws and ordinances. I have affection for, and perhaps affinities to, critics not enslaved by their intents—critics who can surprise their readers, and even themselves. The inheritors of Johnson and Coleridge have been critics like T. S. Eliot, R. P. Blackmur, Randall Jarrell, George Steiner, Christopher Ricks.

The critic must be a skeptic of his own taste—otherwise how could he ever change his mind? Some poets require rereading, or just the laid-up knowledge of experience. At twenty, I was not prepared to read Hardy's poems; at forty, I delighted in them. A critic is like a metal plate that registers electric current. When he's too rusty to carry current, he must be discarded. A critics must ask himself, in his dark nights, *What is this thing we do?* He must be prepared for acts of rescue, prepared to look at dead reputations afresh, prepared to accept what he's loathed and loathe what he's sworn by.

The critic is by nature a parasite—he cannot live without books, that most pathetic of bookworms, the critic. Judging at all seems the strangest part of the business—it's not like checking a spot weld or overhauling an automatic transmission. What might be objective everywhere else is subjective here. (Critics violently disagree, revealing their blood relation to lawyers, congressmen, and other low denizens of public converse.) The critic is not an extension of the publicity department. He isn't paid, if he's paid at all, to write blurbs to please the poet's mother.

The ideal critic would be part hanging judge, part Quasimodo, part bounty hunter, part Paul Revere. Critics can always be overruled by the court of public opinion—but the court of public opinion is notorious for short-sighted rulings. Whatever it is the critic does, it cannot be scientific. Perhaps he should have on his desk a book of litmus strips, or long racks of beakers and retorts (retorts he has aplenty, but of the wrong kind). Perhaps he should own a miner's canary. Open a bad book and the poor thing drops dead.

There's scarcely an aesthetic principle in poetry I haven't rejected and then—for a night of passion or two—embraced. Circumstances alter cases, and cases abhor circumstance (just as aesthetic theory abhors a vacuum). If I prefer a language dense with meaning, darkened by metaphor, devilish in syntax, it will seem that I'll soon be jabbering about lines *iced with ambiguity*, or *deckled with the diligence of diction*. It's true, I do like the weight of Shakespeare's line, Donne's logic, Dickinson's bleak psychology—but I'm as easily convinced by the dead flatness of *The Prelude* or Frost's nattering yarns, at least some of the time. I love these things—except, well, when I love something else better. Aesthetics is too monogamous. I see no little virtue in a critic being promiscuous. If this rules him out as a writer of manifestos, so much the better.

I love Browning's lurid voices, but on a different day I can be seduced by the noodling prose of William Carlos Williams. I would argue that this is what we mean by sensibility (even if sensibility sometimes has little sense). I don't like poetry that plays games for the sake of games; but my head has been turned, when in the mood for turning, by the nettled late poems of James Merrill (our own Callimachus), or the Rubik's Cube organization of Paul Muldoon. I love poems with an intimate sense of rhythm, until I'm struck dumb by some syllabic bit of whimsy and terror by Marianne Moore.

The maker of a good anthology is as close to an ideal critic as a critic can be, and there are few good anthologies whose contents don't fight tooth and nail over what a poem is, what a poem does, and how in hell it should go about that impossible and ridiculous thing, poetry. A perfect critic looks at every poem on its own terms, but not all terms are equal. The perfect critic would probably like everything, or loathe everything—and be almost always wrong, or almost always right. God loves all and the Devil hates all, but a critic must sleep nearer the Devil. For God you must look to publicity departments.

This is not to say that Shakespeare is the same as Herrick. A reader goes to them for different things. It's easy to read too much Herrick, harder to read too much Shakespeare. (A hundred more poems by Herrick would do little for poetry, at least not as much as the discovery of *Loves Labours Wonne* or *Cardenio*.) Yet there are days when Herrick, or Clare, or O'Hara offers what the day is missing, rather than Shakespeare, or Keats, or Eliot.

The nervous sort of reader wants the critic to lay out his aesthetics in every review—as if there were time or space! As if criticism needed disclaimers in small print! Such twitchiness began to infect scholarly writing some years ago, which made Ph.D.'s spout autobiography that rarely proved illuminating or necessary. The workaday critic, with his eight hundred or a thousand words, doesn't have time or patience to hold the hand of a reader not willing to judge for himself. Surely a critic with principles will quote from a book, and the reader will triangulate using the quotation, the critic's reaction, and the reader's own impression. (Quotations are the earnest of the critic's judgment.) If we require trigonometry in criticism, it will be of that sort. Bringing the critic's miserable childhood, or distant ancestry, or pattern baldness, or peculiar cult practices to bear would, I submit, be a waste of time. The review should contain enough gestures toward taste for the reader to give the critic his trust, or brutally to withhold it.

Besides, why should the critic do the reader's work for him? Readers must not fill themselves with the critic's opinion, nod contentedly, then fall into happy slumber to dream of masterpieces yet unwritten. The reader must read radically different critics, consult his own taste, learn which jackals—sorry, critics—he trusts, and, if all else fails, read the book himself. Readers perhaps imagine that critics read books only in climate-controlled, dust-free rooms, wearing state-of-the-art hazmat suits, denied the name of the author until they form an ironclad judgment. Criticism is messy by nature and messy in fact. The art of poetry is a dirty business. A critic is the construction of his errors, his silliness, his sincerity, his doubt.

The Unbearable Rightness of Criticism

When critics play parlor games, they imagine how they would have reviewed the controversial books of the past. Critics are later judged, not by the book they failed to pan, but by the book they failed to praise. Most are certain that, given the chance, they would have recognized the genius of *Lyrical Ballads*, or *Leaves of Grass*, or *The Waste Land*. We pour bile on the heads of the dolts of 1798 and 1855 and 1922 who didn't realize what was there on the desk before them.

When you look at those wrongheaded, purblind reviews long forgotten, however, even the most notorious, it's surprising how shrewd they are. The critics (like the poets themselves) were creatures of their day, and subject to the prejudice of the day. The reviewer is most vulnerable facing a poetry that threatens convention—violations of form and formality tend to provoke the most ill-considered judgments. Yet even there, after you have adjusted for bias, the critic can be uncannily canny about the poetry itself. Such contemporary insight is important not just for its punctuality. The reviews expose how the poets failed the time—or how their time failed the poets. Only by knowing how critics resisted the work can we see what the poetry put in danger.

The first review of *Leaves of Grass* was written by Charles A. Dana, editor of the *New York Daily Tribune*.

From the unique effigies of the anonymous author of this volume which graces the frontispiece, we may infer that he belongs to the exemplary class of society sometimes irreverently styled "loafers." He is therein represented in a garb, half sailor's, half workman's, with no superfluous appendage of coat or waistcoat, a "wide-awake" perched jauntily on his head, one hand in his pocket and the other on his hip, with a certain air of mild defiance, and an expression of pensive insolence in his face which seems to betoken a consciousness of his mission as the "coming man."

The book's frontispiece, a stipple engraving after a lost daguerreotype of the author, displayed a New York rough with his loose clothing and workman's hat—a sailor's open-collared blouse, the moleskin pants of a carpenter, and a slightly crushed soft-crowned hat, called a "wide-awake" supposedly because it lacked the felt "nap." (This is a fair example of nineteenth-century humor, which christened the pilot house of a steamboat the Texas, because it had been "annexed," or added on.) Here was the perfect democrat, a man showing where he stood by wearing neither coat nor waistcoat, while he slouched, hip cocked, staring out boldly at the reader.

The "coming man" was a nineteenth-century notion, perhaps a little touched by religious teleology, but roughly equivalent to what we might call the "man of the future" or, less modestly, the "man with great things before him." Whitman's extraordinary loose-limbed preface to *Leaves of Grass* made grand claims: "There will soon be no more priests. . . . Through the divinity of themselves shall the kosmos and the new breed of poets be interpreters of men and women and of all events and things." Dana distilled Whitman's vision of the poet as a democratic bard:

His language is too frequently reckless and indecent. . . . His words might have passed between Adam and Eve in Paradise, before the want of fig-leaves brought no shame; but they are quite out of place amid the decorum of modern society, and will justly prevent his volume from free circulation in scrupulous circles. . . . [The Leaves of Grass*] . . . are full of bold, stirring thoughts . . . , but so disfigured with eccentric fancies as to prevent a consecutive perusal without offense.*

The idea that poetry has a proper language had been invoked against *Lyrical Ballads* half a century before and would be repeated against

Howl a century after. However irritated Whitman made the critic, Dana detected something in this "odd genius." What fair-minded reader now would claim that Whitman's verse is not "disfigured with eccentric fancies," even if we can't quite believe that his language would have served "Adam and Eve in Paradise, before the want of fig-leaves"? (Surely Dana meant "brought shame," not "brought no shame.") If we are no longer offended, the critic has merely registered the local propriety—as Emily Dickinson did when she wrote Thomas Wentworth Higginson, "You speak of Mr Whitman—I never read his Book—but was told that he was disgraceful."

The young Charles Eliot Norton, later the editor of the *North American Review*, discovered, in a roundup of books,

> *a curious and lawless collection of poems, called* Leaves of Grass, *and issued in a thin quarto without the name of publisher or author. The poems, twelve in number, are neither in rhyme nor blank verse, but in a sort of excited prose broken into lines without any attempt at measure or regularity, and, as many readers will perhaps think, without any idea of sense or reason. The writer's scorn for the wonted usages of good writing, extends to the vocabulary he adopts; words usually banished from polite society are here employed without reserve and with perfect indifference to their effect on the reader's mind; and not only is the book one not to be read aloud to a mixed audience, but the introduction of terms, never before heard or seen, and of slang expressions, often renders an otherwise striking passage altogether laughable.*

The word *lawless* now reads more like a compliment—the laws Norton had in mind have come to seem antiquated, remote, even charmingly naive (and so were not laws but practicalities).

The diction of English poetry has gone through many cycles of contraction and release, when the fashion of one day has hardened into law the next—just as certain styles of clothing have fossilized into custom, like the Prince Albert frock coats and fedoras of some Orthodox Jews. More telling are periods when taste reversed direction, so that fifty years after his death Shakespeare was rewritten for the delicate tongue, and more than a century after that bowdlerized for the delicate ear.

Norton observed the violence in Whitman's violations—the "excited prose," the rejection of the authority of taste, the speech without reserve. It isn't known to what obscenities the Manhattan Island ear was exposed in the "blab of the pave," but Norton was objecting to Whitman's embrace of American slang. Who now could dislike a poet who vilified government, as Whitman did in his preface, for the "swarms of cringers, suckers, doughfaces, lice of politics. . . . It is better to be a bound booby and rogue in office at a high salary than the poorest free mechanic or farmer"?

Norton was embarrassed by Whitman's lack of embarrassment. The judgment is a matter for social history and psychology; even if our ancestors never stitched skirts around piano legs, there was a nicety to language we should now think absurd. We moderns are not yet above such arguments, with the insistent self-censorship of television, newspapers, magazines (even the *New Yorker* long maintained a list of banned words). Television's casual murders, blood sports, and vulgar humor bother few—though its adolescent carnality and cable porn might have jaded even Lord Rochester.

Whitman's critics were disturbed by the indecency of passages like:

> *Limitless limpid jets of love hot and enormous. . . .*
> *quivering jelly of love . . . white-blow and delirious juice,*
> *Bridegroom-night of love working surely and softly into the*
> *prostrate dawn,*
> *Undulating into the willing and yielding day,*
> *Lost in the cleave of the clasping and sweetfleshed day.*

Rufus W. Griswold, Poe's literary executor, exclaimed in exasperation, "It is impossible to imagine how any man's fancy could have conceived such a mass of stupid filth, unless he were possessed of the soul of a sentimental donkey that had died of disappointed love." To Griswold's eye, Whitman was guilty of "gross obscenity"; but the critic could not quote the passages, since he did not "believe there is a newspaper so vile that would print confirmatory extracts." Enraged by suggestions of homosexuality in *Leaves*, he resorted to Latin ("*peccatum illud horribile, inter Christianos non nominandum*"). The anonymous reviewer in the *Spectator* was shocked in 1860 by what he took to be intimations of unrestrained *heterosexuality*.

Norton saw the barbarians at the gates in Whitman's "mixture of Yankee transcendentalism and New York rowdyism" (married, he was surprised to see, in the "most perfect harmony"); yet despite his blue-stocking sensibility he found himself drawn to "this gross yet elevated, this superficial yet profound, this preposterous yet somehow fascinating book." (Whitman's contradictions have perhaps never been better drawn.) The critic's prejudices were largely social, but he understood the poet's means and ambition. Though Norton was prepared to believe that Whitman was what he claimed to be, an American rough, he had his doubts whether the poet was a kosmos. Honest critics doubt that still.

Once we discount Norton's reflexive resistance, his insights seem largely acute, the better for his occasional wit—he wrote his friend James Russell Lowell that the poet "combines the characteristics of a Concord philosopher with those of a New York fireman," continuing, however,

> *there are some passages of most vigorous and vivid writing, some superbly graphic descriptions, great stretches of imagination,— and then, passages of intolerable coarseness,—not gross and licentious but simply disgustingly coarse. The book is such indeed that one cannot leave it about for chance readers, and would be sorry to know that any woman has looked into it past the title page. I have got a copy for you.*

The British, who took to Whitman more eagerly than the Americans, were not immune to exaggerated complaint. The reviewer in the *Critic* thundered that the poems could be compared to "nothing so much as the war-cry of the Red Indians," while the poet was "as unacquainted with art, as a hog is with mathematics" (the critic had forgotten Toby the Sapient Pig, who had made his debut on the London stage in 1817):

> *We had ceased, we imagined, to be surprised at anything that America could produce. We had become stoically indifferent to her Woolly Horses, her Mermaids, her Sea Serpents, her Barnums, and her Fanny Ferns; but the last monstrous importation from Brooklyn, New York, has scattered our indifference to the winds.*

The Woolly Horse was one of Barnum's "humbugs," though a real genetic mutation. The Fejee Mermaid was another humbug, but a fake. Fanny Fern was the first woman newspaper columnist (and therefore freakish as woolly horse or Fiji mermaid), and later a defender of Whitman. Sea serpents were thought to haunt the American coast. The comparisons tell us something of the British view of America in the decades following *Martin Chuzzlewit* and Mrs. Trollope's *Domestic Manners of the Americans*.

Few now recall Martin Farquhar Tupper, author of *Proverbial Philosophy* (1838), a volume of poetic fustian composed in long prosy lines, which sold more than a million copies. A review in the London *Examiner* called Whitman a "wild Tupper of the West":

> *Suppose that Mr. Tupper had been brought up to the business of an auctioneer, then banished to the backwoods, compelled to live for a long time as a backwoodsman, and thus contracting a passion for the reading of Emerson and Carlyle; suppose him maddened by this course of reading, and fancying himself not only an Emerson but a Carlyle and an American Shakespeare to boot, when the fits come on, and putting forth his notion of that combination in his own self-satisfied way, and in his own wonderful cadences? In that state he would write a book exactly like Walt Whitman's Leaves of Grass.*

(During the Gold Rush, a grand jury in San Francisco was sworn in using Tupper's *Proverbial Philosophy*—but this, it must be admitted, was an honest mistake.) The Brooklyn poet may indeed have borrowed some notion of the poetic line from Tupper, or from others who wrote in quasi-biblical cadences—Whitman's free verse was not without precedent. Yet the reviewer saw beyond the defects:

> *He asserts man's right to express his delight in animal enjoyment, and the harmony in which he should stand, body and soul, with fellow-men and the whole universe. To express this, and to declare that the poet is the highest manifestation of this, generally also to suppress shame, is the purport of these Leaves of Grass. Perhaps it might have been done as well, however, without being always so purposely obscene, and intentionally foul-mouthed.*

Filter out the qualms about language, the language not meant for poetry, and the remarks are cunning even while cutting. However scathing the criticism, however it looked down its nose at the upstart American, the droll mingling of Emerson, Carlyle, and Shakespeare was insightful, and the backhanded remarks hilarious—what do we have in *Leaves of Grass* but pages and pages of a man of some culture, playacting the rough? Only the Whitman Whitman wished to be had sheltered a runaway slave or seen the marriage of a trapper and a "red girl." (When Bronson Alcott visited Brooklyn, Whitman claimed to be a house-builder—but Whitman's mother confessed that the poet's brother was the builder and that Walt "had no business but going out and coming in.")

The anonymous reviewer then wrote a burlesque of this backwoodsman, as if his leaves were leaves torn from an auction catalogue:

> Surely the house of a poet is a poem, and behold a poet in the
>   auctioneer who tells you the whole lot of it—
> The bath stone, compass front, open border, fender, shovel,
>   tongs, and poker,
> The blue moreen festoon window-curtain, the mahogany
>   dining-table on the floor,
> The six ditto hollow seat chairs covered with blue moreen,
> Covered with blue moreen and finished with a double
>   row of brass nails and check cases,
> The Wilton carpet, sun shade, line and pulleys, the deal sideboard
>   stained, . . .
> The Tragic Muse in a gold frame.

No matter how trivial Whitman sometimes seems, he is never as trivial as this—and never as giddy (Whitman lacked few things, but among them was a sense of humor). Yet here, here too, what was misguided was not unfair. Whitman was the greatest maker of lists after Christopher Smart, and before Smart you have to return almost to Homer— but Whitman's lists go on and on, as cluttered as the house of a man who can never throw a thing away. The untidy Whitman is easy to love—the reviewer simply had not learned how.

Whitman's old paper, the *Brooklyn Daily Eagle*, did not sentimentalize the poems of its former editor:

Here we have a book which fairly staggers us. It sets all the ordinary rules of criticism at defiance. It is one of the strangest compounds of transcendentalism, bombast, philosophy, folly, wisdom, wit and dullness which it ever entered into the heart of man to conceive. . . . The contents of the book form a daguerreotype of his inner being, and the title page bears a representation of its physical tabernacle. It is a poem; but it conforms to none of the rules by which poetry has ever been judged. It is not an epic nor an ode, nor a lyric; nor does its verses [sic] move with the measured pace of poetical feet — of Iambic, Trochaic or Anapaestic, nor seek the aid of Amphibrach, of dactyl or Spondee, nor of final or cesural pause, except by accident.

It's hard to imagine a criticism, though shocked to its hobnails, more square-shouldered about the poetry. The critic could not quite give the thing a Linnaean designation, but by showing what the verse was not he went a long way toward what it was.

The most difficult book to review is, like a Fiji mermaid, unlike anything seen before — or one that despite superficial similarities to the literature of the day is radically different. Often the author knows he is presenting a work strange and difficult. When Whitman published *Leaves of Grass* anonymously, adding his self-justifying preface, he had done no more than the authors of *Lyrical Ballads* before him. Whitman went one better by also sending his freshly printed book to the most far-seeing literary man of the day, who in 1844 had called for an American poetry in his essay "The Poet":

Our logrolling, our stumps and their politics, our fisheries, our Negroes, and Indians, our boa[s]ts, and our repudiations, the wrath of rogues, and the pusillanimity of honest men, the northern trade, the southern planting, the western clearing, Oregon, and Texas, are yet unsung. Yet America is a poem in our eyes.

Emerson could not have imagined (could not because no one had ever had the gall) that the young author would print the sage's effusive reply in the second edition, issued months later, with an excerpt stamped in gold along the spine — "I greet you at the beginning of a great career." (This is perhaps the earliest example of the purloined blurb.) However shy and gentle Whitman in his codgery years, when he published *Leaves of Grass* he was a bustling, go-ahead young man—restless as a hyena, in the argot of the day, and sharp-practiced enough to write no fewer than three reviews of the book himself.

The "advertisement" to *Lyrical Ballads*, probably written by Wordsworth, was a canny defense of a revolution in poetic diction.

> *The majority of the following poems are to be considered as experiments. They were written chiefly with a view to ascertain how far the language of conversation in the middle and lower classes of society is adapted to the purposes of poetic pleasure. Readers accustomed to the gaudiness and inane phraseology of many modern writers . . . will perhaps frequently have to struggle with feelings of strangeness and aukwardness: they will look round for poetry.*

By "experiments," Wordsworth was referring to those of the scientist. This was not the first time poetry had been called experimental. Henry Pemberton, in *Observations on Poetry* (1738), remarked that epic and dramatic poetry show the "natural effects of different tempers and passions under feigned actions" and "may very justly be compared with the experimental part of natural philosophy" (the term for what we now call science). If experimental poetry still aims to upend convention, the scientific overtone has been lost—perhaps unfortunately, for experiments in literature succeed far less frequently than those in the lab, which rarely succeed at all.

The poems Wordsworth and Coleridge published before *Lyrical Ballads* were typical of their late Augustan day. They gave little hint of such a departure in style and ambition—and the mask of anonymity protected the small reputations they had already gained. With England at war against France, with the French Revolution still in progress (Louis XVI had been executed only five years before), with fears at home about the discontent among laborers and the poor, the notion of overthrowing the high-flown, regal diction of Pope for the humble language of cottage and field might have been called seditious, had people feared poetry more.

It was on the problem of diction that many of the reviews concentrated their wrath. Charles Burney remarked in the *Monthly Review,*

> *Though we have been extremely entertained with the fancy, the facility, and (in general) the sentiments, of these pieces, we cannot regard them as* poetry, *of a class to be cultivated at the expence of a higher species of versification, unknown in our language at the time when our elder writers, whom this author condescends to imitate, wrote their ballads.*

This argument over the identity of poetry—that the poems, whatever their virtues, were not poems—has often been at the center of the attack on the "experimental."

We have become so inured to Wordsworth's and Coleridge's title, it's easy to forget that to the readers of 1798 it meant some scraps fallen out of Bishop Percy's *Reliques of Ancient English Poetry* (1765). *Lyrical Ballads* offered, not a march forward, but a leap backward to the poetry of centuries before—it was peddling the faux antique only eleven years after the publication of Chatterton's fake Rowley poems and but a generation after the Ossian hoax. The difference was that the poems in *Lyrical Ballads* were, at worst, self-conscious imitations of antique style. (Burney overplayed the point—they don't seem *that* antique). It was easy to dismiss imitation while ignoring the means provided for a change more radical—the use, not just of common diction, but of the lives of the poor, of sailors, of shepherds, of the dispossessed. In the end, poetry always ends up republican.

The reaction was what might be expected if Sotheby's started to auction Ethan Allen furniture. Burney continued:

> *Would it not be degrading poetry, as well as the English language, to go back to the barbarous and uncouth numbers of Chaucer? Suppose, instead of modernizing the old bard, that the sweet and polished measures, on lofty subjects, of Dryden, Pope, and Gray, were to be transmuted into the dialect and versification of the xivth century? Should we be gainers by the retrogradation? Rust is a necessary quality to a counterfeit old medal: but, to give artificial rust to modern poetry . . . can have no better title to merit and admiration than may be claimed by any ingenious forgery.*

Ingenious forgery. There is the taint left by Chatterton and Macpherson. Recall that "The Foster-Mother's Tale," for example, would have seemed an allusion to *The Canterbury Tales*—Chaucer had gained a reputation for barbarousness largely because people had forgotten how to pronounce Middle English (Shakespeare's and Donne's "numbers" were also uncouth, compared to the smooth lack of anapestic variation in Pope). This is always the problem with Whiggish criticism—the present has evolved from a savage past, and civilization can be defended only by barring the uncivilized. The sacrifice of the broader subjects available in freer diction is not admitted. The source of *retrogradation*, however, lay in the retrograde motion of planets, which at times move backward across the sky—a mystery until Copernicus. Burney should have known that the apparent drift backward concealed nothing but forward progress.

Where a critic is usually weakest is just where he is most certain—when he lays down the law everyone already obeys.

> *The author shall style his rustic delineations of low-life,* poetry, *if he pleases, on the same principle on which Butler is called a poet, and Teniers a painter: but are the doggrel verses of the one equal to the sublime numbers of a Milton, or are the Dutch boors of the other to be compared with the angels of Raphael or Guido?*

On matters of taste every man is an expert, to himself; and every man a fool, to the experts who come after. Samuel Butler was no Milton, but then Milton was no Samuel Butler.

Despite all this fuss about the upstart poets, marching toward the ill-numbered past, after Burney finally came to the poems he was remarkably reasonable.

> *When we confess that our author has had the art of pleasing and interesting in no common way by his natural delineation of human passions, human characters, and human incidents, we must add that these effects were not produced by the* poetry:—*we have been as much affected by pictures of misery and unmerited distress, in* prose. *The elevation of soul, when it is lifted into the higher regions of imagination, affords us a delight of a different kind from the sensation which is produced by the detail of common incidents.*

This was the point of rupture with the poetic diction of the time. If for nothing else, we can be grateful that the doctor's crack about prose probably fired Wordsworth to compose the longer preface to the 1800 edition of *Lyrical Ballads*, in which he defended poems written in the "real language of men."

At every point where Burney might have glimpsed the book's virtues, he was prevented by a hidebound view of what poetry is; yet he sensed, in the darkened mirror of taste, something he could not quite put a name to.

> *The author's first piece, the* Rime of the ancyent marinere, *in imitation of the* style *as well as of the spirit of the elder poets, is the strangest story of a cock and a bull that we ever saw on paper: yet, though it seems a rhapsody of unintelligible wildness and incoherence, . . . there are in it poetical touches of an exquisite kind.*

There *is* a kind of unintelligible wildness in Coleridge's youthful work (as well as an intelligible wildness)—that is part of its importance, and much of its charm. The critic was right in perhaps every way except the one that matters—he did not understand that the earth had shifted. Just such a quake occurs symbolically in "The Foster-Mother's Tale." (There had been a large earthquake in Derbyshire in November 1795, felt as distantly as Bristol, where Coleridge then lived.) *Lyrical Ballads* failed to fit the definition of poetry because the definition of poetry was suddenly out of date.

Burney went through the book at length, praising where he could, hurling the critic's darts everywhere else ("All our author's pictures, in colouring, are dark as those of Rembrandt"; "Here candour and tenderness for criminals seem pushed to excess"; "Another tale of woe!"). He was bemused when he sensed political radicalism ("if all the poor are to . . . supply their wants from the possessions of their neighbours, what imaginary wants and real anarchy would it not create?"). Burney was a bit too worried by the poets' fondness for criminals and the poems' criticism of the army.

The good doctor certainly missed the point at times, claiming of "The Foster-Mother's Tale" that it "seems meant to throw disgrace on the savage liberty preached by some modern *philosophes*." It's true that the boy in the poem is brought to "heretical and lawless talk" by too much reading, but Coleridge hardly intended a sermon on the danger of books. His sure handling of pathos in dramatic dialogue, which begins in medias res (this "dramatic fragment," a discard from his play *Osorio*, predates his use of fragment in "Kubla Khan"), out-Brownings Browning, half a century before the fact. Yet Burney praised numerous poems, including "The Nightingale" ("Miltonic, yet original"), "Simon Lee," and "The Idiot Boy." And it takes a heart of mush not to admit that "We Are Seven" is "infantine prattle."

Burney may have been right that Wordsworth here and there strained logic. The doctor suggested that in "The Last of the Flock" the Job-like shepherd "had, indeed, ten children: but so have many cottagers; and ere the tenth child is born, the eldest begin to work, and help, at least, to maintain themselves." Perhaps—but Burney overlooked the crushing truth beneath, that in straitened times the sheepholder might have to sell his flock to keep his children from starving. The weepy melodrama hides an uncomfortable truth. Whatever his animadversions, and however narrow the needle through which he was forced to view the poems, Burney frequently succumbed to grouchy praise:

> *The style and versification are those of our antient ditties: but much polished, and more constantly excellent. In old songs, we have only a fine line or stanza now and then; here we meet with few that are feeble:—but it is* poesie larmoiante. *The author is more plaintive than Gray himself.*

Poésie larmoyante—sob-story poetry. (The remark that Wordsworth had out-Grayed Gray would have stung—Wordsworth detested Gray.) There's an uncommon amount of tearjerking in *Lyrical Ballads*, far more than in the border ballads from which they distantly descended— so many are the tears described or evoked that the cock-and-a-bull story of "The Ancient Mariner" serves almost as comic relief. It's hard not to agree that "Tintern Abbey," though the "reflections of no common mind; poetical, beautiful, and philosophical," is also "tinctured with gloomy, narrow, and unsociable ideas of seclusion." *Lyrical Ballads* is an uncomfortably dark book, as was *North of Boston*—when the city looks at the country, it rarely sees how poor and hardscrabble it is. (Poets of eclogue and pastoral often seem willfully obtuse.)

The Waste Land, another gloomy poem, famously confounded early reviewers. Some insisted on reading it through the lens of the author's earlier work (a strategy that would have produced poor results for *Lyrical Ballads* and *Leaves of Grass*, had they not been published anonymously). Some spent a long time talking about anything but the poem: F. L. Lucas offered a long digression on Alexandria, Clive Bell a pointless anecdote about plumping for Eliot by reading "Prufrock" at a country-house weekend in 1916—or was it 1917? Some listed the allusions, at length, or quoted, at greater length. Some, like J. C. Squire, gave the whole thing up as a bad job ("I am still unable to make head or tail of it"). It occurred to few that a poem weighed down by allusion was also a man weighed down by allusion, which in the dreary wasteland of postwar London might have suggested that culture had reached a saturation, where little could be said that had not been said before. And almost no one saw that the real wastes that haunted the speaker (as opposed to the interior desert of a man at the end of his tether) might have been the torn-up battlefields across the Channel. If reviewers resist actually reviewing the book, it tells us something about reviewers, but much more about the book.

When critics tried to come to grips with the poem, however much they disliked it, the results were more telling. Louis Untermeyer was a bad poet and a worse critic, but he struggled resolutely with a poem he had every reason to dislike (later he included it, perhaps a little grudgingly, in his endless string of anthologies). He had a stronger sense than most critics, however, of the inner relation between *The Waste Land* and Eliot's previous work—the traits of Eliot's earliest poems ("an elaborate irony, a twitching disillusion, a persistent though muffled hyperaesthesia") had been merged with the "harder and more crackling tone of voice" of the later, which reveled "in virtuosity for its own sake, in epigrammatic velleities, in an incongruously mordant and disillusioned *vers de société*." The characterizations were not unfair—they were merely misdirected.

The Waste Land, Untermeyer concluded,

> *is a pompous parade of erudition, a lengthy extension of the earlier disillusion, a kaleidoscopic movement in which the bright-coloured pieces fail to atone for the absence of an integrated design. As an echo of contemporary despair, as a picture of dissolution of the*

> *breaking-down of the very structures on which life has modelled it-*
> *self, "The Waste Land" has a definite authenticity. But an artist is,*
> *by the very nature of creation, pledged to give form to formlessness;*
> *even the process of disintegration must be held within a pattern.*

The experimenter who doesn't get the results he expects is more likely to discard them because they do not correlate with the known than to wonder if they don't betray some unknown known, or even some unknown unknown. Untermeyer sought pattern, and was disturbed when he could not find it (pattern was there, but not in the place he looked): "This pattern is distorted and broken by Mr. Eliot's jumble of narratives, nursery-rhymes, criticism, jazz-rhythms, 'Dictionary of Favourite Phrases' and a few lyrical moments." Exactly, but to the critic this was not poetry:

> *Possibly the disruption of our ideals may be reproduced through*
> *such a* mélange, *but it is doubtful whether it is crystallized or*
> *even clarified by a series of severed narratives — tales from which*
> *the connecting tissue has been carefully cut — and familiar quota-*
> *tions with their necks twisted, all imbedded in that formless plasma*
> *which Mr. Ezra Pound likes to call a Sordello-form.*

The critic committed the common sin of projecting an obligation, here the artist's promise "to give form to formlessness" — in *The Waste Land*, the breaking of this promise is the point. Untermeyer understood the poem's defects but not that they were the medium for something more interesting. It was exactly the lack of integration that told the tale, or the tales. Yet more favorable critics might not have been stringent enough to characterize Eliot "as an analyst of desiccated sensations, as a recorder of the nostalgia of this age," and *The Waste Land* as a poem "whose value is, at least, documentary." (Eliot is one of the great poets of city life, and urban manners.) The truths of the bad reviewer are often more troubling than the emollient praise of critics without an ax to grind.

The sins of the critic are almost all sins of damaged expectation. A reviewer like the anonymous J. M. in the *Double Dealer* may have believed that *The Waste Land* was the "agonized outcry of a sensitive romanticist drowning in a sea of jazz"; that "this medley of catch-phrases, allusions, innuendos, paraphrase and quotation gives unmistakable evidence of rare poetic genius"; that the poem would have been perfectly clear to Eliot, "for whom every quotation has an emotional and intellectual connotation of intense significance." To everyone else, however, "it must remain a hodge-podge of grandeur and jargon." Of course *The Waste Land* is that — it is everything J. M. said. The poem merely required readers who could believe that no bad thing.

The decades after such reviews would prove that *Leaves of Grass*, *Lyrical Ballads*, and *The Waste Land* offered poetry a way out of the past — it's always hard for critics to recognize opportunities before some poet has taken advantage of them, and hard even then to admit that they *were* opportunities. The problem was never that the critics did not see, but that they did not know how to value what they saw. That would take no more than time — or other critics.

Once the genius of Shakespeare, or Coleridge and Wordsworth, or Whitman, or Eliot is generally agreed, the critics who backed the wrong horse are generally written out of literary history or held up to ridicule. Yet those critics time makes fools of — John Wilson Croker on *Endymion* ("We almost doubt that any man in his senses would put his real name to such a rhapsody"), Francis Jeffrey on *The Excursion* ("This will never do"), and many another — are often more worth reading than the critics of the day who got it right. We know what the latter critics will say — their taste is what our ears have been filled with; but, unless we read the other critics with attention, we can forget what an uncertain thing a poet's reputation was at the start, forget what withering glances the poems themselves had to overcome, forget that had the nay-sayers had their way literary history might have been different. Reading the reviews that mistook genius is not simply cold comfort for critics whom taste passed by, or an exercise in antiquarian taste. The critics who got it wrong remind us that poets in whom we now see only virtues once seemed full of vices and that, though we may value those vices differently, sometimes it is their presence that makes the virtues virtues.

Verse Chronicle: Shock and Awe

Mary Oliver

Mary Oliver is the poet laureate of the self-help biz and the human-potential movement. She has stripped down the poetry in *Red Bird* until it is nothing but a naked set of values: that the human spirit is indomitable, that the animal spirit is indomitable, that she loves birds very much, that she loves flowers very much, that even her dog loves flowers very much. As for herself—

> *Onward, old legs!*
> *There are the long, pale dunes; on the other side*
> *the roses are blooming and finding their labor*
> *no adversity to the spirit.*

If we trust the landscape of her poems, Oliver lives in a vast nature preserve she polices like a docent, strolling from bush to bush, from beast to beast (I'm told the wildlife of Cape Cod have asked for a restraining order against her).

> *Oh do you have time*
> *   to linger*
> *   for just a little while*
> *   out of your busy*
>
> *and very important day*
> *   for the goldfinches*

> *that have gathered*
> *in a field of thistles*
>
> *for a musical battle . . . ?*

To which the only sane response would be, *Hell, no!* Oliver's humble requests and mousy prayers are sweetly bullying—she sounds like a Dominican converted to the Sierra Club.

For all her love of nature, it's curious that Oliver's birds and wallpaper landscapes are the dullest ciphers—she rarely offers even the smallest detail of description. A field is simply a "mysterious field." Trees are merely "beautiful trees." If there are ravens, they aren't real ravens, but a "miracle // of Lord-love / and of sorrow." This isn't just a failure to imagine the world (all description is an act of imagination only partly tethered to the world, if tethered at all); it's a refusal of the responsibilities of language. She'd rather be a crow:

> *Anyway, my thoughts are all feathery.*
> *I prefer simple beak talk.*
>
> *Maybe it's having wings.*
> *It does make a difference.*

Poets have been seeking transcendence through nature for a long while—the wish is not merely religious, though drawn from faith in nature as an expression of or substitute for the divine. Lots of poets are in love with the ordinary—that's one of the graces of contemporary verse, as it was for Wordsworth, Clare, Bishop, Larkin, and many another. But should the ordinary, after such poetic attention, seem so, well . . . ordinary? It's as if you'd been promised a miracle, yet all that lies on the tablecloth before you is a dead mouse on a garbage-can lid. (Yet think what Bishop would have done with that mouse or that lid!) Poetry teachers say, "Show, don't tell," until they sound like idiots, knowing all the while that a good poet learns what to show and what to tell. Late Oliver shows nothing, tells everything, until you feel like one of Coleridge's wedding guests, buttonholed by an ancient mariner the sailors would have drowned two days from shore.

Thousands of readers, their lives having a poetry-shaped hole in them, read this stuff and are satisfied. Worse, they come back for second helpings. If you're going to be a popular artist with pretensions, when you pledge the reader profundity you ought to offer more than shopworn banalities like "Nobody owns the sky or the trees. / Nobody owns the hearts of birds" or "Instructions for living a life: / *Pay attention. / Be astonished. / Tell about it.*" Yet Mary Oliver is the best-selling poet in the country. When I remember this, I sit bemused, and stir my tea, and decide never to write a poem again. The best seller of one generation furnishes the dusty used bookstores of the next—but what does it say about a country if its best-selling poet is that transcendental fool, Mary Oliver?

Readers complain that it's not fair to review such a guileless poet (readers complain about a lot of things—which is good, because complaint is the first symptom of criticism). But if her poems were without pretensions, they wouldn't invoke Rilke or use an epigraph from Van Gogh or keep looking over their shoulders at Wordsworth. If you never review Mary Oliver, or Ted Kooser, or Billy Collins, or Sharon Olds, you're ignoring half the poetry sold in the country. The worship of simplicities is not a mean thing; but it is made mean when conducted with such hand wringing, such urgent tears, such Victorian sentiment. Those tears are shed all the way to the bank.

Cole Swensen

Cole Swensen's *Ours* might be called a long contemplative rant on gardens, especially the baroque gardens of André Le Nôtre, who created the formal designs at Versailles. Swensen is one of our most diligent avant-garde poets, wrestling like a Laocoön with the shape of her sentences. Poems are often triumphs or failures of rhetoric, and one doorway to a poetry otherwise mysterious is through the syntax it deploys and the syntactical evasions to which it succumbs. The order or disorder of words does no more than leave the lingering shadow of the author—but it tells us more about how he thinks than any annotation of theme or subject.

Swensen's off-center look at shrubbery finds its intellectual sources in thinkers like Derrida, for whom the gaze was always enough for some heavy theorizing, for propositions as difficult to grasp as a will-o'-the-wisp. (This is very different from the meditations of a Roland Barthes, who always returned to the phenomena before him.) Swensen has ideas, which are dangerous things to have; but, unlike a lot of experimental poets, she doesn't browbeat the reader with them. She develops them in gorgeous, hazy images and under-punctuated sentences that rarely know where they're going and sometimes forget when they've arrived.

> Because the kings of France loved Tivoli
> these windows bearing oranges
> globed,
> glowed, and that's how night becomes day without taking
> your eyes off their palaces in winter.

The scene is magical, even if the logic is suspect, the sentence wobbly as a two-legged stool. (Is the antecedent of "their" *night* and *day*, or *oranges*, or *kings*?) These things matter more than the style recognizes—it isn't quite enough to argue that such ambiguities please us through deceit.

The avant-garde aesthetic almost demands some form of one-upsmanship, yet there are only so many ways of torturing syntax or splashing words onto the page. (Certain avant-garde mannerisms have been around so long, Calvin Coolidge could have written respectable poems with them.) If the avant-garde wants to make it new, in Pound's dictum, what can be left to accomplish when the etiquette has been as codified as the place setting for a twelve-course banquet? Most experimental poets still come out of William Carlos Williams's pickle jar or Charles Olson's boot heel.

Swensen has researched her subject thoroughly enough to slather the page with horticultural facts. She composes her verse in short phrases alternating with runaway lines that hurl themselves acrobatically from margin to margin. Her virtue lies in restlessly teasing her material until it yields peculiar insight: "A garden is a window: . . . each pane / recording the faceted plantings / that a single finger traces / in the crisp veil of late frost, / some fortunes turn dust to dust." A deft period or semi-colon would have done wonders for the sentence structure (shouldn't syntax be tended like a garden, too?); but I'd rather cross-examine the Red Queen than argue punctuation with the avant-garde.

Swensen has a painter's eye, bringing her scenes into focus with a twist of the brush: a "forest always just / about to pour over the wall, / which makes the house fuse and the clouds adhere, / leaf by leaf / to the painted world / on a porcelain cup." There's a seductive languor to her best lines, and sometimes a Jamesian sweep of authority. The poems don't quite take advantage of the depth of these descriptions, preferring to improvise on whimsical themes—the garden as mirror, or allergy, or rearrangement of a previous garden, or machine for multiplying, or asymptote, or much else. More modesty might save her from Anne Carson–esque generalizations like "Any garden is a description / of its era's metaphysics" (an era's metaphysics far more likely describes its gardens) or the Jorie Graham–ish pomposities of "Gardens belong / to the class of all things that go beyond." At her worst, Swensen is beguiled by Carson's arch, pretentious titles or Ashbery's brusque absurdity ("We will, / all our hats upon / this sunny day, capsize / in a storm / and with a horse under each arm, Madame"). Whatever meaning adheres to such slapdash phrasing is not worth the ingenuity interpretation requires.

There are too many pages here where the profound is jostled off the page by the pseudo-profound, where the jittery indentations seem all too familiar, as if they'd come from *How to Write Like a Beatnik in Ten Easy Lessons.* As for André Le Nôtre, how can you not like a man "who took three snails and a cabbage / for his coat of arms"? Even Swensen's vices, which include a taste for bogus science and nonsense etymology (*garden* has nothing to do with *garde bien*, and *balustrade*—from *balautium*, the pomegranate flower—is not even distantly related to *ballad*), can't entirely detract from a sustained performance with touches of acidic humor. This long poem makes the garden as strange as the weeds from which gardens come, and to which they inevitably go.

Thomas James

At the age of twenty-seven, some months after the publication of his first book of poetry, Thomas James shot himself with a .45 caliber handgun. In the thirty years since his death, *Letters to a Stranger* has gained a small cult readership. Whenever we read the book of a young suicide, death salts the poems with might-have-beens. It's easy to turn sentimental about those who die young, their promise unfulfilled; and even poets who die before sixty are sometimes treated as if they'd been as young as Keats (an editor once lamented Auden's "own, only too brief, lifespan"—he died at sixty-six).

James' poems are drenched in Sylvia Plath, or rather in her imagery—you feel he must have written with *Ariel* open on his desk. He was hardly the only young poet of the seventies so bewitched. These boyish poems seem incomplete, amateurish at times, full of period mannerism and imprecise gesture. James crams his short, rough-edged sentences with metaphors and similes—there's scarcely a noun without an image clamped to it like a moray eel.

> *Love, the gold mouth has broken open.*
> *Stars are hard as quartz.*
> *The moon hangs like a half-eaten melon.*
>
> *The veined hives bleed in little spurts,*
> *Then thicken. Lambskins whiten*
> *In blue weather.*

This mob of images, few with the melancholy ripeness or feverish rot of Plath's, lacks the shock of recognition that made hers so disturbing. Her images conduct a counter- or double narrative, akin to the double plot of pastoral. Rarely mere window dressing or tinsel, they're shadowed by a muscular and resistant pathology. Whatever lies upon the surface, beneath lurks the psychological disruption to which the images attest. Plath was a disastrous model for someone depressive in his art and suicidally inclined (many of James's poems take place in the recovery ward—he knew those scenes too well). The deadly flourish to her last months of desperate, manic composition might have seemed less a warning than an invitation.

James, whose real name was Thomas Bojeski, obviously found in Plath a secret sharer (I wonder if something similar happened to Hart Crane as he read the poems of Samuel Greenberg). When not scribbling on the ward, he wrote about dissecting a pig or dragging a lake for a body, about a snake-bite victim, the iron maiden, lunch with a hangman, and suicide, suicide, suicide ("The room is livid. / It is like opening an artery. . . . // Scarlet splatters over the buffet"). He had a lurid imagination: the execution of a crippled duck is followed by five examples of decapitation in myth and history.

James's most accomplished poem was in the voice of a mummy of the Twenty-first Dynasty:

> My brain was next. A pointed instrument
> Hooked it through my nostrils, strand by strand.
> A voice swayed over me. I paid no notice.
> For weeks my body swam in sweet perfume.
> I came out scoured. I was skin and bone.
> They lifted me into the sun again
> And packed my empty skull with cinnamon.

The young poet never possessed the burnish of the mature artist, but his last poems reveal a gathering authority. ("I see you," he addressed two aunts, "With your bustles puffed up like life preservers, / Your needlepoint rose garden, / Your George Eliot coiffures, / Your flounces gathered like an 1890s valentine. / You both took heroin." The echo of Lowell sharpens the presence of Plath.) That final access of imaginative power might have killed him—it isn't the hard winter that murders the farmer, but the first blush of spring.

Lucie Brock-Broido, in her somewhat overheated introduction to this expanded edition, praises James's gift for imagery—his cobblestones "ribbed with frost," the peonies' "torches of acetylene," the moon's "facets smudged with soot," the moon "brittle as a wineglass," the "small, improbable moon" (the moon makes all too many farewell appearances). Though this was not yet more than a twitch or tic, James had an Aristotelian eye for metaphor. Brock-Broido claims that *Letters to a Stranger* received just a single review, which rather oversells the romantic myth of genius unrecognized. Though criticism was mixed, the book was reviewed in the *New Republic, TLS, Virginia Quarterly Review*, and elsewhere—it was not ignored. I disagree, often as not, with the editor's readings. The speaker in "Room 101," for example, is not "already dead"; he's a failed suicide, finding himself hardened against the world—if he were dead, he wouldn't lie in a room, day after day, while a nurse brings in "needles, gauze, and pills."

This book is the only world James left the world. As a graduate student, Brock-Broido grew obsessed with him. (She wrote him an eighty-page poem titled "Pornography," with a prose explication, illustrated!) Later she tracked down his friends and eventually his only surviving relative, a sister, with whom she promptly lost touch. It would now be impossible to write the poet's biography, so many of those close to him have died—he has become a tabula rasa, as Chatterton and even Plath became, ripe for projection. Brock-Broido, who undertook this edition as an act of devotion, has added a dozen or so uncollected poems, though she never reveals where she found them. It's no use exaggerating what Thomas James was, a talent only half born, and that half not quite enough for him to be remembered.

Yusef Komunyakaa

Yusef Komunyakaa's *Warhorses* is about war, and scarcely a poem avoids it. It haunts even the field of love, where a lover is forced to say, "Sometimes I hold you like Achilles' / shield." We live in a country now almost permanently at war (an incursion here, a pocket war there, something endless somewhere else), whose political narratives have been infected by the War on Poverty, the War on Drugs, the War on Terror. Love and war have been entangled as long as there has been literature; you could say that the *Iliad* and the *Odyssey* are about a war caused by one dalliance, almost lost for a second, and about a homecoming delayed by one dalliance after another.

Komunyakaa was a soldier in Vietnam, but he never finds quite the right tone for these fictions and meditations of battle—at times he's too solemn by half (if something isn't melodramatic enough, he makes it apocalyptic), at times too lugubrious, falling prey to every kind of sentimentality you can imagine. (It's as if he were influenced simultaneously by Revelations, Jacques Brel, and Stephen King.) Some of his ideas are giddily awful—the title poem is a "performance piece for voices, musicians, & dancers. Two or three seesaws are on the stage." I'm not sure, but I think the seesaws are horses:

> *Horses carried men to grasslands*
> *of the Crow, Shawnee, & Apache.*

Horses carried men to the gangplank.
Horses carried men to Shangri-la,
Nebo, San Juan Hill, & Xanadu.
Horses carried men to the trenches
stinking of mustard gas & betrayal.

Faced with more recent disasters, the poet proves as helpless before the banality of evil as he is before the banality of good. You turn a page and find a poem in two tall columns, one slightly broken at the top — of course! It's a concrete poem about the Twin Towers!

Some were writing e-mails
& embossed letters to ghosts
when the first plane struck.
The boom of one thousand
trap drums was thrown against
a metallic sky.

The purple-hued poetry of the "embossed letters to ghosts" and those heaven-assaulting trap drums doesn't stop there — rescue workers "tried to soothe torn earth," "signed deeds & promissory notes . . . hobbled in broken shoes / toward the Brooklyn Bridge" (this last perhaps due to an unhappily placed antecedent). The good poem on the tragedy of September 11 has yet to be written. It might seem an impossible task, an unscalable rock-face of contemporary prejudice, sentiment, and banality; yet imagine what Auden might have done. His greatest war poem was not "September 1, 1939" but "Musée des Beaux Arts."

The most ambitious poem in *Warhorses*, taking up half the book, is the "autobiography" of Komunyakaa's alter ego, a Vietnam vet who has been a bartender for twenty years, the man the poet might have been with a little less luck. The portrait seems at once too manufactured and too naive — this soldier in a mirror life was wounded by a sniper and won a Silver Star for bravery (Komunyakaa won a Bronze Star, but as a battlefield reporter). The portrait of the soldier's father, who sang cover versions of Nat King Cole and the like, is sensitive to a world now gone, a world of powder-blue suits and Philco turntables; but Komunyakaa can't stop there. When he revisits our racial past, he equates segregating a dance floor with raising a flag (both use ropes) or lynching ("tossing a noose / over an oak limb / at the edge of a field— / a riot of red blooms at dusk").

I like poets who have a historical memory, who know that "shock and awe" is our contemporary version of Greek catharsis. But why succumb to historical judgments so ludicrously misplaced? "Why is our enemy / always dark-skinned . . . ?" asks the aging veteran. This forgets those enemies from the American past, the British, the Spanish, the Germans, the Italians. It's not enough to milk the reader's tears or reinforce his prejudices, never enough to force the poem to yield, in its last lines, a greasy dollop of sentiment—"Yes, / the oldest prayer is still in my fingertips"; "that air made of loneliness & nitrate"; and, perhaps best of all, "Forgive my heart & penis, / but don't forgive my hands."

There are moving moments in this book—peasants during the Russian Revolution "swinging // long-handled scythes against the Russian infantrymen," a Jewish father in mourning "calling / his daughter's name over a loudspeaker." But Komunyakaa is rarely content unless he's hammering a point (the reader is the anvil), and it's always the same point. If you want the moral complexity of Wilfred Owen or Anthony Hecht or Geoffrey Hill, you'll be disappointed. Komunyakaa has nothing but the drive of conviction, which mistakes moral judgment for the ethos of art.

Claudia Emerson

Claudia Emerson's well-behaved, slightly prissy poems deserve more attention than they're likely to receive. They thrive in an oddly narrow register between regret and paralysis, as if the duties we owe the past were enough to kill us. (If there were still maiden aunts, they would write such poems—and they'd sprinkle on the arsenic in double doses.) *Figure Studies*, Emerson's first book since she won the Pulitzer Prize in 2006, is a latter-day variation on *Spoon River Anthology*—she remembers a world of all-girl schools, of parlor gossips and piano lessons, of a mannequin in an attic afterlife after the dress store closes for good.

Everyone was forced to read *Spoon River*, once—but Emerson sees these straitened souls from outside (Masters's townspeople spoke from beyond the grave, which made for a very noisy cemetery). In a small town, every success is resented, every disappointment hoarded—but she avoids the grander failures for quiet lives lived quietly, slightly out of the way, blighted but struggling. The girls' school has a housemother:

> *This life began as mere employment, something*
> *that would pass; she had private joys then,*
>
> *reasons to close her door. This is how she breathes*
> *now, moving sharklike through the halls' courses,*
>
> *sensing the constant blood of wakefulness,*
> *girls' hands swimming—pale fish—into and out of tense*
>
> *bodies held still as water dense with early blooming.*

There's a lot going on here when nothing is going on—the portrait is done in a few discreet strokes. Having private joys no longer, the woman traffics among her charges, a shark arrowing through them, always hungry. They sense they're in danger (are those flowers floating or drowning?)—if not from her, then from the adult world that soon will notice their blooming sexuality.

Emerson knows—the way Masters did, the way Frost did—how lives go wrong. She recognizes what is required of women in such a world. In addition to the mannequin and a female anatomical model (both screaming, Symbol! Symbol!), there is the little girl—always the most beautiful, always plucked from the other girls at the last minute—chosen to be the Virgin Mary in a living Nativity,

> *center stage where a spotlight reveals her*
>
> *gazing marblelike into the manger—nothing*
> *for her to know beyond the fact of being*
>
> *chosen, nothing for her to practice,*
> *having learned already this stillness.*

These lines could easily have become yet another diatribe against the male gaze; but Emerson, like those girls she writes of, remembers when to be silent. She has a confidence in her syntax (too often these days, poets use their syntax like a pile driver), a trust in the unassuming force with which the poems pursue their ends. That's the virtue of patience, of waiting long enough for the ordinary to turn into the unexpected.

Poems that depend on such transformation are risky investments— it's easy to start a poem with a bang, harder to find a place to stop that pays off all the debts accrued and adds something extra, for interest. It's difficult to quote her endings without going halfway back into the poem—like Larkin, Emerson roots the final lines deep in her stanzas, so they are half surprise and half fulfillment.

> *The local boys are, of course, forbidden.*
> *This leaves only the rare visiting*
>
> *father, awkward brother, the headmaster,*
> *the boy who bushhogs the pasture,*
>
> *or the chaplain in his telling collar—starched*
> *tooth at the throat—to remind them.*

This chaplain will remind them by his voice, by his sermons, by his wool-suited authority; but what we focus on is that white tooth, that sharp visible square of dog collar, which manages to shiver into being the hunger of and for religion, the reminder of the primeval mistake by that woman in Eden.

Some of Emerson's poems fall apart while waiting for an ending; some leave their moral lesson too close to the surface. She works best by indirection, making the reader think the poems aren't going anywhere in particular, before they home in like that shark. (The best place to arrive in a poem is the place you didn't know you were heading toward.) She leaps into some poems in medias res and sometimes abandons them there, too. There are touches in this hothouse world of Flannery O'Connor's South, though a South less fraught with hard faith. I'm drawn to a poet who, trying to recreate a childhood memory, asks a friend to burn a piano on the bank of the Hocking River. He's thanked in the acknowledgments.

Sharon Olds

When you open a Sharon Olds book, you know what to expect: lurid vignettes followed by privacies most people wouldn't whisper to their doctor. The body count will be high. The dramatic grammar of an Olds poem is as predictable as a horror movie's—if there's an innocent girl in the first scene, she's sure to be raped or murdered or to die from lead paint by the end. Olds is our most Freudian poet since Plath—if there's any complex or condition, from the Elektra complex to the anxiety of influence, Olds has embraced it as her own.

One Secret Thing is laid out like an autobiography. It begins with scenes wrenched from the Second World War (Olds was born less than a year after Pearl Harbor), though some could have occurred any time afterward, and others might have been recognized by Homer. A family, about to be taken to the death camps, stands exposed in their home, the daughter "with her music / in her hand":

> *They knew*
> *families had been taken. What they did not know*
> *was the way he would pick her cello up*
> *by the scroll neck and take its amber*
> *torso-shape and lift it and break it*
> *against the fireplace. The brickwork crushed the*
> *close-grained satiny wood, they stood and*
> *stared at him.*

Olds loves big scenes as much as Otto Preminger. The shock of this end of innocence, this destruction of art, lies in the premonition of death borne by the crushed body of the cello. In the proofs, this was spoiled by the clumsy handling of pronouns, so it was easy to confuse the victims with the victors. Now it's clear who breaks the cello, but the reader wonders why only one Nazi would be sent to arrest these Jews (the poem has been retitled "When He Came for the Family").

After this phantasmagoria of war come the poet's childhood, youth, marriage, age; but the dominant, dominating figure is her mother. This figure of terror from previous books (apparently she stood only 4'11", no taller than Alexander Pope) seems more confused than calculating.

If there's a fairy tale at the heart of Olds's poetry, it's of the innocent triumphant—she's the Little Red Riding Hood and the Goldilocks of her own poems, and in the end the wolves and bears lie slain around her. In this peculiar merging of fairy tale and Freudian myth, where a parent's every errant impulse has some base motive ("my mother was made of desire leashed"), Olds is the anti-Plath, because she always comes out smelling like a rose (the underside of Plath's influence, which Olds does not escape, is blaming everyone else for your unhappiness). A mixture of eros and disgust lies at the heart of the maze.

> *My mother was such a good kisser.*
> *From where I sat in the tub, her body,*
> *between her legs, looked a little*
> *like a mouth, a youthfully bearded mouth*
> *with blood on it.*

This makes it seem that the daughter wants to kiss her mother's vagina. For the child to survive, the monster must be slain.

You feel sorry for the mother, trying to do the right thing by this small, obstreperous child and getting it as wrong as most parents do. (When she takes her daughter to a doctor, he diagnoses the girl's problem as a "sense / of humor.") As her mother ages, the slow rapprochement between them seems more like mutual exhaustion. After her mother is strapped to a bed in intensive care, pleading to be untied, Olds quietly sings to her, like a mother to her mother—it doesn't even occur to the poet that this mirrors her own famous childhood trauma, being tied to a chair. But then Olds did not inherit a gene for irony. And the pediatrician seems guilty of misdiagnosis.

These new poems sometimes read like rough drafts, the badly constructed sentences collapsing into slightly rabid lists of phrases. When the poet learns she might need a hysterectomy,

> *I bent over,*
> *wanting to cry out, It's my best friend, it's like*
> *having a purse of your own, of yourself, it's like*
> *being where you came from, as if you are your origin,*
> *the basket of life, the withies, the osier*

reed weave, where your little best beloveds
lay and took heart.

Having a purse of your own? Elsewhere the writing crawls with weedy similes: "like a scrimshaw Crusader / chess-piece rotated slowly on its base"; "like the low singing / of a watered plant long not watered"; "like eating hard-shelled animals / at mid-molt."

Olds's virtues have been forthrightness, lack of embarrassment, and a greedy attention to the body (sometimes these were vices, too); but the purposes her virtues served were often narcissistic. (Has anyone noticed how chilly and unlovable her poems can be?) *One Secret Thing* is filled with classic moments: there's a poem, both hilarious and repulsive, about the state of the poet's ass ("this compendium / of net string bags shaking their booty of / cellulite fruits and nuts"), and another where she becomes a fly on the wall, trying to lay eggs on the wallpaper roses while watching a child spanked—spanked to the tune of "Onward Christian Soldiers"! Much of this, nonetheless, feels like a poet taking dictation. Perhaps Olds has mined the ore of her life so long, there's nothing left. Perhaps, aged sixty-six, Sharon Olds has at last grown tired of herself.

Verse Chronicle: You Betcha!

Billy Collins

Billy Collins is funny, everyone agrees. The birds agree, the bees agree, even the fish in the sea agree, Billy Collins is funny. Yet why do I feel, half an hour after closing a Billy Collins book, a sharp grinding in my stomach, as if I've eaten some fruit cake past its sell-by date? His wry, self-mocking poems wouldn't hurt a fly—but they couldn't kill a fly, either, even if they tried. Readers who have whetted their appetites for drollery on previous books may open *Ballistics* and be puzzled. Our Norman Rockwell of sly winks; and elbowing good humor; and straw-hatted, flannel-shirted American whimsy is no longer funny. Worse, some of his new poems take place in Paris.

Billy Collins's method has been to borrow a dry nugget of fact or some mildly absurd observation and see how far he can go. Say you read that the people of Barcelona once owned an albino gorilla, or remember that Robert Frost said, "I have envied the four-moon planet," or find yourself talking to a dog about the future of America. Why, the poem would almost write itself! Collins's gift was to make the poem a little odder than you expected. The problem with his new book is that the ideas are still there, but the poems have lost their sense of humor. Here's what happens to that gorilla:

> *These locals called him Snowflake,*
> *and here he has been mentioned again in print*
>
> *in the hope of keeping his pallid flame alive*
> *and helping him, despite his name, to endure*
> *in this poem where he has found another cage.*

> *Oh, Snowflake,*
> *I had no interest in the capital of Catalonia—*
> *its people, its history, its complex architecture—*
>
> *no, you were the reason*
> *I kept my light on late into the night*
> *turning all those pages, searching for you everywhere.*

There must be a lot of comic things to say about albino gorillas, things that don't require sentimental guff with a twitch of self-pity.

Say you recall the day Lassie died, when, after you finished your farm chores and ate your oatmeal, you drove to town and scanned the books in Olsen's Emporium—and what books they were! An anthology of the Cavalier poets, *The Pictorial History of Eton College*, *The Zen Teaching of Huang Po*. Why, who knew? This is a send-up of Frank O'Hara's "The Day Lady Died"—the book titles mock his purchase of *New World Writing* (as he said, "to see what the poets / in Ghana are doing"). But then what?

> *I'm leaning on the barn door back home*
> *while my own collie, who looks a lot like her,*
> *lies curled outside in a sunny patch*
> *and all you can hear as the morning warms up*
> *is the sound of the cows' heavy breathing.*

And that's it. This labored parody of O'Hara's famous ending ("I am sweating a lot by now and thinking of / leaning on the john door in the 5 SPOT / while she whispered a song along the keyboard / to Mal Waldron and everyone and I stopped breathing") isn't side-splitting at all. The premise has become just another excuse for softheaded mush—Collins doesn't even get round to mentioning (spoiler alert!) that Lassie was played by any number of dogs, that she was *male* (because males have glossier coats), and that, besides, Lassie is immortal and can't ever die.

Collins has managed to be what he rarely was in the past—dull. The ending in many of these new poems falls flat, the speaker gazing at the moon or listening to a bird in hopes of revelation. If Billy Collins can't joke about death, for example, well, who can? When he pokes fun at writers' guides ("Never use the word *suddenly* just to create tension"), or at teachers who ask, "What is the poet trying to say?" he's still our best poet at piercing the pretensions of the whole literary shebang. Get him off the subject, however, and the poems are suffused with mild gloom and misanthropy. He writes of having tea "with a woman without children, / a gate through which no one had entered the world." You think that he's blundered, that he can't possibly be talking about her vagina. Oh, yes, he can! "Men had entered the gate, but no boy or girl / had ever come out"—I'm not sure whether this is wickedly inventive prudery or plain bad taste.

When comedians stop being funny, they must invent themselves anew or retire for good. (Who has ever suffered through Buster Keaton in *How to Stuff a Wild Bikini* and not gone off to drown a few puppies?) A number of poems here mention divorce in a roundabout way, reason enough for a man to take off his rose-colored glasses and book a flight to Paris. Indeed, the most hilarious poem in the book is titled "Divorce," and it's also the shortest:

> *Once, two spoons in bed,*
> *now tined forks*
>
> *across a granite table*
> *and the knives they have hired.*

If Collins can become the bitter philosopher of such lines, there's hope yet. Otherwise, Poetry must do what Poetry does when a poet runs out of gas, or screws the pooch, or jumps the shark—it gives him a Pulitzer and shows him the door.

Thom Gunn

In the forties and fifties, it was almost an act of rebellion to compose tidy stanzas and tidier rhymes, as if the modernists had never existed. The influence of Auden and Yeats (those most seditious of seditious poets) was so overpowering on both sides of the Atlantic that a certain ideological mustiness soon pervaded the poetry magazines, as young poets wrote endless allegorical stanzas on Orpheus, or Achilles, or just about any Greek god or hero you could name. A few of these poems were brilliant; many were good; but the mass proved just period sludge, the sort any age produces—most of it to be washed away on the next tide of fashion.

Thom Gunn could write in this headmaster's manner with the best of them.

> *The huge wound in my head began to heal*
> *About the beginning of the seventh week.*
> *Its valleys darkened, its villages became still:*
> *For joy I did not move and dared not speak,*
> *Not doctors would cure it, but time, its patient skill.*

> *And constantly my mind returned to Troy.*

Gunn's early books, *Fighting Terms* (1954) and *The Sense of Movement* (1957), announced a talent for emotion controlled in muscular, labyrinthine forms. His elegance had a brutish edge, and his brutality concealed a few civilities (his cachet as a young poet came from writing formal poems on bikers and Elvis). It should have been no great surprise when shortly after his first book he moved to California and took up study with Yvor Winters.

Selected Poems reveals how long Gunn labored to overcome the limitations of his virtues. If his early poems seem fussy exercises now, polished into artificial antiquity, the overheated poems on surfers and LSD are simply embarrassing. (The whole of "Listening to Jefferson Airplane" reads, "The music comes and goes on the wind, / Comes and goes on the brain.") Gunn's best work had to fend off Winters in his smugness and rectitude, on one hand, and San Francisco's beatniks and hippies, on the other, but he never stopped trying to treat the incompatible realms of his experience as if they formed a whole.

August Kleinzahler, who edited this volume, has made a judicious and surprisingly conservative selection of Gunn's poems. Though he might have been more generous to the early books (only half a dozen poems survive), the most moth-eaten poems are gone, but so are later poems using the scatty lines of the Beats. I don't miss the loose-limbed verse of Gunn's middle period, or the poems that mentioned Ding Dongs or Charles Manson—or the one from the point of view of a dog. This selection stresses the reasoned continuity of Gunn's work, evident in his formal poetry until the end. (Even late, he could make a lot of metaphysical hay out of a nasturtium found in a vacant lot.) What remain are, for the most part, the poems that take serious things seriously, culminating in the elegies he wrote during the AIDS outbreak of the eighties. Gunn's late poems were often bleak, haunted by losses to time and disease, by the slow recession of pleasure. After the completion of *Boss Cupid* (2000), he seems to have published nothing new before his death in 2004.

You'd hardly know from his poems that Gunn ever worked a day—he took as his gravitating theme a hedonism never wholly gratified. He loved the tightly knit stanzas and clockwork rhymes of the late Elizabethans. ("I want to be an Elizabethan poet," he once admitted, but there's a great difference between being and imitation.) In some ways, he was the thinking man's Stephen Spender, though he wrote a rude comic couplet about Spender. Gunn was a poet for whom feeling blossomed through form (his motto might have been Eliot's remark that a "thought to Donne was an experience"); but he needed the resistance of pattern, the refined difficulty in the made thing. If the cost was too many early poems that began with lines like "Do not enquire from the centurion nodding" or "Lictor or heavy slave would wear it best," and too many gassy stretches of couplet writing, the benefit was the stately movement he could give the passing of passing fancies:

> *Why should that matter? Why pretend*
> *Love must accompany erection?*
> *This is a momentary affection,*
> *A curiosity bound to end,*
>
> *Which as good-humored muscle may*
> *Against the muscle try its strength*
> *—Exhausted into sleep at length—*
> *And will not last long into day.*

Shakespeare and Donne would have recognized that cool detachment, and Dante approved Gunn's vision of the afterlife, where the dead watch the living on black-and-white TV.

Jim Powell

Jim Powell published his first book of poetry twenty years ago and was named a MacArthur fellow, but his books since then have been limited to translations from Sappho and Catullus. Long vacations are not that unusual in poetry—some poets publish only when they have something to say. The longer the time away, however, the better the new poems have to be. *Substrate* is the book of someone who has just been released from a vow of silence and is gabby as a goose.

> *Naked as the day they were born the first time*
> *the newly resurrected blink awake wide-eyed and caper*
> *innocent under heaven*
> *in the final clarity of eternal everyday*
> *like nudists without tennis shoes . . .*

This goes on for another ten lines without stopping for breath. Powell lurches into his subjects, wary of punctuation, eager to get on with things, gripped less by a stream than a flash flood of consciousness. There's nothing too trivial to be set down, and he can spend two dozen lines on a water-colorist brushing a few petals on paper.

It would be mean to suggest that the poet has succumbed to a California aesthetic of the most self-indulgent kind, but Gary Snyder and Robert Hass have a lot to answer for. In the middle of poems recalling a weekend blowout ("danced both days past // exhaustion giddy with the music / and the company, the motion / and the potions, the chalice and the vial") or comforting a woman after the death of Jerry Garcia ("You cut your hair in mourning, your pride, that fully / touched your butt"), you begin to wonder if there's going to be an advertisement for patchouli oil on the back of the book.

After a while, you long for a poem that doesn't buttonhole you about the near extinction of the snowy egret, or the plight of a homeless woman, or the sublimity of California woodlands ("It's time I wrote my 'bearshit-on-the-trail' poem")—and occasionally you get it.

> Contemplating the first smog
> Ruskin thought it the lost souls
> of the French dead
> blowing across the Channel
> from Paris where the Commune's last defenders fell
>
> back fighting, driven through Père-Lachaise
> from grave to grave in a meager drizzle:
> starved workingmen,
> beggars and country boys.

Here the same sympathies that produce drivel about bear shit and the Grateful Dead are turned to deeper effect, and the different effort of weight and solicitude is apparent even in the enjambment. (In a sense, smog *is* the ghost of labor.)

A good part of the book is given over to what is now unhappily called a "project." Many poets believe that the sure path to success is a group of poems dramatizing some long-ago misfortune (three books have been written on the Triangle Shirtwaist Factory fire of 1911); but, once you know the project, whether it's cooking up the life of a Storyville prostitute or staging, yet again, the fall of the Alamo, often you don't have to read the poems. The title sequence here mines the historical sediments of California in poems drawn from yellowed memoir and mildewed report, dragging through the past five hundred years or more of Pacific-slope history. Powell has an eye for the telling anecdote, especially about local Indians, but no idea how to turn it into poetry.

> Firearms no longer terrify them and they are delighted
> by the effectiveness at distance of our Fowling Pieces
> upon a species of large quail prolific
> in coppices, the males with crests reverted,
>
> lead-colored, with ferruginous breast plumage
> and pinkish feet, more savory than those of France, and plumper.

I've read farm bulletins with more plot and verve. Marianne Moore took poems from odd sources, but what poems they were! She discovered a world of moral resource in prose compunction and prose reserve. Powell's found poems, though the originals have been much reshaped, are interesting in their individual ways, but stultifying en masse, full of curious detail and untouched by artistry.

"Substrate" is not, as the publicity promises, a "cultural history of California" but an omnium-gatherum that gratifies fashionable prejudice and succumbs to contemporary mawkishness—the brief extracts possess all too many designs upon the reader. The encounter between strange worlds is almost always between whites and Indians—you'll look in vain for a Sydney Duck or a Chinese whore, a New York capitalist or an Irish fireman. The poems tell us little we don't already know about ignorant sailors, rapacious immigrants, and greedy mine owners, except that apparently for half a millennium Californians have mostly been occupied hunting and dancing.

Katha Pollitt

Katha Pollitt has also taken a long sabbatical between books. Her polished, slightly unmemorable debut, *Antarctic Traveller* (1983), won the National Book Critics Circle Award and was so impeccably well mannered it wouldn't have looked out of place on a shelf at Miss Porter's. Pollitt eventually made her name as a hot-tempered essayist for the *Nation*, though every now and then she still turned her hand to poetry. *The Mind-Body Problem* preserves the stray poems of the past twenty-five years. It's bracing to blink and see a poet go from early maturity to the whisper of old age. These agreeably mortal poems often take a glance backward at youth, then one straight ahead at the mirror.

> *The boy who scribbled* Smash the State *in icing*
> *on his wedding cake has two kids and a co-op,*
> *reads (although pretends not to) the Living Section*
> *and hopes for tenure.*
>
> *Everything's changed since we played Capture the Red Flag*
> *between Harvard Yard and the river. Which of us dreamed that*

History, who grinds men up like meat, would
make us her next meal?

But here we are, in a kind of post-imperial
permanent February, with offices and apartments,
balked latecomers out of a Stendhal novel.

The blunted savagery and look-back-in-bewilderment affability of such lines argue for the civilizing influence of a thirty-year mortgage.

Pollitt's poems are paeans to domestic stability, to the rueful charms of raising children, to the brownstone comforts of the Upper West Side. She's too clever a poet not to feel uneasy at times, harried at the edge of happiness; but the poems rack along, genial in their whimsy and complacent in their discontents. I knew I'd heard their tone before. Then I realized, of course! It was the voice of the *New York Times*'s "Metropolitan Diary," that depressing calendar of heartwarming encounters meant to show that deep down we're all just, well, *people*.

But on 14ᵗʰ Street
the Dominican peddlers sell ocean-blue ices,
plastic shoes, and rugs on which a bulldog
is cheating two beagles and a dachshund at cards
and suddenly out of nowhere the roof of every
flaking office building flares gold as though
it was not going to be demolished tomorrow
and everyone has the same American thought:
Everything is possible.

(*Suddenly*! See Billy Collins.) If occasionally one of Pollitt's poems ends with a quiet shudder, why, by the next poem she's beaming like a white-gloved hostess again. There's nothing wrong with such poems, except that they're so cozy with circumstance, so numbed by prudence, their raw feelings have been smothered. You wonder if the poems haven't been taking Zoloft on the sly. Even when the premise is striking or unsettling, Pollitt lets the reader down with a gentle bump.

The static ambitions of these poems, complicit in their world of things (how *bourgeois* the poems are, given the poet's firebrand past!), are finally disheartening, and no more so than in their repetitions.

Pollitt is a lover of lists, someone who's been making shopping lists all her life and can't stop when she gets to poems. The list is an old device, older than the catalogue of ships in the second book of the *Iliad*. Whitman and Auden sometimes used it to dazzling effect; but, when a poet becomes addicted, when she can't get out of a poem without one or two (if not five or six), you begin to worry. After *marble, murder, saxophones, lipstick, Nero; gold, / palm trees, perversions!; a spoon! // a xylophone! a breast!*; *Mairzy Doats, On The Rocks, At-Eze*; *Mass cards, seashells, / photos*; and *O sweetness, / sunrise, hibiscus, Chinese lanterns, hearts*, the book has scarcely begun. By the end, you never want to read another oddball list again.

Worse, Pollitt feels it necessary to signpost every major turn in her poems (she might as well be driving you along the Long Island Expressway). She opens a poem with some wallflower of a premise but can't come to a conclusion without loudly clearing her throat and declaiming *Still* or *But O* or *And yet* or firing off a rhetorical question or two. (I lost track when I'd counted fifty of the things. Does she have a policy of "Ask, don't tell"?) No matter how tepidly amusing a poem like "Lives of the Nineteenth-Century Poetesses" or "Rereading Jane Austen's Novels" ("timid and queer as governesses out of Chekhov, / malnourished on theology, boiled eggs, and tea"), I'm afraid if you gave the same idea to Billy Collins, he'd do it better. Why does an essayist of such stark opinion and Hotspur passion write poems that wouldn't muss the hair of a Victorian curate?

Rita Dove

Rita Dove has a project in *Sonata Mulattica*, and it's a doozy. A virtuoso nine-year-old violinist makes his debut in Paris weeks before the storming of the Bastille. More than a decade later, Beethoven dedicates a fiendish sonata to him, which the prodigy plays to perfection. They have a spectacular falling out, apparently over a woman, and Beethoven rededicates the sonata to the violinist Kreutzer—this has ever since been called the "Kreutzer Sonata," though Kreutzer refused to play it. The young violinist gradually falls into obscurity and dies in brute poverty.

That this dramatic young man was born to a Polish mother and a black father (who claimed to be, among other things, an African prince) places him in that realm of racial exoticism the Romantic Age required. Whatever prejudices it suffered, the age was less sensitive than ours to race, more curious and less hidebound about differences of skin—there lingered a sense that however noble the savage was, the savage in man could be civilized. It was an age interested in freaks and oddities, in giants and dwarves, in the Sapient Pig and the Mechanical Turk. George Augustus Polgreen Bridgetower was born to his age; but he makes an appealing figure to ours, a boy taking advantage of a world that took advantage of him.

We know all too little about Bridgetower's life—it begins in the fog of his origins and ends in the mysteries of his dissipation. He exists only through frayed evidence—some eighteenth-century newspaper reports; a few sheets of music; a packet of correspondence from Samuel Wesley (the "English Mozart"); mention in Beethoven's letters; and a few appearances in the memoirs of the delightful Charlotte Papendiek, one of Queen Charlotte's household retinue. Dove's poetic biography allows her to embroider the facts, to cobble up scenes that should have happened, to ignore what scholarship might discover, if there were anything left to discover.

In the past, the poet's grand ambitions have outreached her modest gifts. From the beginning of this overlong and sometimes confused sequence, Dove struggles to master the tone, with results frequently embarrassing. She wonders what would have happened had Beethoven not been Beethoven:

> *Who knows what would have followed?*
> *They might have palled around some,*
> *just a couple of wild and crazy guys*
> *strutting the town like rock stars,*
> *hitting the bars for a few beers, a few laughs . . .*
> *instead of falling out over a girl.*

A *couple of wild and crazy guys*! I'm not sure what's dopier here, the dated hipness or the allusion to Steve Martin. It makes you want to write "Peri Bathous" all over again.

Dove has the supreme confidence that comes to most people only after a night of binge drinking, when they clamber up on a bar table and launch into "Danny Boy." In the midst of the biography, she has inserted a short play on the quarrel between Beethoven and his young protégé. Bridgetower declares,

> I'm a natural man, born under a magical caul,
> I'm that last plump raisin in the cereal bowl;
> I'm the gravy you lick from your mashed potatoes,
> I'm creamier than chocolate, juicier than ripe tomatoes!
> I'm older than the ages, yet younger than a minute;
> I'll parade upon a pinhead or waltz upon a spinet.

(I can't ignore the couplet just afterward: "Hell, if I'd been Oedipus, old Jocasta / would've stayed alive just to call me her masta!") Dove justifies the silliness by claiming that this is the sort of humor Austrians admire—if so, the worse for Austria! But why lard the notes with smirking asides like "Ouch! That's gotta hurt" or "Bitter? You betcha"? Or elsewhere throw in inane commentary like "I know, / that sucked; you get the drift"? Or have Beethoven's copyist say to a barmaid, "You've given us some / heavenly head . . . on the beer, I mean"?

Can it get worse? Of course, it can! The playlet includes some "bad girls" singing to the tune of the old Angels' hit, "My Boyfriend's Back":

> Othello's back and there's gonna be a ruckus:
>   Hey Viennese, Othello's back!
> He'll grab your Hooters girl and shout:
> Come here gal, and pluck us!
>   Hey Viennese, Othello's back!
>   Oy, the violin's his only training.
>   Boy, his Wortschatz needs explaining!

I imagine there's a red-light version in which the word "pluck" is not used. I used to think that Thomas Pynchon had written the worst comic songs in English literature, but I stand corrected.

For all Dove's research (she employed an assistant), she still believes the old canard that Napoleon died of arsenic poisoning. There are pointless diversions and diverticula involving, amid much else, the theft of Haydn's head, though this is of no relevance to Bridgetower's life. The only poems here with the odor and rhetorical flourish of the age have been cast in the voice of Charlotte Papendiek, who has the hungry eye of a fashion reporter and rarely forgets to mention a person's clothes. Dove has freely altered and improved the originals, so the genius of Papendiek is all the poet's—but Beethoven and Bridgetower and everyone else are the crudest cardboard compared to the ever watchful, ever alert Assistant Keeper of the Wardrobe and Reader to Her Majesty. After his long neglect, poor George Bridgetower deserved better.

Bridgetower's life might make a brilliant opera—and, wouldn't you know it, someone has already had the idea. It debuted two years ago.

Arda Collins

Arda Collins comes to her first book fully formed, and it's a little scary. The title may be *It Is Daylight*, but the cover is black, and the title page is black—the Goths have at last taken over Yale University Press. Louise Glück, who chose the book for the Yale Series of Younger Poets, provides an intimate, bemused introduction that finds a blood-tie from Collins to Berryman and Dickinson, those poets of airless self-dramatization. It might be more accurate to say that she's a grown-up version of Wednesday Addams, the sort of girl happiest raising spiders or trying to electrocute her younger brother.

These poems take place in the happy, happy suburbs, so of course the unnamed speaker is miserable—if the Welcome Wagon were a hearse, she'd be overjoyed.

At last, terror has arrived.

Next door, the house has gone up in flames.

A woman runs from the burning wreck, her face smeared

with blood and ashes. She screams that her children are kidnapped.

It's truly exciting, and what more would anyone ask?

The blood and ashes, those manifest signs of mourning and penitence, suggest an attention almost religious. In these affectless monologues, even the disasters are deadpan. (Collins has perhaps learned something from Anne Carson, our master of Keatonesque delivery.) The paranoia and numbness that infuse the poems create a world where the speaker doesn't know how to respond to the terrible things that happen. Normality looks odd to her—"Nearby, a gathering of // wives are seated at a bamboo // table. They wear suits and dainty shoes // and little anguish veils across their faces. // They have expensive, sharp silverware." Such portrayals of the lifelessness of the living (the dead, to her, are not dead—they're just tanning) are delicious. When Collins goes too far, it's a devastatingly funny too far—the ladies above "have handmade White House // and Pentagon salt-and-pepper shakers."

Collins is a Nietzschean fatalist, yet the world is a mystery to her, a cipher that can never quite be decoded. It's peculiar when a book's tone and manner are riveting, but its content banal, though even banalities can have irresistible fascination.

I thought how god loves this place;

the grass was coming in, and the crocuses.

What if someone died, or got fired,

or vomited alone in the middle of the night?

The apartments were wood on the outside.

They were stained red like the color of a picnic table.

I was so ugly, I wasn't sure I'd even be able to drive.

At first I thought she'd written, "It was so ugly," but her wording is more telling. This flat deposition (for a lawsuit never to be concluded) displays Marianne Moore's love for the minutiae of being. If Collins has none of Moore's élan or her enchanted gift for description, the younger poet sees the world through strange eyes, and in them the old world is made new again. (If Collins were a Martian, it would all make sense.) Our younger poets were born a hundred years after the moderns; no wonder the lessons of Pound and Eliot and Moore and Stevens seem antediluvian, they've been so often absorbed and re-absorbed (when you teach "In a Station of the Metro" now, you have to explain a lot about the Métro of 1914). Collins, whatever her debts, has learned how to make the ordinary bear the sorrows of hell.

This poet is only dimly aware of her virtues. The book is far too long (though most first books would be stronger at half the length); and the poems become too comfortable with their stark monotone, their theatrical double-spacing, their fiercely prosaic line (Collins has a wicked sense of the demotic—"You go to your piano lesson. You // stink"). More is the enemy of better here. The occasional touch of run-of-the-mill surrealism makes some poems seem to lie on a spur line from the Ashbery factory. Sometimes the poems leave me baffled (I don't get the point of a long poem about a serial killer, or a dreary prose poem about God and microwave ovens). After ninety pages, even lack of affect becomes affectation.

Still, this creepy, irresistible book is a masterful debut. It's impossible to know what Collins will do next, but more of the same would be tedious rather than unbearable. Louise Glück, comparing her to other poets, has apparently forgotten that the abrupt manner, the goggle-eyed guilelessness, and the bloodless tone (like that of a high-functioning victim of Asperger's syndrome) were long ago patented by Glück herself. If the vampires of *Twilight* wrote poetry, it would be this sort of poetry—they long to fit in, too.

The Sovereign Ghost of Wallace Stevens

Wallace Stevens was not quite a teenager when Whitman died. Divided by some sixty years and the Civil War, these famous stay-at-homes were both elbowing representatives of a character peculiarly American. It was cunning for Whitman to pretend to be an American rough, though his rough edges were largely of his own making, and inspired of Stevens to conceal his poetic imagination beneath the wool suit of an expert in surety bonds. One life might be laid upon the affinities of the other: they shared the nonconforming education (Stevens a Harvard man, but a non-degree student), the late access to mature poetry (*Leaves of Grass* published at thirty-six, *Harmonium* at forty-three), the belated recognition and almost bardic status, the vagueness about the private life (we are as mystified by the sexuality of the one as the other). These are the types and conditions of self-invention, the restlessness of an American identity more familiar as lighting out for the territories, both men staying put in a country founded on the idea of moving on.

The poet has interior landscapes in which to disappear, and conformities without that conceal a radical soul within—Stevens was a lawyer, so was his father, so were his two brothers. What is Jaggers or Tulkinghorn but a man paid to keep secrets? (One might say of Stevens that the secret he kept at last from himself was the secret of himself.) Finally, there is the poetry, its achievement an imposed wholeness, Whitman endlessly tinkering with and augmenting *Leaves*, Stevens wanting to lodge his life's work under the title *The Whole of Harmonium: The Grand Poem*.

Just as forged oil portrait or period drama eventually betrays the date of its creation (as if there were a terrible secret it could not contain), poems eventually reveal the terms of their time—we become old enough to read them in their spectral hour, and they become old enough to let us. Here too, Whitman and Stevens form a nexus more than an estrangement: their love of exotic places and foreign words; the multitudes they contained but resisted; their imaginative excess or overplus. One could never confuse two poetries so divorced by influence or design, the poems formed in different periods with different antagonisms. (Yet aren't these the most philosophically addled of American poets?) The shadows of biography give access to something less than architecture but more than accident—the progress of a country that encourages certain types of character, or at least does not eliminate them. At Whitman's birth, the territory west of the Mississippi lay vastly unexplored; and until the Mexican War the far west and southwest were not yet America. The America of twenty-one states had added only seventeen more by the birth of Stevens—when young, he knew a country still barely formed.

We include Stevens in that catchall group the moderns, those poets who changed American verse into something still recognizable a century later. The moderns were rudely different from one another, but they gave American poetry a vast armory of practice not exhausted yet. Their heirs now have heirs (and those heirs, heirs); their legacy of redskins and palefaces, of the raw and the cooked, invented the poetry we call our own—and much that the English and Irish call their own as well. If their impulses were variant, their poetry in part incompatible, and their relations at times hostile, Frost, Stevens, Williams, Pound, Moore, and Eliot largely set the terms for the poetry written afterward. They have generated such a vast secondary literature, had their coldest fires raked over, young Ph.D.'s in waiting must look at the library shelves in despair.

The compelling thing about the moderns is that a reader doesn't have to choose among them—each is a monument to choices made and values discovered. To adore one is not to adore all; but one can adore all, or almost all (my own blindness extends to Williams), without reservation or rank. Part of the invention of self proved to be breaking the contract with the settled assumptions of period verse. It's easy to underestimate that moment in American letters, when certain boundaries and stock notions about poetry were, in geological terms, erased almost overnight. Between 1909 (*Personae*) and 1923 (*Harmonium*), there was a tectonic shift in what a poem had to do to be called a poem.

Harmonium is one of the most violently original, uncategorizable books ever published by an American poet. Critics said Stevens's "diction, in strangeness of effect, lags but little after Miss Sitwell"; that "you are struck by a sort of aridity"; that one poem "defies completely all rational explanations." (The reactions to *Leaves of Grass* had been even more bewildered). Almost a century later, a reader still finds himself lost in the land of the Oklahoma firecat and the Palaz of Hoon, falling among characters like Don Joost and Chieftain Iffucan of Azcan, having wandered into a bizarre world more familiar in Lear's limericks or Carroll's nonsense verse. There are poems that don't start in the right place and poems that stop in the wrong one. Some are cast in plodding end-stopped blank verse, some have a smattering of rhyme, and some indulge in the wild shouts and alarums of "Ohoyaho, / Ohoo," "tink and tank and tunk-a-tunk-tunk," and "Tum-ti-tum, / Ti-tum-tum-tum!" In short, the poems are so strange, so unlikely, sometimes they don't seem poems at all.

One of Stevens's demonic gifts is be able to write beautifully, almost at will:

> You know how Utamaro's beauties sought
> The end of love in their all-speaking braids.
> You know the mountainous coiffures of Bath.
> Alas! Have all the barbers lived in vain
> That not one curl in nature has survived?
> Why, without pity on these studious ghosts,
> Do you come dripping in your hair from sleep?

I might complain about the talking hair, which lies barely within the license of metaphor (in part because the stillness of *ukiyo-e* prints and the almost unreadable whitened faces make every gesture in Utamaro speak—whether the flash of a kimono's design or the melodrama of a woman's most animalistic feature, her head of hair). The final image, however, is redolent of the terror and possession of dreams. Yet later in the same poem, "Le Monocle de Mon Oncle" (surely the smuggest title in modernist verse, and the most madcap), Stevens writes:

The fops of fancy in their poems leave
Memorabilia of the mystic spouts,
Spontaneously watering their gritty soils.
I am a yeoman, as such fellows go.
I know no magic trees, no balmy boughs,
No silver-ruddy, gold-vermilion fruits.

Everything direct and suggestive in the first passage seems padded with horsehair stuffing here, translated into a musty language out of Burton's *The Book of the Thousand Nights and a Night* or FitzGerald's *Rubáiyát of Omar Khayyám*. This is a yeoman talking like a fop. (What yeoman in the past four centuries ever said, "I am a yeoman"?) Part of Stevens's imagination emerged from such baggy, perfumed Victorian translations, though his ornamental phrases out-Burton Burton and out-FitzGerald FitzGerald. Stevens's imagination is more distorted than clarified by his eastern pillow-book fancies (perhaps insurance lawyers were the equivalent of sultans — I suspect their underlings thought so). Whenever he indulges in his visions of Persians or Aztecs or whatever they are, his imagination grows reckless and incontinent.

Disaffected with the modern, especially the modern city, Stevens wrote his fiancée in 1908, "That elevated train coming home with its negroes and cheap people! Dearest, keep me from seeing all that. It is nonsense but it wrecks me." Real life was the nonsense — that's the ugly end of Stevens' aestheticism, the denial of the humdrum, mundane world outside (not just the blacks as a faceless class, but "cheap people"). Stevens never felt the vivifying humanity of subway passengers apparent in the peephole photographs of Walker Evans. Stevens's unpleasant side has often been ignored. He was more generous ten years later, when he wrote, during the draft that followed America's entry into the Great War,

The negroes on the platform ran up and down shaking hands with those in the cars. The few white people who happened to be near took an indulgent attitude. They regard negroes as absurdities. They have no sympathy with them. I tried to take that point of view: to laugh at these absurd animals, in order to understand how it was convenable that one should feel. But the truth is that I feel

*thrilling emotion at these draft movements. . . . It makes no differ-
ence whether the men are black or white.*

This is responsive observation coiled around casual racism (the black
draftees are still *absurd animals* to him—his benevolent feelings seem
provoked more by the draft); such passages measure how narrowly
Stevens avoided a suffocating misanthropy. He wasn't beyond writing
from Cuba a few years after that he "went up to a nigger policeman to
get my bearings and found that the poor thing could not even understand me." *The poor thing.*

The giddiness of early Stevens, the tragicomedy that attends even
his more serious verse, never entirely left him; but like most comic
routines it could not be mechanically repeated without becoming
tiresome or desperate. (As one critic wrote of *Harmonium,* Stevens
"must . . . take in more of human experience, or give up writing alto-
gether.") The poems are so peculiar, critics were awhile catching up.
To love Stevens, you have to love his deformities and even his monstrosities, as you do the wretched, self-conscious lines in Whitman. (A
poet's bad lines are sometimes those he feels he *has* to write in order
to call himself a poet—and are occasionally just the lunatic edge of an
imagination that under similar anxieties produces a masterpiece.) The
poems are lessened and even ruined by such oddities; but, without
the arterial energies they solicit and unleash, the better poems might
be nothing. The license of exaggeration and exorbitance is the guilty
evidence of the pressure of imagination elsewhere.

It's hard at first to know how to take lines like "When this yokel
comes maundering, / Whetting his hacker"—the pleasure for the poet
seems to lie largely in the jointed grotesqueries of the language. The
words parse, but are excess to the lines' reason. (The preposterousness
of such lines has licensed a lot of freakish language since.) So much
of even very good Stevens is cast in this language—half fairy-tale, half
kindergarten gibberish—the reader must embrace the vice as a virtue or simply admire the emperor's clothes, however naked they make
him. Much ink has been spilled justifying stanzas like

> *The lacquered loges huddled there*
> *Mumbled zay-zay and a-zay, a-zay.*

The moonlight
Fubbed the girandoles.

The poem is titled "The Ordinary Women" — just those cheap people Stevens loathed, though he tries to see them transformed. R. P. Blackmur, in his swamp-clearing essay "Examples of Wallace Stevens," defends the poet against charges of preciosity:

> *The loges huddled probably because it was dark or because they didn't like the ordinary women, and mumbled perhaps because of the moonlight, perhaps because of the catarrhs, or even to keep key to the guitars. Moonlight, for Mr. Stevens, is mental, fictive . . . ; naturally it fubbed the girandoles (which is equivalent to cheated the chandeliers, was stronger than the artificial light, if any). . . . I am at a loss, and quite happy there, to know anything literally about this poem. Internally, inside its own words, I know it quite well by simple perusal. The charm of the rhymes is enough to carry it over any stile. The strange phrase, "Fubbed the girandoles," has another charm, like that of the rhyme, and as inexplicable: the approach of language, through the magic of elegance, to nonsense.*

So it's all nonsense and *elegance*, then! Elegance is the vacant form of eloquence.

This argument is unsatisfying in a number of ways. The poem isn't nearly so mysterious. *Loges* has a specific meaning — originally referring to the theater boxes beside the stage, later it indicated the lower rows of a cinema balcony (the *OED* has so far ignored this meaning). Loge tickets could be more expensive than those in the orchestra, sometimes having plusher seats; and it is not likely to the loges, with their spacious and dramatic view of the screen, that these ordinary women have repaired. We know they have no money to spare ("Then from their poverty they rose"), so an evening at the cinema ("They crowded / The nocturnal halls"), with its "lacquered loges" and gilt appointments, would be an escape from care ("They flung monotony behind"). I'm going to assume that these women are watching some eight-reeler rather than a play, because the teens and twenties were the great age of the silent screen — and the everyday refuge of the working poor. The film may be some Douglas Fairbanks feature set in a palace—perhaps *The Three Musketeers* (1921). The Dumas classic certainly has "civil fans" and coiffures in abundance—and there is the famous subplot involving the theft of the queen's diamond brooch ("How explicit the coiffures became, / The diamond point, the sapphire point, / The sequins / Of the civil fans!").

Of course, it doesn't have to be any particular film—Hollywood noted very early the romantic effect of castles and palaces. And the "palace" ("They flitted / Through the palace walls") may be the picture house itself—*Palace* was a common theater name. The film would not necessarily have been silent, of course; big-city picture palaces employed ensembles or even orchestras in accompaniment (the talkies threw thousands of musicians out of work). After *The Birth of a Nation* (1915), major releases were provided with full scores. The classical guitar is not a standard instrument for orchestra, but could be called in as a score demanded. (In *The Mark of Zorro* [1920], Don Diego promises to have his servant play his guitar beneath Lolita's window.) Even so, the "guitars" to whose music these women "flitted" might have been imaginary, heard with the inner ear—a fantasy that begins in the cinema and ends in reverie.

To *fub* is to cheat, a variant of "fob" (Shakespeare has "fub'd off" in 2 *Henry IV*). A *girandole*, according to the *OED*, is a "branched support for candles or other lights, either in the form of a candlestick . . . or more commonly as a bracket projecting from a wall." One might see the former in a palace, or the latter in the lobby of a cinema or on the walls of the auditorium itself. The poem manages to mingle the world in the screen with the architecture of the cinema, but that's surely the point—the viewer is most easily translated from the commonplaces of one world when there are points of contact with the other. (In Keaton's *Sherlock Jr.* [1924], the hero steps into the world of the screen, so the illusion is an old one.) If the moonlight "fubbed the girandoles," the romantic moon—arc light for centuries of lovers—fools or deceives the house lights in the cinema. (This must be the moon in the film, not the one floating outside.) Presumably it is for just such escapist make-believe that the ordinary women pay their dime—the artificial moonlight seems more real than what casts shadows on their way back to their ordinary lives.

The scene these women watch and then enter (having left behind their coughing, their "dry catarrhs") is presumably the "vapid haze of the window-bays" on which such cinematic moonglow falls—only a lighting effect, of course. The counterfeit moonlight deceives the paltry light of their world for an hour or two. (The light that projects through the nitrate film stock to cast shadows on the silver screen—the hazy conic beam caught by the smoke floating in cinemas of the day—would be a kind of moonbeam, too.) This cinematic reading of the poem, I discovered belatedly, was advanced as long ago as 1959 in a lecture by Clark Griffith, according to William Burney, who develops a somewhat off-center variant in his book *Wallace Stevens*. Oddly, critics still treat the poem, in Harriet Monroe's words, as if its "play of whimsicalities . . . seem a mere banter of word-bubbles."

The astonishing thing is that Blackmur, as close to a genius as American criticism has ever produced (excepting only Poe), gave up on meaning so easily, or was just as enchanted by what he took to be nonsense as the women by the nonsense on the screen (even critics want the transports of fiction). It's not even clear if he understood what Stevens meant by *loges*. If they were "huddled," the seats might have been tightly compacted; but loge seats were usually spacious. Blackmur turned this into a bizarre fantasy where the loges dislike the ordinary women and mumble about them—but the loges are more likely a metonym, the more refined cinema-goers muttering at the screen in the same romantic tremor as the ordinary women. The mumbling in the loges, "zay-zay and a-zay, a-zay," is neatly picked up a few stanzas later, when the guitarists "rumbled a-day and a-day, a-day." The viewers sound enraptured, the guitarists merely morose, as if singing an antique chorus ("Alack a day!" or "A-well a day!" may be the phrase referred to).

After the mumbling in the loges, the force of the following stanza ("And the cold dresses that they wore") suggests that the poor women have been transported to the "haze of the window-bays" on the silver screen. The "cold dresses" could be either the thin cotton dresses such ordinary women ordinarily wear, or the sheer gowns of the women on the screen, with whom the poor women identify. At the end of the poem, the movement is reversed, and the women abandon the guitars, and "to catarrhs / They flitted / Through the palace walls." They return to their petty illnesses and daily complaints, leaving the Palace, or whatever palace the Palace projected.

I am at a loss, and quite happy there, to know anything literally about this poem. For Blackmur, the poetry lies in the ignorance, in the near approach to nonsense. (I suppose many readers still feel that way.) It's difficult to know what Stevens would have thought of this, but I suspect he was as mystified by his admirers as they were sometimes mystified by him. No man writes phrases like "fubbed the girandoles" who doesn't want to be taken as a bit of a dandy, an aesthete in yellow kid-gloves—but, unless he's also a kook, he has something precise in mind. I'd quarrel with Blackmur that the words Stevens used in *Harmonium* (*diaphanes, pannicles, carked, ructive, cantilene, buffo, princox, funest*) were always the most exact or exacting available; but, even if so, words have an effect beyond their meaning.

After rattling off a score of such arcane terms, Blackmur claims that "not a word listed . . . is used preciously; not one was chosen as an elegant substitute for a plain term; each, in its context, was a word definitely meant." (He doesn't mention bizarre phrases like "Paphian caricatures," "aspic nipples," "scullion of fate," "unburgherly apocalypse," "musician of pears, principium / And lex," "nincompated pedagogue," "kremlin of kermess," and much else.) A word may be exact without being useful or expedient. Blackmur's case is that the poet's language was not precious, because used precisely—and yet the language of Sir Thomas Browne was precise. If *diaphanes, pannicles,* and *cantilene* aren't precious, saved in their precision to be condemned by their perfume, no word can be. The difficulty is that Stevens thought the poem better if grown from such mannered phrases, or translated into them. Even were the words accurate, they lose more then they gain by their affectation. This is the problem Stevens suffered from the start—reaching after one good, he commits two bads.

Much of Stevens is tedious, refractory, pompous, or ponderous; and even his masterpieces are full of bombast and puffery. As he got older, he fell into blank-verse philosophizing no less like boilerplate than the reams of legal documents that presumably issued from his office. He's a poet whose words you want to get behind—the language is as much an obstacle as a pleasure—but, when you parse those phrases, when you go to the Palaz of Hoon and come back again, you're often a little disappointed. The philosophy of his poems, the grand ones as well as the pleasingly trivial, is that of a freshman class in ontology, epistemology, or aesthetics. Stevens had a high opinion of his philosophical gifts—he was prickly and childish when a late lecture was rejected by the *Review of Metaphysics*. Eliot, who *was* a trained philosopher and possessed the subtlest mind among the moderns—perhaps the subtlest mind in all American poetry, if you exclude Melville—knew enough to leave the philosophy out, or to bury it deeply.

The best poems in Stevens don't require the philosophy (if there's an exception, "Thirteen Ways of Looking at a Blackbird" proves that philosophy is rarely more honored in the observance than in the breach), and the worst are deformed by it. The long poems, those most drawn to Stevens's metaphysical itch, those that feel it necessary to justify their length in terms of abstractions rendered and sustained (but rarely blooded), have made critics the most diagnostic. The critical response to Stevens has itself so often been abstract, so full of critic's legalese, it has made him more a great cloud of being than a man who at times played with words.

I'm not a ready admirer of Stevens' long poems, which permit too large a canvas for his vices, though I would except "Sea Surface Full of Clouds," "The Man with the Blue Guitar," and "Esthétique du Mal"— I hate myself for not loving a monolith like "Notes toward a Supreme Fiction," which has been crushed by the burden of its ideas. The long poems are often drowsy, tropical, and hard to stay awake through (like vast stretches of Tennyson, in their way)—you have to like warmed-over Santanyana to tolerate them. They often seem the last gasp of Romantic tenor rather than the start of something new. Late Stevens, indeed, is sometimes composed as if early Stevens never existed—the *girandoles* have almost vanished, replaced by the metaphysical wallpaper. The long poems have been overrated, perhaps because they are so often about art—critics love poems about poetry and love even better poems about poetics, as if they took more wisdom to write.

Yet even in a poem as tedious as "Sunday Morning," Stevens at the end rises to magnificence:

> *Deer walk upon our mountains, and the quail*
> *Whistle about us their spontaneous cries;*
> *Sweet berries ripen in the wilderness;*
> *And, in the isolation of the sky,*

> At evening, casual flocks of pigeons make
> Ambiguous undulations as they sink,
> Downward to darkness, on extended wings.

Passages like this, and there are scores of them scattered through the work, justify the acres of dull philosophizing, lacking the odor of a necessary world.

Stevens continues to cast a spell over readers, like that other architect of high Romantic nonsense, Hart Crane. The critics who soon talked evasively of "pure poetry" (as Stevens did himself, though nothing is more impure than his hobbledehoy language) were trying desperately to compare Stevens to what had been, which is irresistible and misleading—you need to read Mallarmé to understand him, perhaps, but Mallarmé doesn't take you very far. For such a poet, the only accurate criticism must be comparison to what is yet to come. Stevens is a poet not predictable from the poetry he borrowed from and was inspired by—he became something that could not yet be named, and at last became his heirs.

Like Swinburne, like Hart Crane, like Ashbery, Stevens is reduced by explanation. The incense of the words themselves can be so heady that readers swoon (you can see why, loving the effect, Blackmur was wary of the meaning). Such poets often seem translations of themselves—their poems might just as well be fanciful versions from Hungarian or Langue d'oc. If I prefer poems more complicated the more their effects are exposed (consider Eliot, or Lowell, or Hill—and think of Shakespeare), that is a preference armed as a prejudice. Stevens could write so well without recourse to his dress-up costumes and Masonic vestments (at times he seems decked out in the leavings of a theatrical trunk), it's a pity that you have to wade through a great bog of minor work to get at poems that sharpen the responses of the imagination.

John N. Serio, the editor of Stevens's *Selected Poems*, is one of those fond readers of Stevens who are a little too fond. The poet did not publish his *Collected Poems* until the last months of his life. He long refused to draw a line under his career—and fortunately he abandoned the idea of calling the thing *The Whole of Harmonium*. What the editor has given us is perhaps *The Half of Harmonium*, but it is well judged, defined without being definitive. Few poems familiar to readers have been excluded (I'm tempted to say none at all), and where there is an omission it's filled by something almost as interesting. With Stevens, you could take a lucky dip and get a selection that would spoil a lesser poet.

The table of contents might have identified, as did the fine Library of America *Collected Poems*, the poems added to *Harmonium* in 1931; and the editor might have noted the dates of the poems drawn from *Opus Posthumous*. It is delightful, however, to see the poems surrounded by so much space (the Library of America edition is compactly printed, perfectly legible, but stuffed to the gills). *Harmonium* was a small, squat book, easy to hold in the palm—it's important to return a poet to the eye, when we cannot return him to the ear.

In his rambling introduction, the editor is given to that mode of criticism halfway between a fan's notes and a publisher's blurb. He claims that Stevens "has the uncanny talent to evoke pure being"; but, when Stevens falls into metaphysical guff, it's almost always inimical to his gifts, just the place where he's most given to fustian and empty emotion. The editor writes as if Stevens were an irrational mystic:

> *His poems often had sources beyond the rational and sometimes surpassed even his own cognitive understanding. . . . Stevens's poetic gift to express humanity through his art, although it might have derived from his personal response to the world, his idiosyncratic sensibility, is never mere self-expression. . . . Like all genuine art, it is universal.*

I wonder whether the poet or the editor has taken leave of his senses. Mathematics may be universal. Only when poetry fails to be universal does it become poetry.

The magnificence of Stevens comes at a cost, the cost we pay for Whitman—logorrhea of an uncharming and embarrassing sort, absurd notions, passages too private with their own pleasure, tone-deafness, lofty ambitions insufficiently grounded, and gouts of gimcrack philosophy. The longer the poems, the more likely they were disfigured—even defeated—by these defects. Yet Stevens is our major poet of emotional extinction. There's so little human warmth in his poems (occasionally, rarely, in the comic glimmer), you couldn't toast a marshmallow with it; but the poetry seems the product of, and most terribly reveals, a damaged soul.

The moderns as a group appear, at this distance, far more crippled or stunted than the confessional poets who were their distant heirs and rivals. Eliot suffered nervous collapse and desperate religiosity; Moore a withdrawn adulthood, like an adolescence from whose chrysalis she never emerged; Williams the bouts of goatish womanizing; Frost his egotistic and monstrous cruelties; and Stevens a frozen hauteur and morose unhappiness. Pound is the only one who emerges as a relatively complete man, full of broad loves and generosities, only to degenerate into idées fixes, fascist politics, fetid anti-Semitism, and quite possibly, in late middle-age, progressive dementia.

Unlike the Romantics, the American moderns lived to be old, not one dying before his seventy-fifth birthday, Pound and Frost almost reaching ninety. They survived long enough for time already to have winnowed taste (when we think of the might-have-beens, of Aiken and H. D., our grandfathers had already dismissed them, however much critics have tried to drag them back). After this long century, their classical notions—of the poet's impersonality, of the high ambitions of art, of the sculptural shape of the poem—seem eaten up with romance, even the rot of romance; but what matters is less the way in which their modernity was tainted with a past than in how they reformed a poetry that in 1909 still shared the timidity of English verse.

I wish that Stevens had developed the caustic humor his misanthropy permitted him, instead of the moonstruck fancies to which it drove him. Among the shorter verses added to the second edition of *Harmonium* are "Boston with a Note-book":

> *Lean encyclopaedists, inscribe an Iliad.*
> *There's a weltanschauung of the penny pad.*

and "Soupe Sans Perles":

> *I crossed in '38 in the* Western Head.
> *It depends which way you crossed, the tea-belle said.*

Stevens's affection for such ironies must have been limited. The editor misses these; but they have a tone—an antagonism to convention—brutal and unexpected. They come with a small electric shock. Unfortunately, they're buried with verses that exhibit Stevens in all his vice, like "A perfect fruit in perfect atmosphere. / Nature as Pinakothek. Whist! Chanticleer . . ."

Stevens requires the condition of taste merely to begin, because he's not well served by his weaknesses, or by the time-serving poetry to which weakness gave way. There are wonderful poems that almost everyone likes, including "The Snow Man," "The Emperor of Ice-Cream," "Anecdote of the Jar," "Thirteen Ways of Looking at a Black-bird," "No Possum, No Sop, No Taters"; but there are poems nearly as lovely almost no one mentions — "From the Misery of Don Joost," "Tea at the Palaz of Hoon," "The Man Whose Pharynx Was Bad," "Sad Strains of a Gay Waltz," "Re-statement of Romance," "Anglais Mort à Florence," "Yellow Afternoon," "Holiday in Reality," "Burghers of Petty Death," "This Solitude of Cataracts," and "Bouquet of Roses in Sunlight." I would cheerfully trade "The Comedian as the Letter C," "The Man with the Blue Guitar," "The Auroras of Autumn," and "An Ordinary Evening in New Haven" for such poems; but Stevens is so capacious a poet, he has room for my obtuseness.

We don't usually think of Stevens in terms of the opportunities missed — he remains one of our great poets despite his sins (not because of them), and a model of imaginative industry. Three-quarters of his poetry appeared after the age of fifty, and almost two-thirds after the age of sixty. Still, if he had held a job less demanding, or one that gratified him in different ways, or that didn't require such rococo artifice and moony fantasies (as, all too soon, his marriage did), we might have had a poetry with more social observation and asperity. Or perhaps no poetry at all.

Eliot in Ink

Grover Cleveland was still president when T. S. Eliot was born. His earliest surviving letter was written to his father from the family summer home in Gloucester. The nine-year-old Eliot was deferential, curious in a boyish way, concerned about some missing sunflowers and a broken microscope. A shy child, he suffered from a congenital hernia and once asked his nurse why the naked boy in a book wore no truss.

Eliot longed to be a philosopher rather than a poet. The Great War broke out shortly after he arrived in Germany for graduate study; he escaped to England, unable to pay the family that had boarded him. Eliot was a young man in a hurry, but it wasn't clear where he was hurrying—his life was not a design but a sharp series of accidents. His dissertation was accepted by Harvard, but the U-boats prevented his return for the necessary *viva* (Harvard pursued him for a faculty appointment long after he had given up thought of academia). He had dabbled in poetry at Harvard, and by luck that impresario Ezra Pound soon forced "Prufrock" and other poems into *Poetry* magazine. Still, this dapper young man was unsure of his vocation. He married his wife Vivien three months after meeting her, and it almost became a life sentence. The Eliots were perennially short of money and frequently had to beg from his family. Not until the young poet was unexpectedly hired by the Colonial and Foreign Department at Lloyds Bank did his financial burdens ease a little.

The working title for *The Waste Land*, borrowed from Dickens ("He Do the Police in Different Voices"), reflects the curious lack of cohesion in Eliot's character. The accidental banker spent his evenings writing articles for extra cash, at first for philosophy journals but soon for literary magazines. He did not think himself a poet for a long while, and even then poems came fitfully when they came at all. Laboring at the bank, laboring at prose to keep out of debt, Eliot wrote little verse during his first years in London, because he was simply too exhausted to think about poetry.

After a poet is dead, his letters are the windows to his soul—or perhaps just the cellar doors. These two volumes detail Eliot's struggle to find a career and to shoulder his way into the London literary world, a school of sharks where friends reviewed their friends and publishers reviewed their authors. Most of the early letters were addressed to a small cast: Eliot's parents and his brother Henry (a grinding businessman who later showed striking intelligence and relentless generosity), the local literati, and a few gossipy London hostesses. Among the literary figures, the most impressive were Pound; Virginia Woolf, whose viperish tongue was more lethal than any poison of the Borgias (she found Eliot "peevish, plaintive, egotistical," with a "sepulchral voice"); and Bertrand Russell, infinitely kind even when not trying to bed your wife (it's possible that he and Vivien enjoyed a brief fling).

Many of the letters are merely social, invitations extended or declined, appointments made or broken; but Eliot's hobnobbing life prepared the opportunities that followed, especially the editorship of the *Criterion*, which became the premier literary journal of its day. Eliot had a masochistic capacity for work—the magazine was "run without an office, without any staff or business manager, by a sickly bank clerk and his wife." It was also run without a salary, in the short hours after Eliot returned home each evening from Lloyds. The Eliots' tiny apartment with its lurid orange wallpaper, the terrible isolation from his family (at thirty-five, he still wrote fawning letters to his mother), and all the chatter about chatter—the hothouse atmosphere of London between the wars, and of Eliot's buttoned-up private life, became the vivid background to *The Waste Land*, which more than ever seems a highly personal, even confessional poem, as well as a savage social analysis.

Only at rare moments does the reader get a glimpse behind the curtain of discretion Eliot used to guard his days. Vivien suffered physical ills by the dozen—neuritis, neuralgia, colitis, migraines, and much else that the medical world lacked the tools to diagnose or the medicine to cure. The care the Eliots received verged on quackery—

doctors offered hydrotherapy, galvanism, "manipulation and hand vibration," as well as colonic irrigation, sachets of glands, and injections of Bavarian bacillus. The practice of the day seems little removed from medieval bloodletting and cupping.

Eliot was extraordinarily politic, as a good editor must be, publishing Woolf and E. M. Forster largely as "window dressing." Later, when he had been rescued from the bank by the upstart publishing firm of Faber and Gwyer, he was perhaps guilty of sharp practice in stealing authors from the Woolfs' Hogarth Press. Eliot also wrote a particularly nasty and unjust letter to Marianne Moore that cannot wholly be excused by the crisis in his marriage. (His letters pre-Vivien show a puckish humor almost entirely absent while they were together.)

Eliot's anti-Semitism is luridly on display—he refers to a "Jew merchant" and allows himself pronouncements like "I am sick of doing business with Jew publishers." It's damning that such remarks are made only to those who share the prejudice. Yet he relied on his friends Leonard Woolf and Sydney Schiff, and would have been bewildered to think disliking Jews an unusual prejudice—if Eliot's anti-Semitism was appalling, that of his wife ("horrible Jews in plush coats by the million") and his mother ("I have an instinctive antipathy to Jews, just as I have to certain animals") was even worse. Eliot's benefactor John Quinn was worse still. No one who has read the letters and journals of the time will be shocked—Sylvia Plath was making remarks only slightly milder thirty years later.

If volume 1 of these letters is a Jacobean revenge play, the hero suspecting even his friends of betrayal, volume 2 is a Restoration comedy, with a harried, overworked husband and a fretful wife ever abed. The letters can go only so far in explaining Vivien, who was insightful, doggishly loyal, and dedicated to pushing the interests of her husband— yet this local drama-queen, who briefly considered a film career, was a "teashop creature" who repelled Katherine Mansfield and made Virginia Woolf "almost vomit, so scented, so powdered, so egotistic, so morbid, so weakly." In some strange way, the Eliots made each other sick. It's hard not to think that Vivien used her distress to control her husband, as Georgie Yeats used automatic writing to control hers.

The volumes close with Eliot and his wife temporarily living apart, Vivien having entered the downward spiral that some years later led to her confinement in a mental hospital. A modest man with a streak of vanity, Eliot has not yet emerged from the underworld of marriage (Vivien is all too like Eurydice, and pays a terrible price). He could write to his mother that some believed him the "best living critic, as well as the best living poet, in England," yet go on to tell Ford Madox Ford that *The Waste Land* contained only thirty good lines.

What would have happened had Eliot died of the jaw infection he suffered in 1925, before leaving the bank? His poetic reputation, and to a large extent the critical reputation, might not have been much diminished, though like Keats he would have seemed one of the great might-have-beens of English poetry. Apart from *Four Quartets* (how avant-garde the title once seemed), he published only a few dozen pages of serious poetry afterward.

Eliot's criticism is now undervalued, dismissed by critics without half his sensibility or intelligence. The poems have so long been the foundation of modern anthologies that their reputation has almost as long worked against them (the one indispensable poem of the twentieth century is still *The Waste Land*). Eliot's best poems have almost disappeared beneath dust heaps of commentary, and the dust heaps that lie on those dust heaps. Much of his early work—"Prufrock," the "Sweeney" poems, "Gerontion," even *The Waste Land*—could be called urban eclogues, part of the turn in English poetry from the country to the city. It may take a long time to appreciate those poems afresh, after the poets who struggled against Eliot, whether as allies or enemies, are long dead; but by that time his world will seem as out of date as Pope's does to us.

The letters remind us what an old man the young Eliot was, exhausted by Lloyds, where he worked in cramped quarters beneath the sidewalk, frayed by a marriage unhappily contracted, nervous to the ends of his fingers. He sometimes seems petty, irritable, unpleasant ("Conrad Aiken is here; stupider than I remember him; in fact, stupid")—but many a saint would have strangled Vivien in her bed, and few could have borne his financial burdens. Though the banking world suited his temperament little better than his father's Hydraulic-Press Brick Company in St. Louis, literature for a long while could not support him.

It's possible to read *The Waste Land*, not as a po-faced rattle of miseries by a man who has suffered a nervous breakdown, but as a collection of mocking growls, often at his own expense—"rhythmical grumbling," he later called it. The poem's pitch-black despairs are leavened by the knockabout portrait of a workingman's pub (reading the scene aloud, Eliot was mordantly hilarious), the cynical rendering of the typist's sleazy liaison with the house-agent's clerk, and the mortal comeuppances dealt to Phlebas and others. Emotionally, it is a shockingly cold poem. The famous notes, scribbled out to pad the American edition, are more like Pope's cod learning in *The Dunciad* than the scholar's self-justification for which they are sometimes mistaken (Eliot called himself ill-read). Eliot's poems — especially the pre-Christian poems — have been so weighed down by the concrete overcoat of reputation, their terrifying humor has sometimes been forgotten or misread. With Swift, Byron, and Carroll, Eliot was one of the great comic poets in English.

The first volume of this edition appeared almost a quarter-century ago. After a Rip Van Winkle sleep, the enterprise has been revived, the earlier volume now reissued with two hundred new letters and packets of fresh annotation, with a second volume bringing the correspondence to 1925. Superbly edited, with only a smattering of errors, they include letters from the other characters in this drama, letting us overhear the voices that surrounded Eliot. Still, important though the poet remains, for whom is this vast projected edition aimed? A score of volumes may be necessary for the mobs of letters lying in wait; but, except for Eliot scholars, the books will be more tombstones than monuments.

Knowing a man by the week-by-week crawl through his life is a bit like understanding a locust by examining the dried casing; yet the anxieties boiled down into *The Waste Land* are here available in their raw state. The letters show us the graces this browbeaten life also possessed — Eliot in his thirties, wanting to hear his mother sing "The Little Tailor" again; his brother Henry on a rare visit to London stealing away with Eliot's broken typewriter and leaving his own better one behind; and Vivien calling her husband, of all things, Wonkypenky. Together these volumes are like a long Russian novel that ends in mid-career, terrifying, humiliating, exhausting.

Larkin's Toads

One summer half a century ago, Randall Jarrell and Robert Lowell spent an afternoon on a bench in Kensington Gardens, talking about contemporary poets. "Cal was for Plath that day, and Gunn — and Larkin," Jarrell's wife later wrote. "Randall was for Larkin, Larkin, and Larkin." Philip Larkin has often had that effect on readers — of immediate sympathy, and half-crazed delight. I admit to my own mixed feelings — when I read him I want to run out and press his poems upon strangers, and I want to keep them entirely to myself.

The Complete Poems, with its four-hundred-page armament of apparatus, offers as thorough an edition of Larkin's poetry as any reader will require. Those sated with the poems still have the poet's extranea — the two novels, the jazz reviews, the stray prose, and most winningly (and losingly) the letters. There is even, for those who have not lost the taste, some smutty schoolgirl fiction, a lumpish biography, and a shelf of academic criticism. Yet Larkin for most readers will always be the three mature books of poetry: *The Less Deceived* (1955), *The Whitsun Weddings* (1964), and *High Windows* (1974). Whatever his peculiar world was, it is contained there.

Larkin was a late bloomer. Perhaps his early ambitions as a poet were derailed for a time by his desire to be a novelist. Critics have said what can be said for *Jill* (1946) and *A Girl in Winter* (1947); but nothing will save them from the rainy, dreary, slightly prim things they are — they make Henry Green look like Tolstoy. Larkin was a far more conventional poet before he quit writing fiction — and his moroseness, his paralytic sense of failure, his gloomy appraisal of man (or of the man called Larkin) might in part be the good fortune of sour grapes.

The early poems scarcely hint at the poet he would become. *The North Ship* (1945) is a young man's book (I'm tempted to say a young Oxford grad's—Larkin was twenty-two), full of moony disquietude, with a long run of lovelorn poems and only the thin shiver of sensibility. Some of the verse could have been written by a provincial duffer of 1915. Still, there are lines that don't quite fit, lines that suggest something stirring beneath the dead leaves of Quiller-Couch's *Oxford Book of English Verse*. The poet who confesses to the "instantaneous grief of being alone" or describes himself as "Part invalid, part baby, and part saint" sounds like a man wearing a suit two sizes too small. You begin to hear the voice of that university librarian who kept a stash of porn in his cupboard.

It might have been better for the poet had he waited. Few poets since the Romantics have published good books in their twenties, and even the Modernists were generally at least at the cusp of thirty (Frost forty, Stevens over). Poetry, like mathematics, is a young man's game, critics used to say—but Shakespeare wrote his sonnets in his later twenties or thirties, Browning was thirty when *Dramatic Lyrics* appeared, Whitman thirty-six at the publication of *Leaves of Grass*. There will always be outliers like Rimbaud and Auden; but poetry has become more like fiction, needing the world to lend the shape that form no longer can.

By the time he wrote *The Less Deceived*, Larkin had learned the value of images redolent of the British hinterland—weedy pavements, railway platforms, the trilby hat, the cheap ring made in Birmingham, "docks where channel boats come sidling," Hall's Distemper billboards. His debts to Auden and Hardy began to be paid, instead of merely being acknowledged. The sense of place became important to a man everywhere ill at ease, one who could declare, "No, I have never found / The place where I could say / *This is my proper ground.*"

Women confused Larkin, and sex more than women. ("I had grown up to regard sexual recreation as a socially remote thing, like baccarat or clog dancing," he once admitted—*sexual recreation* is a telling phrase.) His longing fought against his dread of dissolution or panic over property rights (to be married was to be "confused / By law with someone else," an "instant claim / On everything I own / Down to my name"). Was this wariness self-preservation, or mere selfishness? In "Reasons for Attendance," the speaker watches the flushed faces of young couples at a dance—high in their high spirits, reveling in the promise of sex. Even so,

> Therefore I stay outside,
> Believing this; and they maul to and fro,
> Believing that; and both are satisfied,
> If no one has misjudged himself. Or lied.

Many of the poet's unkind and even savage remarks about women (the defaced poster of the girl in the bathing suit in "Sunny Prestatyn" is symptomatic) seem more self-hatred than misogyny. Yet it was not Larkin the misogynist who composed "Wedding-Wind." Few male poets have written so tenderly in the voice of a woman (Frost was another). Though the imagery tends toward irritation and disillusion, at the end it's plain that the farmer's bride has been borne off by a preposterous happiness:

> Shall I be let to sleep
> Now this perpetual morning shares my bed?
> Can even death dry up
> These new delighted lakes, conclude
> Our kneeling as cattle by all-generous waters?

Larkin is one of poetry's great loners—consider Coleridge, who seemed to hate being alone; or that broadminded socialite Byron; or Keats, so good at being a friend; or Auden, who couldn't shut up. ("Loneliness clarifies," Larkin wrote.) Yet a surprising number of Larkin's poems are about happiness—he's a poet of gloom sometimes struck into joy. Elizabeth Bishop had a terrible need to be loved, and one loves her in spite of it; Larkin, a terrible desire not to be loved, and one loves him because of it.

Hope always rides the razor of pessimism in Larkin's poems, and pessimism rarely denies itself the glint of hope—when he gives in entirely to misery, as in "Going, Going," he seems merely a crank. His outright nastiness is usually directed at male louts, mostly businessmen or academics; but he suffered the prejudices of his day and when that day was past liked to shock people with them. His anti-Semitism is no worse than Eliot's, or Pound's, or Sylvia Plath's; but it is no better. He loved to provoke (perhaps his most quoted line was "Books are a load of crap") yet was bewildered when people didn't understand that he had been ironic, or writing in persona—or at least saying so.

Readers were appalled by the poet's *Selected Letters* (1992), where the vile mess that was Larkin was on display; but that was the private Larkin, full of bitter, nauseating remarks about blacks, Jews, women, made often to his Colonel Blimpish schoolmates. The poetry made something less petty out of pettiness. The absence of such malice there, unless due to cowardice (if there's a courage to conviction, there can be cowardice, too), shows how little these things mattered to the poems. Poetry, if it's any good, transcends the life's sorry particulars.

The last books, *The Whitsun Weddings* and *High Windows*, secure the insecurities and perfect the imperfections that formed his style. The Larkin that Larkin became doesn't change—he just becomes more fully himself. If that man is in part a fiction, the character bodied forth would have been at home in Dickens—the poems seem at times the work of Mr. Crummles, at others that of Mr. Tulkinghorn. Yet twentieth-century poetry would have been a lesser thing, a meaner thing, without "Church Going," "I Remember, I Remember," "Mr. Bleaney," "Toads Revisited," "The Whitsun Weddings," "Talking in Bed," "An Arundel Tomb," "The Trees," "Homage to a Government," "This Be the Verse," and "Aubade"—and beyond these the quiet, sometimes overlooked poems like "Faith Healing," "At Grass," "Sad Steps," and a score of others that say something right-angled about the world, right-angled but true.

The main attraction of this scholarly edition is the massive gathering of Larkin's unpublished work. Though most was assembled piecemeal in the editions of *Collected Poems* (1988, 2003) and in *Early Poems and Juvenilia*, edited by A. T. Tolley (2005), more than fifty poems appear here for the first time. If there are scraps yet to be discovered, they have eluded the exhaustive searches of the editor, Archie Burnett.

Alas, Larkin wrote reams and reams of dull poems when young, most no more interesting than a thousand miles of scrubland—all are included here, with notes. The juvenilia make clear how stymied Larkin was by Auden. Larkin was a less attractive and less promising poet before the influence, but he couldn't become a good poet until he had shed Auden's skin. He spent three or four years writing lines like "these are twin headlights of a capitalist's car: / this, the gaslight of a trodden worker who would tread" or "The bank clerk reflects that his pay isn't large: / The professor's had up on a serious charge." (Auden struck a lot of poets dumb. Most never recovered.) Probably the older poet's only lasting gift to his admirer was the blues song, which Larkin turned to hilarious account in "Fuel Form Blues."

You hear the later Larkin before he existed, hear him in "the cold night / Drops veil on veil across the windy skies" or "Your name breathed round the tealeaves and last bun." Larkin possessed a steely modesty, an imperious shyness (until middle age, he was afflicted with a stammer). He survived Auden's robust bullying by lowering his voice, a voice without a sense of destiny, only a terror of fate. Apart from stray lines and some smirking ribaldry ("After a particularly good game of rugger / A man called me a bugger / Merely because in a loose scrum / I had my cock up his bum"), there's little to like in the unpublished work and less to love. Among that little, however, is a brief elegy for his father:

> Because there is no housing from the wind,
> No health in winter, and no permanence
> Except in the inclement grave,
> Among the littering alien snow I crave
> The gift of your courage and indifference.

The chill of indifference is enough to make the reader think (perhaps the poet means only the indifference of the dead), then think again.

Death was Larkin's overwhelming subject (if not sex, or selfishness, or just plain misery)—he was tormented by it when young, and when old wrote his last major poem about it, "Aubade." In the rag-and-bone shop of the unpublished work, there are scraps you wish the poet had rescued:

> An April Sunday brings the snow,
> Making the blossom on the plum trees green,
> Not white. An hour or two, and it will go.
> Strange that I spend that hour moving between

> *Cupboard and cupboard, shifting the store*
> *Of jam you made of fruit from these same trees:*
> *Five loads—a hundred pounds or more—*
> *More than enough for all next summer's teas,*
>
> *Which now you will not sit and eat.*
> *Behind the glass, under the cellophane,*
> *Remains your final summer—sweet*
> *And meaningless, and not to come again.*

Meaningless. There's the final twist of the knife. The previous twist is the quiet pun on "remains"—and the one before that the terrifying volta of "Which now you will not sit and eat." The ending is one small mortal wound after another. The poem was also for his father.

The tender side of Larkin, the side sometimes seen only when displaced, is often revealed as slyly as in the last stanzas of an unpublished love poem:

> *The decades of a different life*
> *That opened past your inch-close eyes*
> *Belonged to others, lavished, lost;*
> *Nor could I hold you hard enough*
> *To call my years of hunger-strife*
> *Back for your mouth to colonise.*
>
> *Admitted: and the pain is real.*
> *But when did love not try to change*
> *The world back to itself—no cost,*
> *No past, no people else at all—*
> *Only what meeting made us feel,*
> *So new, and gentle-sharp, and strange?*

How extraordinary that *colonise* seems (it's not completely softened by the tender-painful "gentle-sharp"). There was something brutish in Larkin, even Larkin in love. The plain monosyllables, unadorned with much resembling an image (compared to Larkin, Frost was a spendthrift with metaphor), create the emotional waste in which love arrives so cautiously. Yet love after drought is often scouring and harsh.

Larkin understood love's annihilation—he's one of the few modern poets (Eliot is another) I can imagine as a Metaphysical.

Archie Burnett deserves a full measure of gratitude for the labors necessary for this extraordinary edition. If such drudgery has a bit of Larkin tedium to it, every good editor must be part Mr. Bleaney. No other poet of Larkin's generation has received such meticulous and exhaustive treatment—and none of the moderns even now, apart from Eliot in Christopher Ricks's edition of the notebook poems. Burnett has provided virtually all a finicky reader could desire—all, and then more than all, for the notes and references and dates pile up like Mr. Boffin's mounds of dust in *Our Mutual Friend*. If a critic has set down an idea about Larkin in an obscure article, Burnett seems to know about it; and if Larkin happens to mention Frinton or rood-lofts or number-plates in a poem, you can be sure that Burnett will discover in which letter, or interview, or on what street corner Larkin also referred to them. The notes are not merely judicious; they are pertinent.

If I have minor quarrels with the edition, which gives us the most accurate text we are likely to have, some are problems of design, beginning with the lack of a proper table of contents. The poems have been cast in a smallish font and crowded onto the page. Among the unpublished poems, so many lack titles that you can slip from one poem to the next without noticing a break—a marginal device might have stopped the eye. No running heads provide relevant page numbers in the notes, so you must hunt up the index, then thumb back through the notes; and if while absorbed there you forget to hold your place among the poems, you're packed off to the index again like an errant schoolboy. Running heads require no expense, merely forethought.

Burnett has traced the drafts in fierce detail, recording variants from late drafts or early published versions, correcting the text where correction is required (Tolley's edition of the juvenilia comes in for devastating criticism), and boiling down the commentary. His notes are a gallimaufry of delightful oddities. I knew that the "Bodies," where Mr. Bleaney worked, was a car manufacturing plant, but not that the name was Larkin's coinage, or that it mimicked a local convention in Coventry, his hometown, of calling a factory by the name of whatever gizmo it happened to make. I knew that the "four aways" were a bet on away games in the football pools, but not that the young Larkin played the pools himself. I'm delighted to learn that "Wild Oats"—

about courting, or failing to court, a gorgeous English rose and her plain girlfriend—was based on experience, and that the poet really did keep two photographs of the beautiful one in his wallet. (Apparently I once knew this and then forgot.) If you want to make a pilgrimage to the lodgings where Larkin lived and on which he based "Mr Bleaney," Burnett will give you the address.

Still, perhaps a few things have been missed. Time tells the speaker in "Send No Money" to wait for the things that happen in life (rather than doing something about them); as he ages, he sees the "bestial visor"—probably his own face in the mirror. How is it possible not to think of James's "The Beast in the Jungle"? Larkin christens a butler Starveling in "Livings," but the note fails to mention the rude mechanical of that name in *A Midsummer Night's Dream*. It's misleading to call 1929 the "first year of the great economic slump"—the American stock market recovered after the crash of late October (the terrible long slide did not start until 1931). Britain's economy remained unaffected until 1930. Though the north of England was crippled, the south suffered only mildly and by the mid-thirties became prosperous. Larkin's poem "Livings (I)" is at best meant to be premonitory.

Americans do not uniformly pronounce the noun "research" on the first syllable, as the note to "Posterity" suggests—usage is mixed, as in Britain. The title to "Sad Steps" comes from the opening of a sonnet by Sidney, but the notes might have observed that Wordsworth long ago made off with the whole line—Larkin's borrowing secures him in a tradition. (Burnett sees that the nonce-word "immensements" in that poem is parodic, but he might have said that the whole passage is a devastating send-up of Romantic overwriting, like Shelley on laughing gas.) American readers might be grateful to be told that "French windows," which appear in a number of Larkin's early poems, are what we call "French doors." Richard Wilbur's "The Death of a Toad" would be a more relevant precursor for "The Mower" than those proposed. The title of "Party Politics" is a pun, not on "political party," but on the common phrase for, well, a party's politics. The missing word in "Address to Life" is undoubtedly "balls"—why not say so in the notes? There are false indentations in "Further Afterdinner Remarks" and a typo ("noone" for "no one"), probably by Larkin, left uncorrected in "You've only one life."

The weakest aspect of the commentary is the sometimes far-fetched attempt to detect echoes of other poets in Larkin. Does "the fields are sullen and muddy" ("The Ships at Mylae") in any way derive from Milton's "Now that the fields are dank, the ways are mire" (followed, two lines later, by "a sullen day")? Besides, shouldn't that be "*and* ways are mire"? What of Vernon Lee's *The Sentimental Traveller* instead: "it winds slowly through the Roman lowlands, sullen and muddy under its willows, going to join the sullen, muddy Tiber"? And does Larkin's "Untiringly to change their hearts to stone" ("Many famous feet have trod") owe a thing to Yeats's "Too long a sacrifice / Can make a stone of the heart"? The metaphor is a cliché. Arthur Mainwaring's "cold Courage turns your Hearts to Stone" and John Clare's "cold neglects have froze my heart to stone" lie a lot closer to Larkin. The editor wastes a fair amount of space on similarly trivial eavesdropping but makes little effort to provide parallels in Auden during Larkin's Auden infatuation—that would at least have been useful. He remarks that Larkin was good at creating Auden's atmosphere without being indebted to specific lines, yet the reader might like to know, when the Auden fog descends, where Auden used "O let" or "pistol cocked" or the sort of list so suggestive in "The cycles hiss on the road." And might the editor not have heard, in the sorrow and emptiness of "Among the littering alien snow I crave / The gift of your courage and indifference" the faint hint of "the sad heart of Ruth, when, sick for home, / She stood in tears amid the alien corn"?

No reader new to Larkin should start here. *Poems*, edited by Martin Amis, is friendlier and far shorter, with a highly personal, hair-raising introduction. I disagree that Larkin is a "novelist's poet"—the descriptions Amis marshals would be contrived in a novel, at least any novel not by Martin Amis. The selection of Larkin's poems is somewhat tight-fisted, *The Less Deceived* in particular being short-changed: among the missing are "Lines on a Young Lady's Photograph Album," "Wedding-Wind," "Reasons for Attendance," "Absences," "Arrivals, Departures," and, most pointedly, "Born Yesterday," a nativity poem for Amis's younger sister. I might drop a few poems Amis includes, adding from other books "Home Is So Sad," "Water," "Sunny Prestatyn," "Sympathy in White Major," and, from the uncollected poems, "Femmes Damnées" and "Party Politics."

Larkin's range was not great; he rarely varied his tone; his métier was the portrait, the meditative lyric, the grumble. Yet how many poets could have written touching poems, as Larkin did, about renting ("Mr. Bleaney"), or retired racehorses ("At Grass"), or a vandalized holiday poster ("Sunny Prestatyn"), or salesmen ("Arrivals, Departures")? Or a poem in the voice of a ruined Victorian girl ("Deceptions"), one very different from Hardy's? Larkin was a misanthrope, but not the way most people are—he merely found life tedious with others in it. His poems are rarely uplifting, or uplifting only after a lot of hemming and hawing and hedging his bets. For all that, for all that he is vinegar's version of Hardy, there are few poets more a guilty pleasure, few who see life with the chill of the born cynic, yet the nervous hope that love may, somewhere, just be possible—if not, perhaps, for him. One of the curiosities of Larkin's poems is how cheerful they leave you—and it's not the kind of cheer to be mistaken for *Schadenfreude*.

There's something nasty in Larkin—yet appealingly, gratifyingly nasty. Lowell and Plath made the private drama a full-blown five-act barnstormer, with scenery chewing and piles of corpses. Larkin, however, was perhaps the poet almost crushed by Freud. He's just some miserable pub-going off-in-a-corner sod who knows things won't get better and rather thinks he doesn't deserve better—life's Osric, perhaps, or Cinna the poet, for what death is deserved except the one most undeserved? It's not Larkin's misery in which one takes pleasure, but the relief his misery offers vicariously. That brings his poems, narrow and squeezed though they are (Larkin and sublimity are as much antonyms as Stoke-on-Trent and Paris), into relation with Greek tragedy, because they offer the ghosts of pity and terror.

Larkin's novels are hard going for such light things; the jazz reviews seem finicky and small, as if he were an HO hobbyist or a collector of moths; the other prose pieces are often lightly hostile, those of a man who wishes he could be anywhere else. Yet Larkin's poems seem exactly right, expressing all that needs to be said, in a manner wholly his own, and neither swaggering, nor vain, nor full of whiz-bangs and Roman candles. It's the late triumph of the middle voice—and in his mildness, his love of back lanes, his dependence on character and characters, he's a lot closer to Frost than is generally admitted (both were rather unpleasant beneath the surface—and in Larkin's case on the surface). You don't wish him a different sort of poet, because he was precisely the poet he could be. In his flaws, his talents were perfected.

When we have shrugged off our prejudices about Larkin, as he was never able to shrug them off about himself (who disliked Larkin more than Larkin?), it may become apparent how central he was to midcentury poetry, a man who saw himself as a ramshackle collection of defects, a man with a prefabricated sense of loss. Such poetry can come after a devastating sea-change like the modernists, when it seems that there's nothing left for a poet to do.

Verse Chronicle: From Stinko to Devo

Charles Bukowski

Charles Bukowski died of leukemia in 1994, but you'd hardly know it. In the years since, his longtime editor has overseen publication of a shelf of books, including three volumes of letters and at least ten of new poems (of which the most recent, published a couple of years ago, was supposed to be the very last). Now comes *The Continual Condition*, as if there will never be an end. You can't blame his heirs for shoving into print all the Bukowski they can, but you'd like some sense of the reserves—are they the size of the Genizah at Cairo? The North Sea oil fields? At this rate, in a few more years he'll have published more books from the grave than he published while alive.

Bukowski was the great littérateur of American lowlife. His father was an American soldier in the Great War, his mother a German war bride. The family settled in Los Angeles, where Bukowski later slaved at odd jobs, working for long stints at the post office as letter carrier and mail sorter; but his true occupations were gambler, barfly, and sidewalk Casanova. Like a lot of angry young men, he had literary ambitions.

Before the advent of oral history, there were few memoirs from what Marx called the *Lumpenproletariat*; and those were sometimes given the gilded touch by editors, when they were not forged outright. Writing well requires some measure of education, but not so much that a man of the mean streets loses his sense of self. Many a writer born to a trust fund has been drawn to the lower depths (as Gorky or his translator had it), as if life there were more genuine, though the poor are bound by the same webs of affiliation, of local debt and local vengeance, found in the Society Register. There have been intelligent tourists enough, like the Orwell of *Down and Out in Paris and London* and *The Road to Wigan Pier*; but a visitor, however sympathetic, tends to sound as if he's slumming.

What Bukowski brought to literature was an unaffected delight in every sleazy pleasure life offered. Dropping out of college, he was just educated enough, and just well-read enough, and had fallen just far enough to take advantage of his milieu. What he lacked in literary grace he made up in pulp sensibility—few have written as badly as Bukowski and still had something to say.

Bukowski fancied himself a poet, among other things; but he rarely spared his poems the attention he gave to fiction. Poetry became a scrap heap where lack of inspiration was no impediment. The poems often read like the diary of someone who once read *Lunch Poems* on a lunch break.

> *it has been a satisfactory night: I viewed an*
> *excellent boxing match*
> *earlier*
>
> *powdered the cat for fleas*
>
> *answered two letters*
> *wrote four poems.*
>
> *some nights I write ten poems*
> *answer six letters.*

Trivia can be its own reward, but after a little of this you want to drink a bottle of Drāno (if you want more, there are now 5,000 pages to choose from). As a poet, Bukowski had the virtues of his prose, only less frequently:

> *"do you like me?" she asked.*
> *"I wish," I told her, "you wouldn't wear all*
> *that mascara, it makes you look like a god-*

damned whore."
"don't you like whores?" she asked.

Despite the irritating lack of capitals, such vignettes are scarcely less effective than Hemingway's. You have to go through a lot of seedy passages to find something telling in Bukowski, usually growled out with dime-novel cynicism: "I don't like us and I never did—is there anything worse / than a creature who lives only to write / poetry?"

A literary culture needs its Bukowskis, if the language is to be freshened and sustained. Without some sense of the rhythm and consequence of speech, poetry becomes an antiquarian exercise. It's a pity that Bukowski's poems are denatured prose whose instance, whose cunning, lies only in these lovingly sordid scenes (I'm charmed that he lived long enough to refer to David Letterman, and that his vocabulary goes from *stinko* to Devo). The poet's hangdog manner, his mournful howls, his constant bellyaching—these are entertaining enough as shtick, though his every second thought turns to bimbos, booze, and the trifecta. Bukowski didn't treat women particularly well (perhaps no man is on oath when recounting his sexual exploits); but, whether mealy-mouthed or boastful, he sounded like an ugly cuss glad to get lucky. He's the antihero's antihero.

Bukowski remained a hard-boiled hack, even after he moved to a good neighborhood—he might as well have stayed in a rooming house pounding out prose on a battered manual typewriter. What distinguish his work, meager though it is, are the gritty and immoral particulars. He's more entertaining than Frederick Seidel because, though he too embraces the disgusting, the sickening, and the vile the way some embrace religion, Bukowski has a sense of humor. There are poets in love with beauty, and poets burdened with telling the truth. If you squint, there's a little Catullus in Bukowski. Perhaps attitude and tone are not enough in poems that rely so much on force of personality; but you can imagine Whitman reading them with a rough nod of recognition.

Franz Wright

Ah, *The Sorrows of Franz Wright*, America's longest-running soap— for hair-raising plot twists and hair's-breadth rescues (and hair-curling acting), you couldn't find better on *The Guiding Light*. Wright has pushed his sorry tale to the center of his poems in a way that makes old-school confessionals like Lowell and Plath and Berryman seem sweetly out of date. He has drunk harder and drugged harder than any dozen poets in our health-conscious age, and paid the penalty in hospitals and mental wards. He presents himself as a latter-day sinner, saved by religion and the love of a good woman, with only the occasional relapse to suggest that his demons are not entirely at rest. For this poet, no good sin goes unrewarded.

The surprise is that some of the new poems in *Wheeling Motel* are tender, considered pieces of work. Of course, there's pissing and moaning in abundance, overwrought piety and breast-beating—Wright can never do something by halves. There are moments, even so, when his flaws work almost like virtues.

> *A strange dog stops and stares quite specifically at me.*
> *There's a message, but no means of transmitting it.*
> *Sooner or later, I'm telling you, even the pity will cut you down.*

> *And you can only armor yourself in death wish for so long, the*
> *blows are not muffled, it will save you from nothing;*
> *and the idiot drive to go on, and actually be glad to go on,*
> *keeps breaking through ruining everything, even*
> *this last chance for some sort of peace.*

Here he approaches the composure so often missing from his work, though soon he's back ranting against Fate, the World, and God Knows Whom ("everyone fucked from the minute he set foot in this world"; "he played it too loud / but fuck the neighbors— // a little intelligence sanity and beauty / won't kill them"). Anger is his oxygen—as many a blogger knows, blacken Wright's name and he'll threaten you with a smackdown in a New York minute.

Rage, even in his best work, descends too easily into intoxicating self-pity: "some subdoormat psychiatrist writing for just what you need lots more drugs // to pay his mortgage Lexus lease and child's future tuition." Wright would like to be a poet of rapture—a desire that has ruined better poets—but his access to the metaphysical proves slightly banal:

Everyone Lord who wakes up in a cell.

Everyone Lord who wakes up in the cancer bed.

Everyone walking the streets with no home and intense frowning
    features of feigned occupation, feigned destination.

Such prayers seem forced and theatrical. Wright's idea of religion is
the cargo cult—there must be something in it for him.

  Not much happens in these unapologetically male poems. There
are predictable scenes in hospitals and psych wards, the mingled affection and resentment for Wright's monument of a father (with nothing
but fury left for his mother), memories of an abused childhood (Stephen Sondheim composed Wright's motto in *West Side Story*—"I'm
depraved on account I'm deprived"), and frequent probing and testing
of the nature of God, carried off with an original mixture of wheedling
humility and arrogant self-belief. It seems odd that the poet has such
a lively black humor—who else would offer, as a Parthian shot, "love,
the next best thing to being dead," or claim to be "composing / a letter
/ to my inner no one"? What do we say when an artist so canny about
life is so idiotic about himself? Ah, that he suffers from the human condition. Still, if a man whose father was a Pulitzer Prize–winning poet
wants to be nothing but a famous poet himself, it isn't rocket science
to guess the dynamic at work. And what are critics but false fathers he
flatters or holds in contempt?

  The arrested adolescence of our Young Werther doesn't sit well on
a man of fifty-six. For all his posing, all his braggadocio, his evocation
of lowlife is much less convincing than Bukowski's—Wright is too literary, too weighed down by the romance with Baudelaire and Rilke.
Yet at times he's able to forget the pretense and produce lines touched
with sentiment but sharpened by beauty:

> *Little cloud of inaudible gnats*
> *in a shaft of morning sunlight,*
> *in the silent sitar-shimmer*
> *blowing through billions of leaves*
> *and their shadows, the middle-aged catfish*

in Walden's emerald
shallows.

The responsibility of address and aspect in half a dozen poems here suggests that all along there has been a mature poet within, just waiting for Wright to grow up.

Beth Ann Fennelly

Beth Ann Fennelly's perky, up-to-the-minute verse has all the disadvantages of charm. The poems in *Unmentionables* skate along in helter-skelter fashion, picking up their subjects as they pass, then dismissing them with an airy wave. Most contemporary poetry is so modest in its ambitions, so sluggish in its designs, so mean in its aftertaste, you wonder why anyone would bother—not the poet, of course, since poets ever hope to occupy some rocky ledge on Parnassus, but the poor reader. A skittish, devil-may-care poet like Fennelly is a partial antidote.

> *Though we vacationed in a castle, though I*
> *rode you hard one morning to the hum*
> *of bees that buggered lavender, and later*
> *we shared gelato by a spotlit dome*
> *where pigeons looped like coins from a parade—*
> *we weren't transported back to newlyweds.*

This is a poet easy in her own skin, delighted by the provocations and exhaustions of sex, but knowing the losses of time—even love has its sell-by date.

Fennelly has a rackety passion for contemporary culture. She stuffs her poems with so many pop-culture references and brand names (Coors, Keds, Marlboro, Oreos, Victoria's Secret), you hope her agent cut a good deal for product placement. The underside, however, is that she's constantly trading better ideas for worse. A poem starts out about cow-tipping (soon to be another Olympic event), just the thing for the poet's tomboyish personality, yet halfway through she loses interest in rural adolescence, with its hints of darkness unexplored, and offers a solemn meditation on . . . 9/11.

> *Somehow, despite the planes clearing fields of cows and flying*
> *into buildings full of red-blooded Americans, it's still so hard*
> *to accept that people who've never seen me would like to see me*
> *dead, and you as well. Our fat babies. Our spoiled dogs.*

This is stupefyingly naive. Thank goodness Congress passed the moratorium on 9/11 poems last term.

Young poets are often seduced by the "project," and there are projects galore here. The French Impressionist Berthe Morisot was a warmly expressive and flowery painter if rarely a striking one, her figures caught in knowing calm and self-possession — had she worked in Denmark, with its cold lights and icy darks, the black-eyed gazes might have registered as psychology. Bathed in the warm glow of France, too many of her subjects look bewildered or smug. Fennelly's biography-lite is routine, dawdling, untroubled by shrewd judgment or sharpened phrase. Often the words are laddered across the page, as if by a disciple of a disciple of Charles Olson, impressionistic in the worst sense. What might be just anecdote embedded in the life of prose, in poetry seems too calculated, as if every happenstance were forced into parable. Fennelly's version of Morisot requires far too many bludgeoning metaphors ("the stretched and primed canvas / of my flesh"), with every shallow insight lit in neon ("I am a puzzlement to myself"; "once I learned this lesson, / I was seared").

For a poet of such energy and sprightliness, Fennelly's work is oddly underpowered, cautious and prosaic in phrasing, choked with clumsy similes. The low moment in the book is another sequence, fifteen dream songs in homage to John Berryman. Berryman's contorted syntax and jazzy vernacular looked dated after his suicide; but distance has confirmed his mastery of rhythm and idiom. *The Dream Songs* has its slack moments — and Berryman's baby talk is hard to take — but his radiant intelligence carries a reader through the dead spaces. He has long been due for a revival.

> *Them lady poets must not marry, pal.*
> *Miss Dickinson—fancy in Amherst bedding hér.*

> *Fancy a lark with Sappho,*
> *a tumble in the bushes with Miss Moore,*
> *a spoon with Emily, while Charlotte glare.*
> *Miss Bishop's too noble-O.*

That's Berryman, Dream Song 187. Here's Fennelly's lazy reply:

> *Of Emily Dickinson, even Charming Billy*
> *Collins writes of taking off her dress . . .*
> *For foreplay, JB, I'll*
> *read your juvenilia. & of bald rhymes:*
> *my students who love you not at all*
> *for a depilatory could wish.*

That trademark inversion sounds, not like Berryman, but like some *Star Wars* fanboy's imitation of Yoda. There's worse: "No sing, no sing to shay. Naughty Henry's / gone away and if I live a peckel / he won't be-O." Instead of driving toward her emotional tie to the dead poet (Fennelly's father, like Berryman, was a hard drinker), she offers page after page of embarrassing pastiche. In her third book, Fennelly hasn't even begun to figure out her gifts. A handful of poems drawn from the poet's past burn with Byronic bravado, as if there were acres of life yet to be lived. Such poems have a don't-look-in-the-rearview fearlessness, though you wish a few more unmentionables were mentioned.

Marie Ponsot

Marie Ponsot has an odd way of looking at things, and it's hard to know if those things were odd to begin with or if it's just her way of seeing that's slant. As poetry has withdrawn from instruction and reflection in favor of observation or confession, poets who cast a strange eye upon the world have proved irresistible. (This might suggest that poetry's function has gone from moral essay to escapism, though surely it has always indulged both—isn't *Paradise Lost* early sci-fi?) Ponsot writes as if some stray thought had just rattled into her head; but, if you compare the version of "Cometing" in *Easy* with the one published last year on the op-ed page of the *New York Times*, you'll see what labor goes into that seeming lightness. Her dyed-in-the-wool quirkiness has antecedents in Bishop and Moore; but Ponsot's darker sense of the comic, of the gloomy, glowing *bizarrerie* of nature, is more reminiscent of a troubled metaphysician like Carroll.

Ponsot's poems, which have been slow to find their audience, are offhand, spirited, and predatory—you think you've taken them whole, but a line or two catches at you just enough to force rereading. She can be a poet difficult to quote. To a garden:

> For these few spring weeks you're a sprawl
>
> of flowers, you green the summer toward its rest
>
> in fruited autumn. Yet it's winter that's best,
>
>
> yes, to imagine joy, next. The winter test.

That's the close of a sonnet, or quasi-sonnet (Ponsot's rhymes and me-ter are often in pleasant divergence from a fixed scheme). The diction is as curious as an outfit patched together from a Romantic charity box—William Allingham's *fruited autumn*, the Keatsian verb *green* ("Have not rains green'd over April's lap?"), the luxuriant *sprawl //* *of flowers*—but it has gleeful individuality. The lines are edged·with meaning, not thrust toward it but happening upon it by the way. You realize, gradually, that the darks here reveal a religious nature—how-ever lovely the garden in summer and autumn, winter is the retreat into the wilderness. The garden makes us realize the joys of patience, of longing for fulfillment—that might be called the discovery of faith.

Ponsot's poems work best when they sidle toward their meanings—the few poems that buttonhole the reader seem amateurish. Is the sub-ject TV coverage of the war in Afghanistan? "Achilles is not there, or Joshua either. // Rachel is not there, nor Sojourner Truth. // Iwo Jima flag boys? not there. // Twin Towers first defenders? not there." She doesn't slip often into such pompous hectoring, but when she does she's got chalk to spare and the laser pointer to go with it.

The poems in her new book have been set double-spaced, a harm-less craze that afflicts many poets under forty. Ponsot, who is eighty-eight this year, gains nothing as a dedicated follower of fashion. I've heard young poets say they like the "space" or "air" this introduces to the poem; but how long before some poet wants every line in boldface twenty-four-point type, or given its own page? The liveliness in Ponsot's work comes from the cunning of her lines—she doesn't need to blare them out like TV ads.

Her poems have always been hit or miss. A delicate run of observation may be followed by some bright banality. (Does a reader really need to know that the "plane's nose always gets there first"?) In this alone, she resembles Les Murray, a poet of great appetite who's often tone deaf. Ponsot lets her lines come dangerously close to cliché before saving them with a little twist of perception. To seize that risk, sometimes poems have to fail. It's hard not to admire a poet, however, who finds so many poems in odd corners. Her subjects can be as kinked as her delivery: here a soliloquy by a turkey, there Herr Grimm talking to his brother about "Hansel and Gretel," then poems on Peter Rabbit's sister, or pet dogs, or waste pipes. She's caught by the mean, lovely detritus of life—and sometimes, fortunately, that *is* life.

The poems in *Easy* are late work, a little undernourished or contorted in meaning; but there's hardly a page not touched by this poet's unpretentious flair. Many whole books lack lines as warmly idiosyncratic as "Green states its claim" or "they've put their old-time pre-TV faces on," or the "vastness of empty unlistening // others call sky." You hear in her the hyperactive thought of Dickinson, quickened with the abundance of her own perception, and the longing of Hopkins, that patron saint of rapture, though she seems more doubtful about the other world.

Joanna Rawson

Joanna Rawson's subjects have been smuggled in from the headlines— illegal aliens trapped in a boxcar in the desert; a young woman walking through Baghdad, strapped to a bomb (the sections of the poem tick backward from six to one); pilots back home practicing strafing runs. If you read just the titles in *Unrest*, you'd be forgiven for thinking the poet a war correspondent: "Kill-Box," "A Summer under Occupation Reports Its News & Weather," "Provisional Endings during

Wartime." These pieces contrast the horror of war or the terror of dying immigrants with the cozy life of the poet and her family, the lushness of nature, the quiet certitudes of the garden. As rhetoric the contrast is powerful, as argument cheap and nasty:

> *About this garden that's disintegrating.*
> *About this dry teasing heat yesterday's accumulating*
> *cumulous [sic] clouds meant to fix.*

> *The last iris slaves on.*

> *About this spiral of dust starting to rise into the air like a startled*
> *girl's throat.*

> *And these birds that crane their heads into the drought*
> *that just this morning blew the heads off the purple thistles.*

(*Cumulous* is a word, but you suspect Rawson means *cumulus.* Since she has *miniscule* elsewhere, her publisher needs a new copy-editor.) These lines come in the poem about the suffocating illegals, so the startled girl isn't metaphor; but the lines soon slip into bad taste: "How long did the banging on it go on? // Exactly what sort of noise did the collateral spray of their one last bang on this hot / communicating wall make? . . . // Haven't we asked these questions of boxcars?" It's not just that "collateral spray" (so forensic—very *C.S.I.*); it's that the poet has dragged in the boxcars of the Holocaust.

Rawson might reply that, when you're trying to shock an audience numb to violence, any rhetorical device is fair—the coquettish under-playing ("Isn't it starting to get a bit hot in here?"), the staccato narration ("Paid a *coyote* $1500 each for the ride. / The hatch locked from outside"). The coyness risks an insulting comedy, however, and the breathless fragments are cheesy attempts at moral emergency. Despite the long arm of her empathy, the poet can have little idea what dying immigrants or a suicide bomber are thinking.

Rawson's juxtaposition of the weedy American garden with strafing runs suggests that everyone is implicated, everyone guilty. She favors bardic statements warily circling a theme—the lines are often provoc-ative, mysterious, laggardly, as if they can't summon up the energy for enjambment. The poems work better in sidelong ways ("most of what goes wrong in a garden // does without meaning to, / without malice"). When juxtaposition becomes judgment, however, the poet's guilt seems a highly privileged one; the acts of rhetoric and attention, so striking singly, prove empty when they offer only complacent outrage.

There's another problem. Rawson's style has Jorie Graham's thumbprints all over it—mile-long lines and stunted stanzas, theatrical pauses, a highly caffeinated obscurity, and a tedious minute-by-minute record of consciousness. Influence and imitation are necessary to poetry, and nothing new is written without significant debt to the past; but to borrow so much, as if Graham's style could be worn like a Halloween costume, risks denying the poet's own impulses. Taken to extremes, imitation is the sincerest form of sycophancy. One Jorie Graham is more than enough.

Though the richest parts of Rawson's imagination are drowned in the sludge of the older poet's style, she writes of the natural world with original grace:

> The gilded larches deliver their knock-down argument in favor
> of the reckoning summer-singed light.

Her homely detail may conceal something devastating:

> Out of nowhere it occurred to me it must be the iris causing
> this grief.

> So all season I've studied the setting-down of inconsolability
> upon our house and almost had it chalked up to this cut
> flower's perfect mercilessness.

Graham often implies that the irrelevance of the personal is relevant, even culpable (there's something almost Jungian in the notion). Almost a quarter of Rawson's book is given over to episodes from some occupied zone, but the reader emerges no wiser about where that is or what it means. There's an endless poem about a garden, a dead horse, and the fighter jets tested nearby; but the connections are vague, slippery, and far too contrived. Rawson's guilts and accusations seem unlocated (don't Iraqis and immigrants love gardens, too?), as if there were evil afoot, somewhere, as if bad men were in charge, somehow.

John Ashbery

John Ashbery, that charming old fox, that master of flimflam and bunkum, has been up to his tricks so long they seem almost new. It's hard to remember that he published his first pamphlet when Nixon was a newly minted vice-president. Ashbery has long been a master of American vernacular, his language as fresh as whatever comes waltzing down the catwalk, yet his poems betray only the smallest awareness of the historical present—it would be hard to know whether the country was at war or peace, in profit or panic, wearing flip-flops or white spats or hoop skirts. Except for the carbon-dating of idiom, his poems might have been written before Gadsden's purchase.

Ashbery has published a dozen books of new work since turning sixty. This exuberant fecundity has in raw numbers long outdistanced the late poems of Stevens or Hardy, but that very facility exposes the contradictory nature of Ashbery's recent achievement—the poems seem entirely novel, but also slightly mechanical, as if they'd emerged warm from a cracker factory. Yet the eighty-two-year-old Ashbery doesn't sound eighty-two—his poems reveal nothing of the gravitas of age. His elegies, if that's what they are, are the most unelegiac elegies in English—if you weren't watching for them, you might miss them entirely. There has been no summing up as the curtains begin to close, at least none not also a comic routine. No, every couple of years Ashbery comes strutting out in tie and tails, freshly barbered, shining with bonhomie. What other poet his age would toss into his poems (or prove so engaging when he does) *trial period, sticker shock, in real time, glad rags, same old same old*, or *I'm outta here*? He seems younger by the minute, as if he were aging backwards.

The poems in *Planisphere* are no great surprise, for Ashbery has become as reliable as an old song-and-dance man who can still carry a tune and hit his marks, night after night. The rambling sentences, the ear-to-the-pavement demotic, the rimshot logic, the feeling that you're overhearing a slightly demented monologue—all these have been characteristic of his poetry for twenty years or more. Perhaps after he turns a certain age, you don't buy the poet, you buy the brand.

> Is it possible that spring could be
> once more approaching? We forget each time
> what a mindless business it is, porous like sleep,
> adrift on the horizon, refusing to take sides, "mugwump
> of the final hour," lest an agenda — horrors! — be imputed to it,
> and the whole point of its being spring collapse
> like a hole dug in sand.

There's no imitating this, though many poets have built minor reputations trying. Yet would the poem be much different if "spring" were replaced by *Congress* or *love* or *death*? Or *Donald Duck*, for that matter?

Ashbery long ago took the shock out of Dada and made it as toothless and housebroken as poor Rover. (Ashbery! He house-trained Dada!) When was the last time an Ashbery poem upset anyone? The aggressively nonlinear, absurdist verse of his twenties and thirties was written half a century ago. The last true avant-garde book was *Flow Chart*, twenty years back — and it was terrible. The unhappy truth is that Ashbery has become as mannered as a diplomat, capable of politesse and an agreeable smile, but little else. Yet when you compare him to other poets in the same vein, how pedestrian they seem. Ashbery is own man, with no dog collar upon him — and isn't that what we have expected of American poets, from Whitman forwards?

Much of what Ashbery has denied his poetry (the ordinary logics and meanings, the drive toward conclusion) are things it's hard to imagine giving up — and I'm glad not everyone has. But I'm secretly pleased to know that poetry can exist without them, just as I might be delighted that a man could live without a brain, or a heart (when you enter Ashbery's world, you're as close to Oz as you're ever likely to get — and you'll get no extra credit for guessing who Dorothy is). When I read a tall stack of new poetry books, the young poets so desperate to say something, the older poets saying the same old things, Ashbery seems like the sorbet course in a long meal.

The poems in this new book have been arranged, with a cheerful nod to chance, alphabetically by title, which makes the book a kind of alphabetical tour of Ashbery's imagination. Doesn't the heart lift a little at titles like "For Fuck's Sake," "Giraffe Headquarters," "Idea of Steve," "Not My Favorite Shirt," "The Plywood Years," and "Um"? Not that the titles have much to do with the poems, not that you couldn't fling them at poems completely different and be just as happy. The best poem is a list of movie titles that begin with "They," and perhaps the next best a floundering rehearsal of the plot of a thirties horror film called *The Tower of London*, a jumble of half-remembered details and half-forgotten actors.

> *Richard's bride was unlike the Queen*
> *in the play* Richard III. *She was played by*
> *Barbara O'Neil, who played Scarlett O'Hara's*
> *mother in* Gone with the Wind, *though she wasn't old*
> *enough to be. That's the way I remember it. Wait, she was*
> *actually Edward's wife.*

Wait! It's his usual meta-commentary on memory and age, on the Brownian walk of association that somehow, canting off in one direction, then another, gets you somewhere.

There are passages in *Planisphere* that seem to have been written while Ashbery was comatose ("*Spray-on sex*, he botanized. / That could never happen. // He's being held by Egyptian matrons") and one sentence that just about defeats me ("If we enjoyed spring spells later / it was because the motoric finish / spalled"). There are perfunctory metaphors galore; there are poems that start with everything and end with nothing; and there's the terrible suspicion that, for all the debonair grace, Ashbery's poems are missing something profound at center. Yet American poetry would be a more tedious business without a crackpot like that ever intriguing, ever frustrating Mr. Ashbery.

Verse Chronicle: Trampling Out the Vintage

C. K. Williams

C. K. Williams has long been our bard of secret shame, of psychological rupture, of the gaffes and faux pas that illustrate in small the disaster of being human—and who does not learn forgiveness by starting with venial sins? (You feel that he worships not Whitman but Erving Goffman.) Williams has remained a bleaker and more lurid version of Frost, with self-loathing added. His vignettes seem to occur by accident—they *just happen*, like the instigations of malign Fate. A child asks a grieving family an unforgivable question; the poet sees a deformed thrush the mother bird will soon abandon; something unsaid passes between a man and woman on the Métro—such moments lie outside the customary, cushioned life. In that instant of guilt or mortality or regret, Williams has discovered his ground—he dwells on things, then grinds them into poems.

The tabloid epiphanies in *Wait* sometimes occur in hyper-clarified vision:

> *On the sidewalk in front*
> *of a hairdressers' supply store*
> *lay the head of a fish,*
> *largish, pointy, perhaps a pike's.*
>
> *It must recently have been left there;*
> *its scales shone and its visible eye*

> *had enough light left in it*
> *so it looked as they will for a while*
>
> *astonished and disconsolate.*

A poet elsewhere so depressing shouldn't be this droll and insightful, though Williams is not simply Thurber in tragic mode. At best, he records his pocket dramas, finds some small lesson, and leaves it there. Despite the hypertensive, cobra-like lines now characteristic and even tiresome (if no longer monogamously employed), he's old fashioned enough to like homilies, to find human behavior both fascinating and repellent. We're so skittish now about judging people, it's refreshing when someone breaks the taboo, even if Pope's *Moral Essays* will never make the best-seller list again.

Williams still takes adolescent delight in provoking the reader's disgust: "A basset hound with balls / so heavy they hang / a harrowing half / inch from the pavement." *Harrowing?* He could at times be mistaken for Frederick Seidel, our other Tacitean poet of late empire (soon the dog is licking its balls; and then, like an Annunciation, a Ducati motorcycle appears). The weakness of these new poems lies not in their voyeuristic fancies, their relish in shock and discomfort, but in turning that social eye to Public Issues, to Man's Inhumanity to Man. Whether Martin Luther King revisits the slums, or Dostoevsky is scolded for his anti-Semitism, or the Great Blackstone saws a lady in half ("when we learned that real men were supposed to hurt women"—yes, real men in top hats, waving magic wands), the poems trade all their psychological subtlety for a little retro breast- and brow-beating.

When he's not standing on Adrienne Rich's soapbox ("nuclear rockets aimed at your head, racism, sexism, contempt for the poor"—you'd eat a cake of soap to make him stop), Williams is illustrating some lesson from the Jorie Graham School of Subtlety—"Don't we know yet that history / spins like a compass needle / but quivers remorselessly into place? / How can a child not cry to the night? / How can the prescient dog not howl?" *How can the prescient dog not howl?* Only Schrödinger's cat knows for sure, and I confess I was laughing too hard to ask it. A few poems on the Iraq War have been written in Power-Point, like most war poems these days. You wish the poet were confident enough not to settle his arguments the way the hammer settles them with the nail.

Williams's writing can be so acute, so sharp-edged and darkly humane (he's as gloomy as Robinson, that psychologist of American pastoral), it's surprising that his new poems are blandly indifferent to style, as if he'd traded poetry for the talking cure. What but poetic deafness could make so many passages read like sociology texts ("That what is often specified by the inheritors of those thrice-removed sanctifications, that certain other groups, / by virtue of being in even potential disagreement . . ."), or literary journalism of a paralyzing dullness ("Dillard is erudite, tender / and wise, and she can be funny"), or the doltish burbling of airline magazines ("I came to love Mexico when I lived there, the gentleness of its people, its prodigious history and culture")? Too many lines have been scraped together from pointless, stuttering lists of synonyms ("That dip in existence, that hollow, that falling-off place, cliff or abyss / where silence waits, lurks, hovers, beneath world, beneath sense"), as if the drudges at Roget's would otherwise be unemployed.

A dispiriting number of these poems have been provoked by literature. I'm glad Williams can get worked up about Dostoevsky's sins this late in the day; but only in the chaos and belittlement of memory does this poet find the petty cruelties, the failures of charity, that make his poems distinctive. He stands before the decaying wreck of the ocean liner on which he once sailed to France:

> That such a monster could be lifted by mere waves
> and in the storm that hit us halfway across
> tossed left and right until we vomited
> seemed a violation of some natural law.
>
> At Le Havre we were out of scale with everything;
> when a swarm of tiny tugs nudged like piglets
> at the teat, the towering mass of us in place,
> all the continent of Europe looked small.

Williams draws our eyes to the scene, and lets us work out the rest.

Tony Hoagland

The title of Tony Hoagland's new book, *Unincorporated Persons in the Late Honda Dynasty*, is the funniest thing about it. Along with Billy Collins, Dean Young, and a giggle of others, Hoagland has thrived among the gentle practitioners of gentle humor, sometimes with a gentle dash of the gently surreal, who have given American verse a New Age school of stand-up comedians. (Their motto: *Humor, or else.*) His new poems celebrate that great American religion, shopping, and that great American temple, the shopping mall. The art of American consumption was part of our literature long before *Babbitt* and *The Theory of the Leisure Class*—Henry James knew all about the golden bowls of the Gilded Age, Trollope's mother went broke starting a Cincinnati bazaar (right idea, wrong location), Mrs. Lincoln's dresses almost bankrupted her husband, and even Whitman was astonished by the ready commerce and "gay-dress'd crowds" along Chestnut Street. You might say that the subject of Americans and what they buy, from Thomas Jefferson's rare books (or, when he went on a spree, the whole Louisiana Purchase) to O. J. Simpson's Bruno Maglis and Carrie Bradshaw's Manolo Blahniks, is an embarrassment of riches, or just a bunch of crap: "the little ivory forks at picnics and green toy dinosaurs in playrooms everywhere; // the rooks and pawns of cheap $4.95 chess sets made in the People's Republic of China."

There's not a lot to say about American consumerism that wasn't said by Veblen, even if shopping is a Darwinian metaphor for the manners and mores of American life. Hoagland wisely turns his eye to all those lives impoverished—or, who knows, made infinitely richer—by that endless buying, buying, buying. Still, when he thunders on about the "late-twentieth-century glitterati party / of striptease American celebrity" he sounds as if he's channeling Billy Graham channeling Billy Sunday. Denouncing Britney Spears is like invading Rhode Island.

Hoagland has a superficial ease and charm—he's likable, and his poems are likable, but they're often less than they promise. He's a wonderful collector of the junk with which American furnish their lives, but it's hard to turn junk into poems. Hoagland is the Updike of American trash, forgetting nothing—but he hasn't figured out how to recycle rubbish into art. All too soon, Spears will seem dated as a Stutz Bearcat or a man shouting "Twenty-three skidoo!" There's a quieter and more unsettled poet inside all this bric-a-brac:

> And when we were eight, or nine,
> our father took us back into the Alabama woods,
> found a rotten log, and with his hunting knife
>
> pried off a slab of bark
> to show the hundred kinds of bugs and grubs
> that we would have to eat in time of war.
>
> "The ones who will survive," he told us,
> looking at us hard,
> "are the ones who are willing do [sic] anything."
> Then he popped one of those pale slugs
> into his mouth and started chewing.

Hoagland doesn't quite know what to do with the complicated feelings this evokes—it's smug for him to say, "That was Lesson Number 4 / in *The Green Beret Book of Childrearing*." (Things could have been worse—he might have turned the scene into *Deliverance 2*.) In the silent desperation here, the real subject might have been the father's misplaced expression of love.

Hoagland is skittish about love, though he knows that romance is often absurd and comedy the catharsis of fear. His hymn to American courtship scares me:

> It is just our second date, and we sit down on a bench,
> holding hands, not looking at each other,
>
> and if I were a bull penguin right now I would lean over
> and vomit softly into the mouth of my beloved.

This goes on to peacocks and walking-stick insects ("she might / insert her hypodermic proboscis delicately into my neck"), but you get the idea: Man is the animal who spends a lot of time thinking he's not an animal. Like so much of Hoagland's work, the poem softens into sentimental mush; yet for a moment the poet has seen the darkness in love, the animal passions released and endured.

These whimsical, mildly satirical poems about modern anomie, composed with far too much corn syrup and partially hydrogenated vegetable oil, want to rouse primal fears, then comfort the reader with a warm glass of milk. Sometimes this arch joker forgets the point of humor—a poem on the D.C. sniper, which starts with the mystery of God (that riddle ever invoked when life is cruel or unfair), comes all too close to ridiculing the dead. Next he'll be making fun of Holocaust victims.

Keith Douglas

Keith Douglas was killed by mortar fire outside a French village three days after D-Day. His unit of Sherwood Rangers had taken casualties on Gold Beach the day of the landing. A student at Oxford, Captain Douglas joined the army at nineteen, just after the declaration of war. Though he had survived the murderous tank warfare of North Africa, he confessed to a friend that he would not return from Europe alive.

Douglas was a poet in the period style, or in a number of period styles (his tutor at Oxford was Edmund Blunden, and his apprentice work has the musty whiff of Georgian verse). The poems vary wildly, a job lot of gestures and rhetoric more borrowed than invented—the early verse suffers from too much moonlight and too many dead girls, and even the later sneaks in a unicorn or two. When there's a riveting image ("That church, amputated by high explosive, / Where priests no more lift up their murmurous Latin"), Douglas is soon dragging in princes, a peasant lass, and the moon (that "magic painter"). Poets are stuck with their period, but what Auden made of that period was far more cunning and irresponsible and subversive.

War transfigures the artist even while trying to kill him. What the shock of combat teaches can swiftly be lost if the poet yields to noble rhetoric or regurgitated patriotism. War's random violence brought out a more serious and sardonic poet in Douglas: "John Anderson, a scholarly gentleman / advancing with his company in the attack / received some bullets through him as he ran." The cruelty of the matter-of-fact sounds like John Crowe Ransom. The poem shortly begins to gush, and then Zeus arrives to turn it into heroic elegy—yet that suspicion toward the heroic casts a shadow over the rest. The raw brutality and hardship of the Egyptian campaign gave Douglas a subject not dragged from books or fantasy. Dead soldiers

> rest in the sanitary earth perhaps
> or where they died, no one has found them
> or in their shallow graves the wild dog
> discovered and exhumed a face or a leg
> for food: the human virtue round them
> is a vapour tasteless to a dog's chops.

These canine Valkyries fascinated the young officer (the "wild dog finding meat in a hole / is a philosopher")—he even drew sketches of the beasts. Soldiers are often uneasy with their own detachment—death at first seems an overwhelming fate, then just an unhappy accident, the dead to be avoided if possible.

You need to go a long way to find the good lines in these poems, and when you do they're surrounded by bad ones. Douglas's hobbled style never found a sustaining language—you might say that clumsiness came naturally to him, though most poets have to labor for their graces. Still, the erotic undercurrent to his descriptions promised a poetry more subtly pointed, more sensual and disturbing, than any he lived to write. The scene is an Egyptian tea garden:

> Slyly her red lip on the spoon
>
> slips in a morsel of ice-cream; her hands
> white as a milky stone, white submarine
> fronds, sink with spread fingers, lean
> along the table, carmined at the ends.
>
> A cotton magnate, an important fish
> with great eyepouches and a golden mouth
> through the frail reefs of furniture swims out
> and idling, suspended, stays to watch.

The metaphor is overelaborate, but the development of observation owes something to "Sweeney among the Nightingales."

Douglas wrote only a few poems after returning to England in 1943, where the Rangers trained for D-Day in amphibious tanks, with mock landings on the British coast. He looked after his men, took tea in Cambridge, and occasionally went to a dance. He also worked on his memoir of the Battle of El Alamein and engaged in a hopeless correspondence with a young married woman he fancied. Perhaps he'd written all the poems he had it in him to write.

Simplify Me When I'm Dead, a reprint of the selection made by Ted Hughes almost half a century ago, is a convenient abridgment of a poet who almost never wrote a good poem; but it should never have been weighed down with Hughes's charmless, hucksterish introduction. The book is desperate for a few notes, which could have been borrowed from *The Complete Poems* (1987), a book with a longer and more acute introductory essay by none other than Ted Hughes.

The poetry of World War II has suffered critically in comparison with that of the Great War, though the cause isn't clear. Sassoon, Rosenberg, Brooke, Gurney, and others have their gifts; but except for Wilfrid Owen none merits close attention, and even Owen is an acquired taste. The war poetry of Randall Jarrell, Richard Wilbur, and Anthony Hecht is more devastating as art, and to those soldier-poets of the later war should be added the civilians W. H. Auden and Robert Lowell, the latter a conscientious objector. (Among poems, *Four Quartets* and *The Pisan Cantos* should not be excluded.) Perhaps it's time to reexamine the old prejudice, which was a prejudice before many of the best poems of that war were even written.

Don Paterson

Don Paterson's poems are nervy, prickly, sometimes elliptical—oh, and did I mention that they're Scottish? When so many poets try to be plain as a tire iron, plain as a jackhammer, it's a pleasure to have to work out meanings, always presuming there's something to be worked out. Paterson is loyal to the traditions without being slavish about them—he likes the binding obligation of rhyme and meter, but wants license to kick up a little dust now and then. For a poet so often in debt to Frost and Hardy, he's mockingly up to date.

Rain is composed in a minor key—moody, elegiac, the poems lie in the shadow of things not always mentioned. Paterson's restless new book is full of fables and allegories, with a few songs that live in the misty border country of the ballads. He has pared away the complications of feeling in *Landing Light* (2006), as if simplicity offered both comfort and protection from death. The new style comes at a price, but it's odd the price should so often be great dollops of sentiment. A man sets up a swing for his boys:

> *I spread the feet two yards apart*
> *and hammered down the pegs*
> *filled up the holes and stamped the dirt*
> *around its skinny legs*
>
> *I hung the rope up in the air*
> *and fixed the yellow seat*
> *then stood back that I might admire*
> *my handiwork complete.*

The poem is more devious than this (in parts perhaps impenetrable), its subject choosing not to have another child. Paterson likes leaving the moral or lesson implicit—his lines hang there, strangely unfulfilled. Yet the sing-song meter and dime-store rhymes keep dragging poems with the mystery of Hardy back to the children's verse of de la Mare. The questions of innocence and experience might evaporate if the sentiment didn't leak even into verse more adult: "The sea reached up invisibly / to milk the ache out of the sky"; "One thing makes a mirror in my eyes / then I paint it with the tear to make it bright." The book ought to come with linen handkerchiefs from the broken mills of Glasgow or Aberdeen. When does the *faux-naïf* become simply naive? You can try so hard for simplicity you turn your poems to porridge.

Paterson's overlong elegy to the poet Michael Donaghy, who died at fifty, is written in stately pentameter, withheld in judgment and desolate in reminiscence; but he keeps milking the grief as if it were a cow. The night

> *reached into the room*
> *switching off the mirrors in their frames*

and undeveloping your photographs;
it gently drew a knife across the threads
that tied your keepsakes to the things they kept;
it slipped into a thousand murmuring books
and laid a black leaf next to every white;
it turned your desk-lamp off, then lower still.

The last image, of the darkness getting darker, doesn't need the "mur-muring books" and the thickening pathos that precede it. A prefatory apologia in Scots (Paterson writes well in the old literary language) is more moving in four lines than the elegy itself.

Just when you think you have this poet's measure, he'll do some-thing loopy, like an ode to a young goddess of techno—it's an extended joke, stuffed with electronic-music jargon and the results of too much Googling, the sort of thing Paul Muldoon might have dashed off at a bus stop. (In Muldoon fashion, Paterson later pulls thirty-five renku out of a hat.) Don't try Natalie Beridze's tunes, however, unless you have a hankering for robo-hymns and techno-Muzak. You're delighted that a poet would think of such nonsense—then you're half sorry he did.

Paterson, who moonlights as poetry editor for a London publisher, has translated Rilke's *Sonnets to Orpheus*, written books of aphorisms, and in recent years been drenched with a shower of awards. He's as protean as many British poets—they write plays, libretti, novels, trans-lations, songs (you're surprised they haven't been asked to rewrite traf-fic laws or contribute the occasional slogan to a Marmite campaign). In the compact literary world of the United Kingdom, even if not so united any more, the opportunities and commissions can be distracting.

The better poems here, like "The Bathysphere" and "The Lie," cre-ate an allegorical world that turns ours topsy-turvy. They build their mysteries slowly and allow the reader no way to escape their crushing conclusions. "The Lie" might have been written by Kafka—"I'd risen a full hour / before the house had woken to make sure / that everything was in order with The Lie." There the poet pays his debts to literature in order to make something entirely his own.

Derek Walcott

The scene might have come out of Chekhov, it's so touching and strange. The aged poet, confined now to a wheelchair, sees across an airport lounge a woman he'd lusted after sixty years before (Chekhov would have made that a railway waiting-room). Wrinkled now, "treble-chinned," she has lost all the unbearable beauty that once so inflamed him. She too is confined to a chair. They sit together, ruined by time, exchanging the nothings of conversation—and yet in him a familiar heat begins to stir.

The poems in *White Egrets* show Derek Walcott's usual command and authority, however weakened the poet by the terrible roil of age, by the "quiet ravages of diabetes." The years have stripped him of some of the arrogance that at times made his verse an exercise in armor plating:

> *Down the Conradian docks of the rusted port,*
> *by gnarled sea grapes whose plates are caked with grime,*
> *to a salvo of flame trees from the old English fort,*
> *he waits, the white spectre of another time.*

The lines are still deliciously rich, but the sea grapes and the flame trees and the rusted port are on standing order from the local prop-warehouse. His familiar scenes have come to resemble Potemkin villages.

Walcott's new poems fall easily into his resonant murmur (occasionally snoring or wheezing now), knitted in rhyme falling often into quatrains, tightened into pentameter and then unknotted again. At eighty, a poet has every reason to survey his past, marking the toll paid in loss and regret, the dead loves and dead friends roughening the memory, when he can recall their names. (He finally realizes that he's a terrible painter—the painter is always the last to know.) However much he may hope to live "beyond desires and beyond regrets," that peace seems not a day closer than death.

Whenever a poem starts to flag, Walcott pastes in lush strips of Morris wallpaper, natural description so deliriously gaudy you forget it's just pretty nonsense. It hardly matters if the poem is set in Stockholm, London, Barcelona, Pittsburgh, Amsterdam, on his own Caribbean island, or in the hill cities of Italy:

> Roads shouldered by enclosing walls with narrow
> cobbled tracks for streets, those hill towns with their
> stamp-sized squares and a sea pinned by the arrow
> of a quivering horizon, with names that never wither
> for centuries and shadows that are the dial of time.

One landscape looks awfully like another in a world reduced to a single glossy issue of *National Geographic*.

Perhaps too much of this book worries the same quarrels that have marked this long career, quarrels now like superannuated hounds drowsing by the winter hearth: the seductive tradition of English literature vs. the artist's greed for originality, hatred of empire vs. respect for old ways now lost, the longing for travel vs. love of his small island. The arguments were never won or lost, just overtaken by a different world. Walcott's verse lives for the antique regimens of the Cold War (his history book stops short around 1960). People worry about a lot more than the British Empire these days.

A poet of great gifts can make all sorts of mistakes and not fail, while a poet of mediocre talent can do almost everything right and not succeed. Perhaps Walcott has earned the right to slip in a few flat passages and over-extended metaphors. Or to drop into preachy editorials ("I watched the doomed acres / where yet another luxury hotel will be built / with ordinary people fenced out"). Or to indulge in giddy Byronic rhymes like *lose her / Siracusa*, or *dressmaker / Jamaica*. I wish he had long ago retired that word *empire* (once more the schoolroom map is red with the old British possessions), wish that in almost every book the flash of the sea weren't compared to coins or the surface to a sheet of tin or the flight of birds to arrows—I thought this time he'd neglected the last, but there it is on the final page. In one short sequence, an egret devours ticks with an *electric stab*, has *stabbing questions* and a *stabbing head*, and will soon be *stabbing at worms*.

Solemn, stately, by turns guarded and grandiose, this is verse of an old-time eloquence, tormented by the emptiness such moody sonorities fill, since every bellow is now a bellow against death. *White Egrets* is Walcott's best book in a long while, precisely because he has nothing left to prove, the writing now just the medium for mortal restlessness, a withering record of the humilities and humiliations of age. These may be the last songs of a David now heavy with years, the man from Gath a distant memory, and the old goat longing for pale-eyed beauties to keep him warm.

Anne Carson

Anne Carson's book in a box carries all her rattletrap learning, her risky ingenuity, her peculiar voice infused with the gravitas of the Greeks and the kookiness of the Jazz Age (if she's not the Medea of contemporary poetry, she's the Betty Boop). Carson is a queer fish, an unconventional—you're never sure what she'll do next, only that it will be riveting and fatiguing by turns, or perhaps both at once (some of her work rivals those early Warhol films whose tedium drove the audience nearly to suicide).

Nox weighs two pounds, is thick as a volume of Proust, and comes in a specially made clamshell case. This replica of the scrapbook memorial Carson constructed for her brother, who died a decade ago, consists of almost two hundred pages pasted together accordion style. If you're not careful, it will leap from your hands and go spilling down the stairs like a Slinky. On the surface, Nox is a meditation on Catullus' Carmen 101, which ends triumphantly, sadly, "ave atque vale." The book progresses by fits and starts, her private recollections triggered by a word-by-word lexicon of the Latin text, supplemented by fragments of letters, torn snapshots, postage stamps, pencil rubbings, crude drawings. Every patch of prose, and the photographs and whatnot besides, has been pasted or taped or stapled to the page, at least photographically. For a hundred bucks, you can get the limited edition—if it offers real Scotch tape and real staples, you should snap it up.

Carson tells us only so much about her difficult brother (he fled a prison sentence, traveled on a false passport, died under an assumed name), as if there were privacies that could not be breached. Like a good classical scholar, she knows how suggestive the fragment can be. Coleridge knew it; Pound knew it—indeed, it has become an avant-garde cliché, yet we have to rediscover it every few years. The poem records the losses suffered even during life, when people are driven apart by their own strange whirlwinds.

Carson rakes over the sparse material remains of her shared past. The deckle-edged Kodak snaps, some cut or mutilated, are powerful because ordinary: one shows the wintry yard of a cottage, her mother and the two children standing stiffly in the cold. The photographer's shadow falls—forlornly? domineeringly?—upon the snow. Is that the father, hardly more than shadow here? Her memories are cautious, as if she doesn't want to give too much away (what is given can no longer be hoarded). History, she muses, is always something survived. The overpowering loss is made no better by knowledge that any literary memorial must be inadequate, that healing gestures do not heal.

Carson is a canny, thinky writer (in the past, she has often out-thought herself), who at times has all too much to say about what she says. If one of her themes is the grief of history, the other is muteness, the silence of the past beneath her brother's long silences. Even as an adult, she hung on his every word, like a younger sister still lost in hero worship. The piecemeal dialogue she records is strange, almost oracular, the torn letters part ransom note, part evidence of terror or fury (history is salvage law, too). Carson has left her misspellings and mistypings intact, as if the rawness of sorrow were more important than correction. The hesitations and interruptions and irritations of this strange book serve like *Moby-Dick*'s passages of cetology—delay is power.

A long book that offers only a dozen pages of poetry ought to feel empty (there's probably more Latin than English here), yet *Nox* is im-possibly full. The lexicon entries, though the reader may be tempted to skip them, become a kind of found poetry, a meditation on mean-ing, on ambiguity, on transience, and even on love, for who looks so closely except in a kind of rapture? Catullus wrote Carmen 101 for his own brother, who died in the Troad, site of the ruins of Troy. Though the Roman poet visited the grave, Carson didn't enjoy even that con-solation—her brother had been dead weeks before she heard, his ashes already scattered on the sea. The book tries to make up for all those ab-sences and lacunae, a cenotaph for the uncomfortable, unhappy man whose life brought suffering and whose death, suffering once more.

For decades Carson apparently tried to translate the Catullus (drafts are pasted to some of these pages), but *Nox* turns the raw matter of grief into a meta-translation. Often with avant-garde work, the formal fuss and bother can't conceal the humdrum, homely sentiments at heart. With too much experimental poetry, where there's smoke, there's . . . well, just more smoke. Carson's poetry has always suffered from a weird affectlessness (in readings she employs that as a superb form of deadpan); yet here the flat, toneless lines, laid out like Wittgenstein's *Tractatus,* have the exhaustion of grief endured. This deeply personal, dark meditation on death and memory justifies the nuttier projects on which Carson has lavished her talents. The final page is a smeared and illegible scrap that seems to be another draft of the translation denied us—it looks like a tombstone half eroded by time.

Frost's Notebooks: A Disaster Revisited

Robert Frost's *Notebooks* were published three years ago to rapturous approval. Frost is still an American icon and an American nonesuch, the last major poet to find a public audience—his poems said more about the American character that any poet's after Whitman. Though Frost's America seems distant almost a century after the publication of *North of Boston*, he remains the most quoted American modern. The notebooks gave a rare look inside his workshop, showing the painstaking and sometimes clumsy way his poems and essays and talks were put together. Reviewers for newspapers and magazines, working to short deadlines, usually take on trust the labors of scholars. Still, it was hazardous for the *New Republic* to call the book "expertly edited and annotated" without apparently checking the editing or annotation, or the *TLS* to declare the edition (apart from one minor cavil) a "superb job" and a "labour of love," saying of the notebooks that "anyone who dips into them has reason to be grateful to their editor."

Late in 2007, a review by James Sitar in *Essays in Criticism* accused Robert Faggen, that very editor, of committing monstrous errors of transcription, some so embarrassing they made him—or Frost—look like an idiot. A few months later, after six months in press, my own review in *Parnassus* condemned the edition in similar terms. Both pieces claimed that Faggen, though in many places a canny reader of Frost's diabolic hand, had offered hardly a page that did not need revision. The errors ran to the thousands, many of them major; and a good proportion gave readings nonsensical or preposterous. Who would believe, had a scholar not said so, that Frost wrote "picktie exhibition," or a "hide [linigue] for harriners," or "Columbus brooch alone awhile," or "In colleness or in the quest of fruit," or "all he is parinian," or "use of lipstitch and howdy," or many like acts of myopic absurdity?

Where Faggen was not making nonsense of Frost's sense, he was misreading with suicidal creativity: Frost's "brought up to date" became "brought up dull"; "if I blame your Bently" became "if I become your Bently"; "any of us" became "angry"; "belong to the highest class" became "belong to the highest clan"; "It seems poor spirited" became "It runs poor spirited." On and on it went. Faggen showed a hapless gift for transcribing words that were not there while overlooking the words that were. Lines perfectly legible were called illegible and left untranscribed. Punctuation was invented on some occasions, ignored on others. Words Frost had misspelled were mistakenly corrected, words he had spelled correctly bizarrely misspelled. Though Faggen declared that everything in the notebooks was included, entire lines were missing, as well as a whole page found by James Sitar. The editor showed a genial talent for transcribing his own editorial notes and private queries, as if Frost had made them. The phrase "When spoken to unsympathetically attack ally as by a hostile lawyers" should have read "When spoken to unsympathetically as by a hostile lawyer." The two extra words were Faggen's initial attempt to read "unsympathetically"—he simply forgot to remove them. This is among the damning evidence that the editor failed to proofread his text against the original manuscripts.

Sitar minutely examined four notebooks housed at Boston University and Dartmouth; I used xeroxes from half of the forty or more at Dartmouth. We worked independently, without knowledge of each other's discoveries. When the New York Times picked up the story, Faggen responded with scholarly hauteur. "My practices are in harmony," he announced, referring to one mistake, "with those of most other editors of Frost's manuscripts: I let his misspellings stand. This is not an error. In short, we have here a matter of critical judgment, the sort any responsible editor must exercise. And I maintain that most of the passages about which Mr. Logan raises questions fall into this category." So it was all due to a difference of opinion or poor Frost's misspellings. Faggen later wrote the editor of Parnassus in high dudgeon, darkly threatening legal action.

Faggen assured the *Times* that "any project of this nature and magnitude is bound to invite criticism and undergo changes and improvements, a great many of which have been incorporated in the forthcoming paperback edition." This technique, entirely fitting for a Frost scholar, is called *stonewalling*. It's true that scholarly editions sometimes have to correct a handful of errors in subsequent printings; but Faggen's tone is curiously dismissive, if he already knew that a "great many" corrections were necessary.

An editor is a beautiful drudge, the sort of drudge to whom all readers must be grateful. It's a pity that modern English departments hold editors in such contempt. Very few departments teach the first thing about editing manuscripts, preferring that graduate students scribble some airy nothing in the latest critical jargon. There are not many second chances in scholarship—though a good edition may last a century, a bad one may not be replaced for a generation or more. New editions of Shakespeare are issued by the hour; but half a century after Eliot's death we are just getting round to scholarly editions of his work, and the last modern edition of Drayton's poems was published before Eliot died.

Now at last the long-postponed paperback edition of the *Notebooks* has appeared. It should first be said that Faggen has used his delays wisely, repairing a good many of the freakish readings he blithely defended (a "great many" changes in fact meant thousands). Numerous pages show that he has sometimes radically altered the earlier text—the new edition contains, in other words, every evidence of the pernicious and corrosive errors he once blandly denied. Take, for example, the now infamous transcription of a bit of Frost's Yankee wisdom. (Curly brackets mark words Frost wrote above the line.)

> *Thus there is another rule of life I ~~never~~ {always think of when}*
> *I see a player serving two or three bats once before he goes to the*
> *plate to fan pitcher with one bat. Always try to have arranged that*
> *you were doing something harder and more disciplinary [~~illegible~~]*
> *than ~~what you~~ the picktie exhibition you ~~have before you~~ are about*
> *to make of yourself.*
>
> [Faggen 1]

It should have been obvious to a child that something had gone wrong here. *Serving two or three bats? Fan pitcher? The picktie exhibition?* I offered the following corrections in my review (changes to Faggen's copy are marked by underlining):

> <u>Then</u> there is another rule of life I ~~never~~ {always think of when} I see a ~~m~~ player <u>swing</u> two or three bats <u>at</u> once before he goes to the plate to fan <u>the pitches</u> with one bat. Always try to ~~ha~~ have arranged that you were doing something harder and more disciplinary ~~that~~ than ~~what you~~ the <u>public exibition</u> you ~~have before you~~ are about to make of yourself.
>
> [Logan]

Here is Faggen's new version:

> Then there is another rule of life I ~~never~~ {always think of when} I see a player swing two or three bats at once before he goes to the plate to face the pitcher with one bat. Always try to have arranged that you were doing something harder and more disciplinary [~~illegible~~] than ~~what you~~ the public ~~exibition~~ you ~~have before you~~ are about to make of yourself.
>
> [Faggen 2]

This is much better. It follows my suggestions almost exactly, and in one place improves upon them—Faggen is surely right that Frost wrote "face the pitcher," not my "fan the pitches" or Faggen's original "fan pitcher." Still, the editor has missed two small strike-outs, claimed a perfectly legible word is illegible, and oddly struck through the word "exibition," though it is uncanceled in the original. He has reduced some ten errors to three. They are not important errors, perhaps; but then he has had two chances to get the passage right.

Take another bewildering excerpt, some doggerel about Christopher Columbus.

> Colundres! Christophes! No less!
> What no one left alive but you
>
> He boards again
> ~~Columbus boards~~ in I [illegible]
> Till someone comes up over [side]

> *The meekly [?vaunt] single file*
> *Columbus brooch alone awhile*
>
> [Faggen 1]

The editor who believes that sensible old Robert Frost wrote things like *Colundres! Christophes!* or *Columbus brooch alone awhile* simply isn't thinking. Frost occasionally misspelled a word or botched a phrase, but the notebooks show he did not write nonsense. This was my proposed transcription:

> <u>Columbus</u>! <u>Christopher</u>! *No less!*
> *What no one left alive but you*
>
> ~~Columbus broods~~ {He <u>broods</u> *again*} *in* <u>Spanish pride</u>
> *Till someone comes up over side*
>
> <u>They</u> *meekly* <u>vanish</u> *single file*
> *Columbus* <u>broods</u> *alone awhile*
>
> [Logan]

I kept Faggen's couplet order, though here and elsewhere he ignores Frost's instructions for inserting marginal additions. Here is the editor's second try:

> *Columbus! Christopher! No less!*
> *What no one left alive but you*
>
> *He broods again*
> ~~Columbus boards~~ *in I Spanish pride*
> *Till someone comes up over [side]*
>
> *The meekly vanish single file*
> *Columbus broods alone awhile*
>
> [Faggen 2]

This, alas, is only a little better than his original. He adopts many of my readings, including "Spanish pride," but in the same line continues to transcribe "broods" as "boards" (the word is clear and unmistakable), fails to mark correctly the phrase Frost wrote in superscript (*He broods again*), and leaves intact the "I," which was his earlier misreading of the "S" in "Spanish." He then keeps "side" in brackets for no reason, and takes "They" for "The." On the following page of the notebooks, he continues to offer "They've named it for Americas" for what is obviously "They've named it for *Americus*" (i.e., Amerigo Vespucci—Americus was the Latin form of his name, feminized to America because continents were by custom given women's names).

Consider the third passage I examined, in which Faggen transformed Hanno the Carthaginian into "Hannof the Carlingian" (the notes had the name correctly, but the transcription was cheerfully grotesque—there's no "f" to be seen, and "Carlingian," whatever that might be, cannot possibly be the word on the page). In his revision, Faggen has done fairly well through most of the passage, making some twenty corrections on the page, all following my version, though he misses a word and misplaces a phrase, misspells another word, and somehow renders "all to the good, *if* I was chasened" as "all to the good. I was chasened." Worse, at the end of Frost's draft, Faggen at first offered this (I have extended my earlier transcription by one sentence):

It would go on tell how the sailors getting impatiently with her intractability were permitted ~~to skin her~~ by Hanno to skin her and take her hide home for a trophy of one of the earliest voyages in the Atlantic. They they hung it up in the temple of Ashtaroth as hide [linigue] for harriers. Tunique ought to be rhymed somehow with Runic—Runique.

[Faggen 1]

~~so~~ *It would go on <u>to</u> tell how the sailors getting <u>impatient</u> with her intractability were permitted ~~to skin her~~ by Hanno to skin her and take her hide home for a trophy of one of the earliest voyages <u>into</u> the Atlantic. ~~They~~ <u>They</u> hung it up in the temple of <u>Astaroth</u> as <u>a</u> hide <u>unique</u> for <u>hairiness</u>. <u>Unique</u> ought to be rhymed somehow with <u>Punic</u>—<u>Punique</u>.*

[Logan]

Faggen's second trial is better, though not by much.

> *It would go on tell how the sailors getting impatiently with her intractability were permitted* ~~*to skin her*~~ *by Hanno to skin her and take her hide home for a trophy of one of the earliest voyages in the Atlantic.* ~~*They*~~ *they hung it up in the temple of Ashtaroth as hide unique for hairiness. Unique ought to be rhymed somehow with Runic—Runique.*
>
> [Faggen 2]

The first sentence has been left unchanged despite the obvious mistakes. *Getting impatiently?* Elsewhere "*Astaroth*" is still "Ashtaroth" and "*a hide*" still "hide." "Runic-Runique" has been left uncorrected, no doubt because Frost's capital P's are slightly malformed (he sometimes dragged the end of his stroke—and in "Punique" he started to write a lowercase "p" and changed his mind). A little thought would have suggested that "Runic" makes no sense—Hanno came from Carthage, not the snowy wastes of northern Europe. In the jocular poem Frost imagines, the rhyme will be *unique / Punic* (or "Punique," his Ogden Nash–like joke). Ho-ho. Having forgotten the Punic Wars, Faggen barrels on, often in error.

There are so many additional passages to choose from, it's difficult to select the best examples. Here's part of a draft of the unpublished poem "Old Gold for Christmas":

> *You're one fool walking so you can't yourself*
> ~~*It's where I wanted*~~ *{I want to claim} claim my residence.*
> *[jllegible phrase]*
> *The house is not much but the barn is standing.*
> *There! Midnight I suppose or one o clock.*
> *The city should be careful it does*
> *Blowing its lights out all at once* ~~*so suddenly*~~ *on {on people}*
> *Like eighty candles on a birthday cake.*
>
> [Faggen 1]

This has been left uncorrected in the new edition—Faggen has not even bothered to change the hilarious "jllegible phrase." Here's how the passage should appear:

You're <u>on foot</u> walking so you can't yourself
~~It's where I live and~~ {I want to} claim my residence.
<u>{The next election if I have to vote}</u>
The house is not much but the barn is standing.
There! <u>midnight</u> I suppose or one o clock.
The city should be careful <u>what</u> it does,
Blowing its lights <u>all out</u> at once ~~so suddenly~~ {on ~~one breath~~
    ~~on people~~}
Like eighty candles on a birthday cake.

[Logan]

This should be mortifying, since in transcribing an earlier draft Faggen has *on foot* correctly; but the lines are representative of the problems throughout—words misread, words missed entirely, words inverted, words not read at all, and one word duplicated where it stands alone on the page. The "jllegible phrase" is difficult but not impossible to read, even in a smudged xerox.

Here's a difficult excerpt from Notebook 1, which Faggen initially rendered as follows:

The pod {may be an Egrets} [~~illegible~~] carapace
From many flowers one [illegible]
But yet so bursting full of fertile seed
[?Found] Then {sound for} the stackling sake
The moon [illegible] talking is the worse the late

[Faggen 1]

The moon talking! His second try is little better:

The pod [~~illegible~~] {may be an Egrets} carapace
From many flowers one [?such] ace
But yet so bursting full of fertile seed
[?Found] them {sound for} the state's [~~illegible~~] sake
The more [illegible] tally is the worse the take

[Faggen 2]

He has given greater attention to rhyme here; but, almost indecipherable as the handwriting is, Frost wrote something nearer this:

The pod [?~~is our lone~~] {may be a [?<u>lonely</u>]} carapace
From many flowers one [?<u>servile grace</u>/?<u>sowing race</u>]
But yet so bursting full of fertile seed
<u>Count</u> *them ~~if but~~ {<u>someday</u>} <u>for</u> the <u>statistic's</u> sake)*
The more <u>the</u> tally is the worse the take)

[Logan]

The problematic *lonely* in line 1 is written over another word, perhaps *car* (a false start at *carapace*), making deciphering difficult. *Egrets,* however, makes no sense. Yet the line "From many florets one lone carapace" occurs the page before. I found belatedly that Frost kept other drafts of this passage in Notebook 23, where "Count them if but for the statistics sake" suggest the accuracy of my transcript. Why did Faggen not notice these drafts and use them? He seems to have puzzled out one word at a time, without thinking that words must make phrases and phrases, sentences—or even that individual words ought to be in the dictionary. That's the only way to explain how, in both editions, Faggen records another version of the last line above as "The more the rally thing the worm the tale"!

Or consider these lines:

He knows exactly where to draw the line
Between the good for nothing and the bad
He's they ~~were kept at their expense~~
[~~illegible line~~]
Better that good for nothing kept them
~~At your expense than that we had to keep them~~
[~~two illegible lines~~]

[Faggen 2]

Frost was here trying to draft a particular thought. In the first edition, Faggen offered "He knows sadly" and "He's ~~there were kept~~," so he stared hard at this and made two changes, though the latter is nonsensical. The passage should read:

He knows ~~just w~~ exactly where to draw the line
Between the good for nothing and the bad

He'd ~~rather they~~ ~~were kept at their expense~~
~~He'd rather people kept themselves~~
Better <u>the</u> good for nothing kept them<u>selves</u>
At ~~our expense than that we had to~~
~~Than that we kept them~~
At our expense than that we had to keep them

[Logan]

As elsewhere, words and strikeouts are missed or misplaced, a canceled word is canceled no longer, and legible lines are called illegible.

You wish Faggen had given some pages a closer look the second time. Take this short excerpt nearby:

Are right don't preach it now
For I'm a pilgrim can't [~~illegible~~] ~~with you long~~
[illegible line]
He has a singing voice
Yes that his song.

[Faggen 2]

"Can't" was "can" in the first edition, so Faggen did give the passage further scrutiny. The lines ought to read:

<u>All</u> right <u>dont</u> preach it now
For I'm a pilgrim <u>I</u> ~~cant tarry~~ ~~with you long~~
<u>I must be going—I can tarry but a night</u>
He has a singing voice
Yes <u>thats his son</u>.

[Logan]

Or, to take a final example, here's Faggen's original transcription of a bit of Frost's light verse:

A thousand years ago in Rome
And I was in a catacomb
~~Upon a rosmary shelf~~
Stretched out upon a strong shelf
I had entirely to myself

I lay apparently becalmed
From having died and been embalmed
With toes upturned arms composed
And you would never have supposed
What I lay there a thinking of
Of many things but mostly love
Venus with who wrote Anchises lay
So far from having had her day
Her reigning was just begun
She was is the one and only one
The element of elements
That all the universe creates
That when the elements were brutes
Was observing was

[Faggen 1]

This remains unaltered in the new edition. It should read:

A thousand years ago in Rome
And I was in a catacomb
Upon an [?ossuary] shelf
Stretched out upon a stony shelf
I had entirely to myself
I lay apparently becalmed
From having died and been embalmed
With [illegible word] {toes upturned} arms composed
And you would never have supposed
What I lay they there a thinking of
Of everything but mostly love
Venus with who with Anchises lay
So far from having had her day
Her regency was just begun
She was {is} the one and only one
The element of elements
That all the universe cements
That when the elements were booked
Was obviously was overlooked

[Logan]

More than a dozen errors, many of them comical. Again, there are words and strikeouts missed entirely, and readings that invent nonsense where sense was there to be seen. Frost usually drafted his poems metrically, so setting down a line like "Upon a rosmary shelf" or "Her reigning was just begun" ought to have warned any editor with an ear that something was amiss. Faggen also seems not to notice when Frost was drafting in rhyme. Frost made mistakes (here he forgot to delete "they" in one line and "Was" in another), but he was not subject to the sort of errors with which the editor burdens him. *Venus with who wrote Anchises lay?* A few lines further, "To *hydrogen and* [?*oya*] *oxagen*" is transcribed simply as "To." Lines nearby show similar lapses, as if the editor had started his labors and been interrupted by the doorbell.

Faggen has corrected about half of the painful nonsense I pointed out in the review, in each case embracing my proposed revisions: the newspaper he called the *Tribute* is now the reliable *Tribune*; "to consider bear one year" now "to consider *fear* one year"; "In colleness or in the quest of fruit" now "In *idleness* or in the quest of fruit"; and his "lipstitch and howdy" now "*lipstick* and *powder*." The editor has accepted that Frost wrote "dig your *grave* in if *you died*" not "dig your rave in if your dead"; "all he is *poor man*" not "all he is parinian"; "wild *heaths* and deserts" not "wild hearths and deserts"; "go to wrack and *ruin*" not "go to wrack and mine"; "two rows of rock *maples*" not "two rows of rock samples"; and "He might {have} *parroted* the thinking folk," not "He might {have} arrested the thinking folk."

Unfortunately, Faggen has failed to adopt readings just as obvious, so we still have "History that coming / I [~~illegible~~]" instead of "*His son thats coming's / Is State Police*"; "Who are you marring with now?" instead of "Who are you *marrying me to* now?"; "And if I did today" instead of "And if I *died* today"; "Lets not be persona!" instead of "Lets not be *personal*"; "And put in y in some fold of her dress" instead of "And put *it by* in some fold of her dress"; and "got know down" instead of "got *knocked* down." He perversely continues to maintain that Frost wrote "Sog Magog Mempleremagog" instead of the Biblical "*Gog Magog Memphremagog*." (The glacial Lake Memphremagog lies north of Vermont, above the Magog River.) Frost's capital "g" is plain; it lies on the notebook page just above the identical "g" of God. Faggen's idea that "Sog" was a joke is a nifty defense, but would need some shred of evidence.

Worse, Faggen is still certain Frost wrote "No one ever took a wife for wise except by mistake in reading old print Wife Wife." The type form of the old "long s" looked like an "f" with part or all of the crossbar missing—the running titles in the First Folio seem to include plays called *The Tempeſt* and *Meaſure for Meaſure*. Frost took great care in his notebook entry to print out the words "wife wife"—in other words, in an old book "wife" might have been mistaken for "wise." Ha ha. The poet went to a lot of trouble for such a dull joke, but it has been entirely lost on Faggen.

Among blunders I did not mention in my review: "The works . . . they can say" should be "The *worst* . . . they can say"; "rise on skipping stones" should be "rise on *stepping* stones"; "taken sure of" should be "taken *care* of"; "the Post office has recently appeared" should be "the *post* office has recently *agreed*"; "The mining of them that nod and not" should be "The *misery* of them that *read* and *read*." If Faggen believes Frost wrote any of the things he transcribed so recklessly, he's beyond salvation. To take another lucky dip in the voluminous sack of errors, Frost wrote "*tell* my daughter," not "till my daughter"; "*in* the street light," not "I the street light"; "any *state* in the union," not "any sate in the union"; "*Such* is his social . . . fancy," not "Struck is his social . . . fancy"; "the *city* should be careful," not "the really should be careful"; "all the people they to sleep have *bored*," not "all the people they to sleep have poured"; "*with* our {new} *novelties*," not "will our {new} novel"; and so on. Not one of these ridiculous lapses has been corrected. Many of the mistakes remaining are small, and few possess the high comedy of those in the first edition; but, when you multiply them, page after page, you still have a gruesome monument to the scholar's nemesis, Error.

Even after superficial acquaintance with these notebooks, the editor's governing philosophy should have been that Frost tried to make sense. There are moments of distraction and slips of the hand; but only at hazard can an editor pretend that Frost was an ungrammatical and illiterate moron who could write "A propiting toward old prodigal romance" or "Then {sound for} the stackling sake" or "Of all empodered in our pachyderm" or "That is not gathered to abidale"—three of them on the same page! The poet did on occasion misspell a word or botch a phrase; but the incompetent transcriptions the editor defended he has now often silently corrected, if not always convincingly (the third example, for example, is now "If all [?unpacked] in our pachyderm"—it should be "*Of* all *embodied* in our pachyderm"). He has even humiliatingly been forced to revise most of the longer quotations in his introduction. (In the acknowledgments, he tries to correct which notebooks Boston University holds, only to get them wrong in a new way.)

The paleographer, that miserable soul, delights in spending his mortal hours among *a*'s that look like *u*'s, *t*'s that could pass for *l*'s, *p*'s acquainted with no letter in any human alphabet, and words, whole words, that beg to be mistaken for twins entirely unrelated. If he does not love such things with his horny heart and weary eye, he has no business in the business. The finest corrections here show a flair for reading a hand sometimes fiendishly difficult (at worst it makes a doctor's prescriptions look legible). Unfortunately, Faggen is rarely thorough, and the resulting patchwork of readings reliable, almost reliable, and grossly mistaken makes the edition unusable. He simply lacks the attention and finicky care necessary to make his transcripts perfect. It's bemusing to compare a page of these editions and find twenty or thirty corrections—my favorite being "He made a sort of fling latched on me" reborn as "He made a sort of *flying tackle* on me" (in another draft of this line, Faggen rendered the phrase "a f lying Lachle").

Harvard must have asked the editor not to increase the size of the volume. A missing line has been squeezed in here and there (as well as the whole page noted by Sitar), but there's still no sign of the fragmentary draft, probably of a poem, Frost left on both sides of the torn page in Notebook 31. Rather than attempt some more sensible system of numbering the notebook pages, Faggen has soldiered on with his comically ambiguous system—in Notebook 47, there are forty sheets that might be known as 47.1r (that is, Notebook 47, page 1, recto). For the purposes of the index, the editor has simply thrown in the sponge, so you learn only that Thoreau is mentioned somewhere in the wastes of Notebook 47—it's up to you to thumb through the thirty-seven pages of this edition to find him. Why didn't Faggen simply use the volume's page numbers? "Thoreau, 655." Done. The index has been expanded by a full page, but there are still entries missing or inadequate—good luck if you want to know where Frost mentions Lenin, or Warren Harding, or Richard Bentley. And why, even after the error was pointed out, is Walter Pater still William?

There is still some mystery surrounding so-called Notebook 47, a bundle of unrelated and miscellaneous sheets. The note regarding its location has been left unrevised, so the innocent scholar who thinks all the pages lie at Dartmouth will be surprised when he shows up at Hanover; a buried footnote reveals that some pages are at Virginia (there was no good reason for these caches of orphaned sheets to be married in shotgun fashion). Still, if you were curious about the page where Frost said that in public women should not be permitted to wear "lipstitch and howdy," you'd be hard up. Dartmouth has no knowledge of this page. I suggested that Frost probably wrote "lipstick and powder," and as noted the reading has been corrected. Though I'm delighted that a reader, without ever having seen the page, can decipher Frost more accurately than Faggen, I'm sure scholars would like to know where it is held.

This is a tale of scholarly hubris, editorial incompetence, and academic cowardice, a sorry tale whatever moral you attach to it. The first edition bore every sign of haste and monstrous carelessness, a deaf ear to meter, and an unhappy inability to look for the sense of a passage or to compare it with drafts elsewhere in the notebook, or even on the same page. Alas, this is sometimes still the case.

Here a scholar has tacitly admitted to making thousands of errors, many of them ludicrous and humiliating in nature. This paperback edition amounts to a wholesale rejection of the earlier volume, which was defective in just about every way imaginable. Since the *Notebooks* has now in many places been corrected (even if not half so well as necessary), you might think the editor would mention the fact in his introduction, or that Harvard would blazon it on the title page. Alas, about these crowds and mobs and throngs of corrections there's not a single word. The poor reader will ransack this freshly dry-cleaned edition in vain for any sign it isn't exactly the text published in hardcover three years ago. Will Harvard now offer to replace the condemned hardcover edition free of charge, particularly in the university libraries on whose shelves that calamity now sits, waiting to ambush any unwary young scholar?

The difference between Frost and the other modernists is that Frost seemed to like people. His private life was messy and sometimes cruel;

but his poems care about people's cares, are troubled by their troubles. He might have viewed this whole sorry episode with sangfroid, just another sign that men and women are often guilty of vanity, pride, and unwitting self-delusion. That might be called the human condition. Frost would have invented a rueful phrase to cover it.

Heaney's Chain

For a poet, life after the Nobel can be pottering, or bookkeeping, or simply keeping busy—it's rarely full of radical departures or stunning new poems. Eliot called the prize a "ticket to one's own funeral," and indeed it proved the funeral of his poetry. Even pottering can be difficult when you are constantly in demand to judge this prize or sign that public letter, to give a blurb to old X or a recommendation to young Y. For a poet, all life can be a distraction from the Siren call of the page. When you read that Seamus Heaney has a secretary to help him answer correspondence, you wish he had half a dozen, and perhaps a few armed guards. Yet apart from Pasternak, who was bullied by his government, no poet has ever turned down the poisoned chalice.

Heaney is the most popular literary poet since Frost, who managed to convince most of his readers that he wasn't a literary poet at all, that he booted up poems while mucking out a spring or driving a buggy—and perhaps, in a way, he did. Readers often love in Heaney what they loved in Frost, the unassumed and unassuming wisdom. Heaney has rubbed shoulders, as Frost did, with some of the most important literary figures of his day; Heaney has spent a long share of nights in hotels and on the road, as Frost did; yet often they write as if, just out the window, the cows were bawling to be milked and the first green shoots were sprouting in the fields—and as if neither man had spent more nights in a hotel than the Queen of Sheba.

In *Human Chain*, the poet is again a child in the world of things, his attention drawn to objects common as a coal sack:

> *Not coal dust, more the weighty grounds of coal*
> *The lorryman would lug in open bags*

And vent into a corner,
A sullen pile
But soft to the shovel, accommodating
As the clattering coal was not.

In days when life prepared for rainy days
It lay there, slumped and waiting
To dampen down and lengthen out

The fire, a check on mammon
And in its own way
Keeper of the flame.

This isn't lump coal, the top screening from the mine, but the bottom-deck "slack coal" sometimes called Smith's coal, the cheap bits and grindings that fall through the other meshes. This refuse coal trims the cost of the fire (hence the mention of the Bible's Mammon). "Keeper of the flame" is its own droll joke, as if the coal, like the poet, honors the dead. Heaney is not a plain poet, at least not as plain as he seems—the poems often have to be prodded and stirred to yield their meanings.

At times the Ireland of Heaney's poems seems trapped in amber. The boom years of the Celtic Tiger and the bursting of the bubble afterward have made little impression on his work. Yet this love of the things of this world has made a world, even if one somewhat sealed off. (Susan Sontag once said to an American novelist that he was living in his own theme park, and Heaney's Ireland is sometimes like Disney Dublin.) *Human Chain* is a gallery of *things*—of the binder and the baler ("the clunk of a baler / Ongoing, cardiac-dull"), of the heating boiler and the mite box and the gold-banded fountain pen, possessions that also possess, things that seize the people who use them, like the boy

Who would ease his lapped wrist

From the flap-mouthed cuff
Of a jerkin rank with eel oil,

The abounding reek of it
Among our summer desks

My first encounter with the up close
That had to be put up with.

Given the poet, given the future, it's hard not to think that the Troubles lie there before him. That would suit his passive temper. At ease
with forgotten manners, at ease with a sentence winding toward two
final prepositions, Heaney manages to stiffen his syntax with an Anglo-
Saxon rectitude of rhythm; yet, where most poets live by eye, Heaney
likes to press the reader's nose into the carnal stench of things.

This love of the way things work, this delight in the hard practical
craftsman, is very different from Auden's boyish romance with mine
equipment (Auden loved such machines partly for the rust). Heaney
likes to see a task efficiently done, and his poems are full of characters
who know a job of work. Like Virgil's *Georgics*, his poems offer a quiet
master-class on how a farm used to be run, the homage of someone who
returns again and again to the Irish fields that bore him.

> *"Lick the pencil" we might have called him*
> *So quick he was to wet the lead, so deft*
> *His hand-to-mouth and tongue-flirt round the stub.*
>
> *Or "Drench the cow," so fierce his nostril-grab*
> *And peel-back of her lip, so accurately forced*
> *The bottle-neck between her big bare teeth.*
>
> *Or "Catch the horse," for in spite of the low-set*
> *Cut of him, he could always slip an arm*
> *Around the neck and fit winkers on*
>
> *In a single move.*

Perhaps we give too much respect to a poetry lost in pastoral—it's
the strain of Romanticism most palatable to contemporary taste (palatable, and often deeply conservative). A lot of modern poetry comes
out of Wordsworth's leech-gatherer, and at times Heaney drags in too
many old grubbers with dirt under their thumbnails. Lewis Carroll
wrote a howling parody of "The Leech-Gatherer," and I doubt he

would let the Irishman off any more lightly. Yet Heaney's nostalgia is rarely simple—he understands the cost of love too well.

Heaney has Frost's avuncular voice, the bootstrap wisdom, the delight in the natural world caught and rendered; yet he's not really a teller of tales, and his poems are slow to draw the homilies beloved by Frost—the endings are hesitant, unrevealing, morally ambiguous. One of the great virtues of Heaney's poems is patience—when he lingers over a description of a shopcoat, he gives the thing edge and weight. (Frost never paused for such descriptions and had an aversion to ingenious metaphor.) However much this is poetry, it is not "poetry," the long-winded sentimental bombast that makes schoolchildren run screaming from poems ever after.

For decades Heaney has been a model citizen in the state of literature. He has produced useful translations (most popularly, *Beowulf*, a best-seller), idiosyncratic anthologies, a respectable body of criticism, and, every few years, a new book of poems. He's unlikely to be remembered for more than the poems, and among the poems unlikely to be remembered for much written in the past ten or twenty years. (If I am not a fan of his *Beowulf*, I realize I have a generation of Old English teachers against me.)

There's a state of innocence poets need, a state hard to reach when they've been frog-marched out of Paradise to the memorial dinners and honorary degrees of experience. Many of Heaney's new poems start with the old flair and dash, but after a few lines lose their way and sputter out. The late work has been solid, composed to a high level of craftsmanship; but the poems are like footnotes to poems already written, with all his mastery but little of his passion and less of his subdued outrage. They become that evil thing, poems written for the sake of writing poems.

Human Chain is far from Heaney's best book—the short and short-winded sequences rarely smolder like a peat bog afire underground. He's still good at the character sketches from the Irish hinterlands, the deft evocations of common objects (the evidence of the ordinary bewitches him), the elegies and funerals that increasingly have dominated his work. Troubled by the losses memory is heir to, most moving on his father's decline and death, the poems are evocations of a life now past.

Heaney still has the great virtue of never saying too much, of letting the poem do so much work and no more. He can make buying a copy of book VI of the *Aeneid*, that sturdy companion of young Latin scholars, as haunting as the visit to the Underworld within. For a poet of such ambition, Heaney has long given modesty a good name.

Heaney's Ghosts

Even though no one reads poetry any more, poets are still in demand. Those who wear the albatross of the Nobel Prize, like Seamus Heaney and Derek Walcott, are on permanent call for lectures, readings, blurbs, and book launches, while suffering a blizzard of invitations to serve as judges, receive honorary degrees, or read the manuscripts of nervous young poets. If the job required kissing babies and opening supermarkets as well, it would hardly be worth doing.

Somewhere in the midst of the fur-trimmed academic gowns and soapbox punditry, the poetry can get lost. A poet of the hedge and ditch has to remember the rank smell of ploughed earth. For some four decades, Seamus Heaney has served as a reminder of a pastoral world almost forgotten, the culture of the small farm and the turned penny that even in Ireland has become increasingly rare. Behind him stand Frost, a farmer only briefly and disastrously, and much further back Virgil, who was probably no more than an armchair ploughman.

The Irish poet Dennis O'Driscoll had the bright idea of sitting Heaney down for a marathon series of interviews; and with Irish cheek he persisted, though Heaney had already been called the "most over-interviewed of living poets." O'Driscoll has a day job in Irish Customs, which sounds like a joke—if any country already has too many customs, it's Ireland. The interviews took place mostly on pen and paper, but Heaney is a master at making prose an informal conversation; and by fits and starts he completed, over the course of six years, this Cook's tour of his childhood and his poetic career.

Heaney has so frequently read in contributor's notes that he was born in County Derry in 1939, he claims he has almost stopped believing it. (A few old men alive then would have been babies during the

Great Famine.) His answers to questions about childhood do have a slightly warmed-over, rehearsed feel—and when he explains, early in this iron anvil of a book, which side of the family home was devoted to the kitchen and which the stable, you realize you're in for a very long haul. Questions like "What kind of traffic is on the road in the forties?" and "Did your mother cycle sometimes?" suggest that, if this is O'Driscoll's audition as Heaney's biographer, he won't be able to fit the life into fewer than twelve volumes.

Every few pages, however, Heaney condenses memory into a moment of poetic resonance, with all his charm and cunning—the schoolmaster cyclist battering by on his "racer," or the whole large Heaney family tumbling out to push a car. The family shed was sheathed mostly in flattened tar-barrels, just as the childhood seems sheathed in the magical ken of things—the thatched roof much favored by mice, the pump Heaney has called the "omphalos" (after the stone in the temple of Apollo at Delphi), the small windbreak of old hawthorns, the reeking dunghill, all in the manner of a "small, ordinary, nose-to-the-grindstoney place." The childhood has its own peculiar logic, like a fairy tale's. The interviewer sometimes knows the right question, asking if the house depended on rainwater. You feel that he has reminded the poet of things half forgotten. O'Driscoll says modestly that the questions provoked Heaney to write a few poems.

A reader jaded by memoir might still find it curious to know that the Heaney stove would have been stewing up feed for the animals, with scones rising on the griddle, an ever-boiling kettle, and pots choked full of washing. After he vanished into boarding school, the family traveled back in time, moving into a home with a traditional turf fire and an open hearth. The fascination is not that such stray facts have sometimes inspired Heaney, but that this particular life turned into poetry, when the life of the next farmer's son down the road did not. The muse does not rise from every patch of local mud.

Heaney's rural childhood fell during the Long Weekend between the War of Independence and the Troubles of the late sixties. The Heaneys were Catholic in a part of Northern Ireland where farmers both Protestant and Catholic lived side by side. The family was not Republican; and the poet has maintained a peculiar, sidling relation to the fraught politics of the counties that make up that thorn in the neck of Ireland. His school map showed the six counties of partition and almost nothing else, as if they were their own island.

Heaney was not immune to the hurts offered in a province where Catholics were viewed with beetle-browed suspicion. He suffered the "old Northern Ireland reminders that I'd better mind my Fenian manners." At Queen's University, where he wrote his first poems in "Hopkins-speak" (too much could be read into his early debts to that most Catholic of Catholic poets), there was still at times an informal apartheid. The interviews are particularly thorough on Heaney's discovery of his contemporaries there (less thorough on his obligations to the poetic tradition), and the shouldering and elbowing among members of a famous workshop of poets called the Group.

The "need to voice something that hadn't got voiced," the experience of the Northern Irish Catholic, lies behind the great pressure Heaney feels to record and testify, though in his later books the ground has been too well covered, the imaginative mechanics grown a little worn from overuse. It's not surprising, for a poet who does not want to be overwhelmed by politics, that his poems have been driven toward symbolic experience. If Heaney too often talks of poetry metaphorically, by reference to barrel making or cement mixing or some other far-fetched labor, that may be no more than the poet's inability to explain the unexplainable except by homely analogy—or it may be an unconscious desire to justify poetry in the world of drudgery. Education removed him from the grim labors of the farm—his poems have been a long struggle to atone.

Heaney, who can read and speak Irish only haltingly, knew from the start that the "linguistic experiences that threw my switches were in English," as was true for most of his generation of Irish poets. A writer is sometimes chosen by his language—and in Heaney it's not the language once spoken by Irish bog and boulder. The imposition of English still rankles a little, as does being called a British poet. That's a dangerous thing to call an Irishman, whether he's a poet or not.

Though Heaney was surrounded by politics of the most violent sort (friends, a cousin, and a pub owner who lived down the street in Belfast all were murdered), he refused to be closely involved—a leader of Sinn Féin once browbeat him for not writing about the cause. The poet needed few excuses for moving out of Belfast in 1972, during some of the worst of the sectarian murders; but those offered ("The apprenticeship was over . . . ," he says. "The required thing was to step away a bit"), prove no less shifty and unconvincing than Auden's for emigrating to America in the shadow of World War II. Yet this ability to stand aside freed the poems from the powerful undertow of Northern Ireland's violence, where the victors, if there were any, were often victims.

It is good to remember that this poet has been—has sometimes been forced to be—a smiling public man: cautious in judgment, a born diplomat, but clever at speaking behind his hand. (The slyest moments here are his backhanded judgments on fellow poets.) Heaney earned his keep at the podium for some years, and for more than a decade was a professor at Harvard. The academic language of "deconstruction," "hegemony," "postcolonial," and that scare verb "privilege" still infects his speech and is not placed in ironic quotations. You could say more generously that in whatever pub Heaney happens to be, even when the pub is Harvard, he keeps his ears open.

Heaney's ambition glowers like a turf fire beneath his genial manner, a blaze revealed in the dispiriting number of tetchy comments about critics. No matter the honors accrued, the resentments are alive: one review was a "hatchet job," another may have been "payback." He always examines a negative review "to see if it's salutary objection or shitty backlash." Apparently it is mostly the latter. Perhaps without a thin skin a poet can't be sensitive enough, though there have been poets with hides a howitzer couldn't penetrate. The richness of these interviews comes in part from the weakness of character inadvertantly revealed. A poetry of warmth and humility has been drawn around a personality at times icy with conceit—this is disturbing, until one remembers Robert Frost.

Heaney's poems come from a specific place, while Frost, the other major pastoral poet of the last century, sometimes seems so dislocated from place, his poems are already halfway to allegory. (As the Irish poet wryly admits, however, for all his poems about fishing, since his teens he has rarely picked up a rod.) We go to Heaney's prose not for the ripeness of atmosphere that infuses the poetry, but for all that cannot get into the poem—namely, how a poet views his craft. He is always sharp-eyed at spotting the psychological fractures in the verse line: "Every good poem . . . ," he says, "could conceivably be an epitaph."

Heaney is a rationalist who wants access to the pagan past—his view of the poet is virtuous and metaphysical, as if there were still Irish bards wandering the countryside like tinkers. A reader can get a little weary of the references to the numinous in poetry, to the poet's "fidelity to the mystery." (To say that "poetry is a ratification of the impulse towards transcendence" makes it sound too much like faith healing.) Ghosts tend to be housebound; and in a peculiar way Heaney has become the revenant of his own life, prone to dropping by. He is best at the long memory of the senses—the "old breadcrumby smell of the porch" at school, for instance. The interviews permit, even encourage, a gout of reminiscence; but in poems memory must be measured out slowly and more carefully, like old brandy.

The interviewer is as dogged as Kafka's magistrates—his questions are courteous, rarely silly (O'Driscoll has read more of Heaney's obscure addresses than the poet can probably remember writing), but almost always a trifle dull. If they rarely excite Heaney to memorable speech, he occasionally finds the proper burr—in his childhood home, the upper bedroom held "three of those big iron-frame beds that would eventually end up as makeshift gates, brass-turreted jobs, real old jinglers, as broad as ruck-shifters." He recalls of some gardening tools, "You'd see this lean-to of seasoned shafts that could have been spear shafts stacked against the wall." There stand Ajax and Achilles.

The most consequent poet of our age has long borne the burden of being called the finest Irish poet since Yeats—with the not-so-sly implication that he's not as good as Yeats. Five hundred pages of chat, even with Yeats, would be a good deal too many. This book underscores how much a poet like Heaney is used by his past to make its claim, but perhaps no book can explain the indelible mystery of his work. The secret can't be found in interviews, because they are the wrong place to look. In the end, this interminable inquisition does what it should—it sends you back to the poetry, the poetry of a man who has lived in the rectitude of language and the doubts of the tongue.

Verse Chronicle: Weird Science

Maxine Hong Kingston

Since *The Prelude*, the poem-memoir has been surprisingly rare, especially in a day when lives are scarcely lived before they're committed to Facebook or laid open like fresh corpses in blogs. *I Love a Broad Margin to My Life*, Maxine Hong Kingston's breezy and peculiar new memoir, is cast in verse, which to a prose writer must seem a wonderful idea. Writing verse is so easy, after all—why, it just spills down the page like Jackson Pollock's dribbles. You break the lines wherever you like—never too long, never too short—and soon a humble-jumble work briefer than *The Great Gatsby* is splashed across two hundred pages or more.

> *I am turning 65 years of age.*
> *In 2 weeks I will be 65 years old.*
> *I can accumulate time* and *lose*
> *time? I sit here writing in the dark—*
> *can't see to change these penciled words—*
> *just like my mother, alone, bent over her writing,*
> *just like my father bent over his writing, alone*
> *but for me watching.*

This may not be distinguished poetry; but it's thoughtful, tender, sensitive to those deadlines in life that become the deadlines of art—we're all going to die, usually sooner than we wish. Kingston has been drawn to her heritage yet slightly suspicious of it—the difference between the China she longs for and the China that exists is already the shadow of loss.

A memoir that stayed close to the contrary whims of nurture might have proved capable of analyzing the insistent will of nature. Unfortunately, after a few pages Kingston gives up any sustained self-portrait, treating the reader instead to trivial anecdotes, breast-beating over the Iraq War, slapdash notes from a trip to China, and some freeform spirituality that would embarrass Gary Snyder:

> I swirl,
> galaxies swirl. Rocks alive, mountains
> alive. Soul through and through rocks,
> mountains, ranges and ranges of mountains.
> Bright Smile of Spontaneous Joy. Lift
> the sides of your obstinate mouth, and start joy.

I begin to think that brooding has been much underrated.

Kingston is a soft-boiled soul, faintly embarrassed at being well off, full of liberal guilt and unconscious smugness, and without the least idea how to make the world better, except by giving a little money here, protesting a little there (she was arrested outside the White House), and spreading a lot of New Age guff wherever she can: "I have been a man in China, and a woman / in China, and a woman in the Wild West. / (My college roommate called; she'd met / Earll and me in Atlantis, but I don't / remember that.)" When Kingston indulges in such loopy nonsense, you're tempted to laugh at the whole state of California, or at least the pocket duchy of Berkeley. I wish she'd given more space to her practical, grouchy husband Earll, who says things like "The Church is a gyp."

Kingston has resurrected the insufferable male hero of her novel, *Tripmaster Monkey*, who serves as her alter ego on the journey through China; but she is not a writer coarse or funny enough to thrive in picaresque—she has little of the charm of Thoreau (the memoir's title comes from *Walden*), who made minutiae burn with the heat of existence. Instead, her tale batters along, knocking about the page like a drunk man's walk through memory.

Kingston is alert to people caught between two worlds—the scenes in China are far the most vivid, especially a visit to her mother's home village (the poet's early memoir, *The Woman Warrior* [1976], though full of naive sentiment, has held up better than anything she has written since). She and her imaginary counterpart tour a monastery and other villages, one apparently composed entirely of artists; but she behaves like a city rube, jaw agape at all she sees, reminiscing in a childlike stream of consciousness. She's allowed to plant a rice field:

> *Oooh, the mud, the pleasurefull* [sic]
> *mud, my free and happy toes. You trace*
> *in water a square, and at each corner embed*
> *one rice plant. Oh, my hands*
> *rooting and squishing silken luscious mud.*

I'm surprised her hosts didn't drown her. Kingston possesses only rudimentary Chinese, and the villagers are all the more eager to take her money—her whirlwind progress seems a grotesque form of colonial tourism. Poetry has done her no favors, allowing an imagination already disorganized to practice its defects in rambling and self-dramatizing anecdotes. Free verse looks easy to the outsider, as if it just fell off the lap of prose—if you're going to write a long poem, however, perhaps you ought to possess some ear for the poetic line. Kingston is a prose writer who lives with ghosts (as well as a mob of banalities), writing in a form she doesn't understand. Poetry is also her China.

Thomas Lynch

Thomas Lynch is better known as a mortician than as a poet. His essays on the business end of the end of life are sardonic, anecdotal, full of the rituals of American death. For almost forty years, Lynch has run the family funeral home in a small Michigan town not far from Detroit. Now in his sixties, he's a dry and slightly morbid observer of the life of death; and he brings to *Walking Papers* the qualities useful to his day job: solemnness (even glumness), formal bearing, and a sharp eye for the bottom line.

There are many occupations guaranteed to bring a chill to conversation—after serial killer, mortician is probably the most effective. (When asked his vocation, Auden used to reply, "Medieval historian," after which he was left alone.) Lynch's early poems were a little less burdened by his dark trade. Now he's too eager for the graveyard pun or, if he's trying too hard, the Billy Collins premise that sucks all the air out of a poem. When a poem begins, "What sort of morning was Euclid having / when he first considered parallel lines?," it almost writes itself, down to the dollop of gooey feeling at the end. The only problem is that all the pleasure is front-loaded; working out the poem is about as interesting as solving a quadratic equation.

Lynch's new poems are dogged, slightly ponderous, not ruinously bad but not ruinously good, either. Corpses, however, make him positively cheerful; after the "charred corpse of the deacon's boy," the "white maple coffin / covered in sunflowers," and the remark that "corpses do not fret their coffin boards" (mortuary humor, at Wordsworth's expense), you realize that he takes a secret delight in death, and in the reaction to death:

> Upright over corpses it occurred to him—
> the body outstretched on a pair of planks,
> the measly loaf and stingy goblet,
> the gobsmacked locals, their begrudging thanks,
> the kinswoman rummaging for coppers—
> it came into his brain like candlelight:
> his lot in life like priesthood after all.

Perhaps there ought to be a verb in that last line (Lynch's punctuation and syntax are surprisingly wayward for a poet so meticulous), but the sharpness of observation finds a slow revelation here—those who deal with death are sin-eaters, allowing the living to keep living.

Given to bouts of Midwest Babbitry, Lynch will say that the public library provides "sweet fodder for our hungry minds," which sounds like a slogan for cornflakes. Or he'll claim that a silence is "dumb welcome to my own mum thankfulness," a line unsayable unless you already have a broken jaw. There are fossilized versions (I almost wrote "embalmed") of what Merwin was writing forty years ago:

> There was this hollow after your going
> as if the air you'd lately occupied
> having waited for you these long years sighed
> at your leaving; as if the light were lonely.

Some poems are so preachy, you wonder if Lynch has been ghost-writing for Adrienne Rich. The public reaction to the Iraq war is reduced to "joking, dancing, / carrying on / as if nothing / mattered. As if / nothing was wrong. / Neither the dead / nor the damaged, / the litany / of woe and toll: / to currency, / economy, / the poor planet, / the armed forces, / the price of oil." *The litany of woe and toll!* When you've waded through the desultory sonnets and a plodding sequence to members of the late Republican administration ("The Names of Donkeys" eventually gets round to George W. Bush and Guantánamo), you feel as if you'd gone ten rounds with a lead pipe. If a poet has no particular verbal gifts, he's dependent on an odd point of view, or a warming tone, or—always the refuge of a scoundrel—something to say.

Lynch now lives part of the year in Ireland; and the Irish poems are lushly detailed and animated, broader in sympathy, less miserable—perhaps a man who works so much around death is different at a distance from his labor. There's death in Ireland, too, of course—this poet can hardly get away from it—but the black humor is more generous and humane:

> After half a morning's massive labors
> they'd got her out the back door to the haggard—
> a heap among the spuds and cabbages
> of putrefaction and composting grief—
> and knowing that the job was incomplete
> they set to work with spades and dug a ditch
> of such surpassing depth and length and breadth . . .
> it was after dark they shoved her into it.

Perhaps the only thing worse than not taking death seriously enough is taking it too seriously. That last line is as sharp as anything by Seamus Heaney.

Eiléan Ní Chuilleanáin

Eiléan Ní Chuilleanáin's new book, *The Sun-Fish*, is set in some misty vale inhabited by Yeats's Cuchulain, some fairies and elves, and a whole lot of peat. The poems live in this century, mostly; but they carry the freight of another day:

> her grandmother remembered in old age
> Her long hair down, her wide shoulders bare
> Before her basin in the early light
> While the cat lapped a basin of fresh milk,
> And how as a child she watched without moving.

Ní Chuilleanáin loves this stillness, the timelessness of an Ireland both passing and passed—stately, measured, the poems unfold in their own time, making very little concession to the reader. They're full of material things, things with density but no specificity, as if she dealt only in the Platonic cat, the Platonic milk, and the Platonic grandmother. Sometimes her miniature worlds are pregnant with mystery; yet, even when they're a puzzle box no one could open, they don't wheedle or ply, never bristling with the privacy or privation of Geoffrey Hill's poems. Ní Chuilleanáin can write about the extinction of a species in a melancholy, private way, where other poets would be mounting the soap box. Her poems invite being read, while seeming not to care what the reader makes of them.

Though little known in this country, Ní Chuilleanáin has long had a major reputation at home. Fast nearing seventy, she was for many years overshadowed by Seamus Heaney, Michael Longley, and Derek Mahon. Her poems are so strange, written with such cool detachment, shrinking at times as if they wanted to disappear, it took longer for their quiet virtues to be appreciated. Ní Chuilleanáin is a watcher, not an actor—fewer than half her poems are in the first person, and you feel that given half a chance she'd vanish from the others in a blink.

> Shaped like a barrel with asthma, her black skirt
> Bunched at her waist, she kneels or squats
> At every spot reputed to be holy.
> Her two daughters wait and gossip until
> She scrambles up and they move a few yards on.

The old woman is making a religious pilgrimage, but the poem manages to make that almost irrelevant. The grown daughters fret, the saint is never named (it must be St. Fionán)—the little drama of personality and landscape is barely a drama at all. The detached tone can be surprisingly hard to read—is the poet being grave, or puckish, or a little of both? However removed these figures from the world of cheap airfares and crashing banks, such a woman has survived into the days of the Celtic Tiger, as if all Ireland might still be soiled with the superstitions of a lost age.

Too often a note of preciousness steals in, as if the things of the world were valued too highly (not every cashmere sleeve or bone-handled knife deserves a special glow): "Who can explain / Why the wasps are asleep in the dark in their numbered holes / And the lights shine all night in the hospital corridors?" Or: "When the cat wakes up he will speak in Irish and Russian / And every night he will tell you a different tale / About the firebird that stole the golden apples." These lines have the winsome, *faux-naïf* tone that made Randall Jarrell's poems so hard to bear. The voice hardly varies, and you could fall asleep in the middle of one poem and without knowing it wake in the middle of another.

Having been put together in unexpected ways, as if the parts had been shuffled or slightly mismatched, the poems are so quiet and subtle, you have to read them twice before they come into focus, if they're to come into focus at all. Indeed, these poems love being inconclusive—conclusion would violate the anxieties never laid to rest.

> She used to love the darkness, how it brought
> Closer the presence of flesh, the white arms and breast
> Of a stranger in a railway carriage a dim glow—
> Or the time when the bus drew up at a woodland corner
> And a young black man jumped off, and a shade
> Moved among shades to embrace him under the leaves.

Ní Chuilleanáin's studied view and her nods toward Irish folklore sometimes suggest a poet who is haunting, but also trying too hard to haunt. Yet how rare it is when a poet immersed in other voices—there are whispers of Yeats, of Heaney, even of Hardy—speaks with a voice resolutely her own.

Kimiko Hahn

The shelves devoted to the poetry of science are almost as bare as those devoted to the science of poetry. The most famous example after Lucretius' *The Nature of Things*, one of the most tiresome books in classical literature, must be Erasmus Darwin's *The Loves of the Plants*, a bit of Augustan daffiness in which the plants prove more sexually voracious than any nymph of the Earl of Rochester's. Kimiko Hahn's *Toxic Flora* (a pleasantly anti-Romantic title) attempts to use the black arts more deeply and deliberately, relying for inspiration on the science columns of the *New York Times*.

Many poets love science in an amateurish way. The problem with writing a poem on the cabbage looper moth or the loggerhead shrike or the exoplanet Gliese 436b is that poetry labors to convey dry-as-dust information—the science is therefore usually limited to allegory or symbol. (Too often when poetry takes up science the science sounds like theology.) Hahn's method amounts to sketching some scientific quarrel or discovery, then nattering on about it until she swerves for a few lines into her private life. The results can be slightly disturbing. She compares a snail-eating caterpillar on Maui to a "mother who rips open another mother // for her unborn child," but this doesn't quite prepare the reader for the ending a few lines later: "My mother is from Maui." Rather than a stunning and clinching revelation, the line seems both too much and not enough.

Hahn's secrets and resentments are so deeply buried, the scientific anecdotes rarely winkle them out, more often providing some far-fetched analogy the poet pounces on like a Pomeranian. I like the idea that lovers are just as mysterious as fossil harvestmen and families as poisonous as the *Heliconius* butterfly, but I begin to wonder if the mild traumas of the poet's life really need science to explain them. The ligature is usually so fanciful, the logic so cryptic, the reader is left to puzzle over the strained connections. Planets are formed of disks of dust and debris, she writes,

> *giving rise to zodiacal light*

> *and a reason for developing sharper telescopes:*

the father spanking the ten-year-old
just out of the shower

and because she already had breast buds

she didn't want anyone to look.
Years later, the whole family still thinking it was funny . . .

The connection isn't the male gaze, but the creation of a world, a life, from the dust of old events. The incident is troubling, but that colon leaves far too much unsaid.

Marianne Moore was perhaps the last American poet to use the minutiae of science to dramatic effect; but her poems seem testament to an almost moral curiosity, as well as the application of a fine imaginative pressure to matters otherwise unpoetic. If a seventeenth-century theologian thought that the dusty rings of Saturn were Jesus's foreskin, Hahn feels obliged to rant away like, well, another seventeenth-century theologian: "maybe the rings are the uterine linings from my dried up uterus, / maybe the rings are saliva from apologies never uttered . . . , // maybe the rings are baby teeth, wisdom teeth, vomit, and shit."

The slightly slipshod nature of the enterprise is made clearer by the columns from which Hahn draws (poets feel naked without a "project" these days, even if it's no more interesting than draft legislation on petroleum leases). In the helpful appendix listing the original articles, entries are missing or misdated—once she even lists the wrong article—and the facts from the columns themselves have sometimes been sloppily transcribed. Worse, much of Hahn's poetry is only lightly rewritten from the *Times* prose, which explains the slightly denatured style—too many poems look like desperate note-taking in Bio 101. In "Brooding," the *Times* reporter's "Then a graduate student, he pulled up a trawl bucket from the dark midwaters of the Monterey Canyon . . . and found a mass of squid eggs" becomes Hahn's

As when a student
hauling a trawl bucket from the black mid-waters off Monterey

found a mass of squid eggs.

In "The Blob," the newspaper's "Chunks of the monster were hacked off and shipped to the museum that later became the Smithsonian" turns into Hahn's "Chunks were immediately shipped to the nascent Smithsonian." The original article's "a link between the vocalizations and the particular syrinxes behind them" appears in "Defining *Syrinx*" as "a link between such vocalization / and the particular syrinx behind it." In "Sustenance," the report that a "species of moth in Madagascar . . . alights on the neck of a sleeping magpie . . . and sticks its long proboscis between the bird's closed eyelids" is now:

> *The Madagascan moth alights on the sleeping Magpie*
> *insinuating its proboscis between the closed eyelids.*

There is "found" poetry, to be sure; but elsewhere Hahn has italicized the passages she quotes, however inaccurately, implying that the rest has been transformed. Marianne Moore was far more austere in her borrowings and correct in her acknowledgments. None of Hahn's light-fingered musings can be called plagiarism, not exactly, since the poet is more or less open about her sources (with the exception of "The Search for Names," adapted from an unacknowledged Wikipedia entry). Still, such lazy use of the originals would earn her an F in any freshman comp course.

Paul Muldoon

Paul Muldoon is a force of nature. Though he has lived in America for more than two decades, he's still the most influential Irish poet after Seamus Heaney—a lot of young English and Irish poets come out of his vest pocket, though they're not half so clever as the real thing. Muldoon turns sixty next year, but it would be too much to expect this perennially boyish writer to slow down. *Maggot*, his eleventh collection, is full of poems that have more bells and flashing lights than a pachinko machine; yet the arty wordplay of his late manner can be exhausting. Though he's still capable of writing a poem that's moving and serious at once, his heart's not in it—he'd rather be lighting off firecrackers and tying tin cans to the tails of cats.

> *On a grassy knoll two Tritons dressed as tramps*
> *are doing the Versailles vamp*
> *while, high above the rumble,*
> *another is aiming to put his stamp*
>
> *on something, anything. The Nereid as a flitch*
> *of halibut, caught without a stitch*
> *on this holiest of days. Not to worry if we fumble*
> *as we bait and switch*
>
> *in a storm sewer that might turn a mill*
> *never mind a rumor mill.*

At first this seems simple free association. Muldoon's recent poems have been driven by such gusts of rhyme, lost in such whirlpools of puns, it's easy to read them as high-octane nonsense. The passage is in fact part of half a dozen sonnets working whimsical turns on François Boucher's *Arion on the Dolphin*, taking in big hair, a doo-wop chorus, Teflon, a dog-paddling dog, Versailles, and the assassination of JFK. Even Thomas Pynchon would be jealous. (The rococo painting, already self-parody, was a failed commission for Louis XV.) The lyre-strumming Arion, "eye-linered and lip-glossed," is compared to a "rock god"—rock music, that is. The sonnets are partly about power, partly about arrogance, and partly about boy-kings who die before their time. Hyperactive, hypnotic, his mind going four ways at once, Muldoon is forever stealing into the underworld of words, as if across languages and centuries all words were secretly related—he long ago sold his soul to the devil who wrote *Finnegans Wake*.

A phrase in Muldoon may scuttle in and out of a poem, meaning something different each time (the storm sewer above is later "where the third of the shooters / waits in the wings for the motorcade"). If the reader is intolerant, the poems will have no subject but their own dervishy whirls (there are more metamorphoses in Muldoon than in Ovid)—but these queer and infuriating arabesques are the medium for a poetic imagination far more complicated. You know you're in Muldoonville when you meet a postmodern detective, or when Edison's electrocution of an elephant is equated with torture by the KGB, or when a series of short lyrics is not about love—it's about auto accidents.

There's not much feeling in Muldoon's new poems, but for a few lines he can still fetch the past through the dammed-up resistance of memory.

> A sky of china clay in which something very like a star
> flared as over Bethlehem
> and where the Star
> of the Sea herself was obscured by a plume
>
> of ox breath. Christmas Eve. My mother boiling onions for sage
> and onion stuffing. The tinsel
> bought in Omagh from an Eastern sage
> who still went door-to-door.

Alas, he can't sustain it—too soon the Medicis come marching in, and a Sisyphean Santa Claus, and a puss that rhymes with a "little bloody pus." The consequence of this wild, allusive, hypomanic style is a curiously flattening of tone—every line seems blared by a tin horn, every poem a dance of the seven veils done by West Point cadets.

Such poems make me laugh, and despair, often both at once. The poet invents a seven-line stanza in which lines two and seven reappear as lines one and six of the next, line three rhymes on the word "dark," while line four always ends in the phrase "acid remarks." And line five? Line five is by turns, and in strict order, "to all and sundry," "at the Christmas party," or "in the third-floor Ladies"! It's a tour de force, but all his poems are tours de force, if they're not coups d'état. The poems owe so many debts to the form that actually saying something seems accidental—Muldoon is brilliant at such things, but the results are often a disaster.

Patience is not a virtue with Muldoon's work, it's a necessity. An extended and somewhat clumsy villanelle that you're sure is the most terrible nonsense may turn out a day later, when you think again, to be a portrait of the limitations of the Age of Discovery. You can labor over a Muldoon sequence, buy a box of a dozen decoder rings, yet after long study find that the poet is having a cyst removed from his testicles—all you have to show for such make-work are Muldoon's balls. Indeed, the better you come to know a Muldoon poem, the less interesting it seems. Without the tricks, the substance is often trivial.

The poems of this Artful Dodger have become little slot machines of half-baked half-rhymes, phrases shuttling and shuffling like a great Manchester loom—all for something that looks as if Stevens's "Sea Surface Full of Clouds" had been run through a blender. The pity is that Muldoon (Pulitzer behind, Nobel perhaps dead ahead) has more mind than a gaggle of poets together. You could not hope for a richer use of language, or one at times more empty.

Gjertrud Schnackenberg

Gjertrud Schnackenberg's husband, the philosopher Robert Nozick, died of cancer almost nine years ago. *Heavenly Questions* is a book of grief and the ways of grief. The poems return again and again, in harrowing detail, to the scenes of his illness. Schnackenberg is a poet richly drenched, even drowned, in the classics; but, however much her mind strays to the myth of Theseus or the battles of the *Mahābhārata*, the battleground here is the operating theater and the recovery ward. Lines and phrases are often repeated, as if every poem were the ghost of a pantoum, as if the poet found herself practicing a litany she is unable to abandon.

The best passages have the visual precision and leaps of perception that have long characterized her work:

> *A bleaching coral reef with pockmarked walls*
> *And shining heaps of gouged-out tesserae—*
> *Like seashell litter, slowly ground to sand,*
> *In violet-blue, in white, in basalt green,*
> *Vermilion, mica leaf, along the floors*
> *Like ex-mosaics chiseled from the walls.*

Unfortunately, such lines are rare. Schnackenberg is attempting something very difficult, as she did in her last book, the *Throne of Labdacus*, in which her retelling of the myth of Oedipus was mesmerizing in its leaden progress.

The fierce privacy of grief after an inconsolable loss cannot easily be turned into poetry. Grief is far more difficult to render than love, which even schoolboys can do in touching fashion—grief is the emotion that reduces us to silence. Schnackenberg's marriage was proudly intellectual (the couple's bedside reading was apparently vetted by a Great Books committee); but, though the poet shapes her sorrow through science and philosophy, she is never wildly comfortable with abstractions.

> The vein of graphite ore preoccupied
> In microcrystalline eternity.
> In graphite's interlinking lattices,
> Symmetrically unfolding through a grid
> Of pre-existent crystal hexagons.
> Mirror-image planes and parallels.
> Self-generated. Self-geometrized.

Self-geometrized! Even the numbing pentameter cannot help such a word (when Eliot used "Polyphiloprogenitive," he was joking). Too many lines sound like attempts to versify a microbiology textbook: "A break-site underwent a subtle change, / A hidden break-site in a chromosome; / A break, without apparent consequence." Her losses wither when cast into such desiccated language.

The most moving passages chronicle the dying husband's last days and last hours, his illness filtered through a dream vision of the Hagia Sophia or a contemplation of chess in the *Mahābhārata*. The numerous invocations of the ship of Theseus are composed partly of the famous paradox of identity (if each individual board has been replaced, is it still the same ship?), partly Ariadne's curse (when Theseus forgot to raise a white sail, his father believed him dead and killed himself), and partly the scene in the *Paradiso* where Neptune watches in wonder as the keel of the Argo (the very first ship, but sailed by Jason, not Theseus) passes overhead. The mazes of these poems often have no thread to guide the reader out.

Unfortunately, Schnackenberg describes her husband in such gushing fancies of love ("My magic stag lay in a trance induced"), the real man vanishes:

> How could I memorize his gentle ways.
> The way he mingled friendliness with passion,
> Plain dealing, open-handed, unafraid.

The swift, reflexive generosity.
His striking conversation, magic ease
In seeking what the other could, then more,
In understanding, warmly understood.

This is no longer a dying philosopher but a paragon without port-folio. Schnackenberg can hardly write of this "wonder-wounded hearer, / Facing extinction in a mental mirror" without making the reader wince. Worse, her language is overstuffed with generalities and immensities. You can't turn a page without getting smacked in the face with the "nucleus / In micro-desolate eternity," "black heavens pouring out infinities," "dissolving oceanic memories / In other future ocean-vanishings," a "sound trapped in the graphite magnitudes," or "exploding outward into gaping stars."

The poetry is often beautifully restrained, the fortitude with which she bears her husband's multiple operations and his final release into death wholly admirable. Schnackenberg is unsparing about her loss, and the terrifying emptiness that follows. The poems are moody, dyed in grief, burdened with sorrow, and unutterably dull:

Once upon a time, war drums aroused
Chaotic gongs, and horns wailing for war
Were summoning the pieces to the board,
And chariots in slow motion grinding past
On mammoth wheels carved with battle scenes
Were drawing toward a clutch of soldier pawns
With spears like lightning springing from the ground.

Such soulful, dreary writing, unmemorable as it falls through its verse paragraphs, is the merest echo of her early work. Schnackenberg's po-ems have always had a slightly drowsy quality, but now they seem to fall asleep before they start. *Heavenly Questions* (the title comes from an ancient Chinese poem) is a serious work of grief. I would rather read mediocre poems by Schnackenberg than good poems by almost anyone else, but that does not make this heartbreaking book any better.

Verse Chronicle: Blah Blah Blah

Richard Wilbur

The perennially boyish Richard Wilbur may be the first American poet to write decent verse at ninety—most poets have trouble at seventy, or fifty, or thirty. Sophocles wrote *Oedipus at Colonus* at ninety, but poems of grace and depth are more likely to be written when the poet is still young and foolish. Wilbur was never the darkest of American poets—a kind of moral sunniness was always breaking in. He was sunny the way Frost can be sunny, though Frost is sunny only by cutting out three-quarters of his poems. Wilbur was the Frost left over, the Frost of most high-school anthologies.

Anterooms is a thin book, fattened with more blank pages than is healthy. In these not quite two-dozen new poems (with a handful of translations and a fresh flurry of riddles by the late Latin poet Symphosius added as makeweights), Wilbur has made a belated virtue of brevity and simplicity. Some oddity of syntax or the quirky way one word leans against another opens the lines to a world more hesitant, more despairing, full of those anxieties Wilbur poems were once good at fending off.

The poems are at times so simple they could be mistaken for the linsey-woolsey of light verse, but at best they have the severity of memories long abided. In his twilight work, Wilbur has embraced Frost's narrow, homespun diction, with a consequent gain in the register of emotion.

> *Sometimes, on waking, she would close her eyes*
> *For a last look at that white house she knew*

In sleep alone, and held no title to,
And had not entered yet, for all her sighs.

What did she tell me of that house of hers?
White gatepost; terrace; fanlight of the door;
A widow's walk above the bouldered shore;
Salt winds that ruffle the surrounding firs.

Is she now there, wherever there may be?
Only a foolish man would hope to find
That haven fashioned by her dreaming mind.
Night after night, my love, I put to sea.

This is more haunting the more one reads it: the dedicated pauses, with the delayed rhyme on *sighs* (taking full advantage of the *abba* quatrain), the dream house slowly revealed, the yearning for the death that is life again. Wilbur's beloved wife of sixty-five years died four years ago—the gentleness of his longing is almost unbearable.

Wilbur's first poems were published when Roosevelt was president— the verse manner was so staid, that could have been Teddy, not Franklin. The poet's mastery was recognized from the start—in the decade after the war, he was a kind of cavalier's cavalier; but that appreciation came with the reservations of a critic like Jarrell, who called him "delicate, charm- ing, and skillful" (it's not clear whether that was in ascending or descend- ing order of sin). Hilarious though Jarrell's review was, he seemed to be criticizing Wilbur for everything Wilbur was not—and what he chiefly was not was Lowell. The younger poet's despair tended to be puckish, however tangled in the moral order of grand opera. It tends that way still:

In this great form, as Dante proved in Hell,
There is no dreadful thing that can't be said
In passing. Here, for instance, one could tell

How our jeep skidded sideways toward the dead
Enemy soldier with the staring eyes,
Bumping a little as it struck his head,

And then flew on, as if toward Paradise.

The poetry of the Second World War now looks more durable and ravaging than that of the First, though sometimes written by soldiers a lifetime later. I wish Wilbur had more often used the shock so naked here, and the black humor somehow beyond shock — it's the cynicism of soldiers themselves, when they try to forget death.

Most of Wilbur's work since about 1960 has been undernourished — after he devoted himself to translation, the Baroque manner degraded into mere fussiness and plasterwork. He lost the metaphysical unease that cut through the complicated rhyme schemes and prissy, over-worked diction. Pound recognized that poetry is distinguished in part by melopoeia, the music of language; but language too sweetly musical can be sickening.

The poems in *Anterooms* are often well-worn homilies, without Frost's rough charm (it's impossible to understand Frost without understanding his charm). Though the riddles once more display Wilbur's wearisome elegance, riddles are a form with both feet already in the grave. Mallarmé and Brodsky, however, have rarely had finer translators — reading such pieces, I'm not wholly resentful that Wilbur spent much of his maturity translating the plays of Racine, Corneille, and Molière. To a crowd of middle-aged formal poets, Wilbur can do no wrong (every new book calls for a Fourth of July celebration); but his publicity machine is working a little hard to call this minor volume a "major event in poetic history." Perhaps such praise should be reserved for *The Waste Land*, or *Lyrical Ballads*, or, hell, Shakespeare's *Sonnets*.

Yusef Komunyakaa

There's a lot of gushing in Yusef Komunyakaa's new book, as if his emotions came at a discount from Costco. His best work has been taut, bristling with constraint, the saying urgent with meaning and the having said an achievement, not an indulgence. The populist strain in Komunyakaa, the wish to play to the rafters, has long fought with his love of classical literature and classical reserve. In *The Chameleon Couch*, the populist gets the upper hand.

Komunyakaa knows how to construct a complex poem, having learned more than a little from Derek Walcott. One piece starts with the poet making love; but something haunts him, following him along beaches, onto an airplane, until he realizes it's the image of Cape Coast Castle in Ghana, a notorious center of the slave trade. He recalls his visit to that benighted place; yet, just where the poem gathers its resources for revelation, the only justice poetry offers, he lets an imaginary governor hector an imaginary woman captive:

> There's a tyranny of language in my fluted bones.
> There's poetry on every page of the Good Book.
> There's God's work to be done in a forsaken land.
> There's a whole tribe in this one, but I'll break them
> before they're in the womb, before they're conceived,
> before they're even thought of.

Fluted bones! On and on the deadly bombast runs, from "I own your past, / present, & future" to "I'll thoroughly break you, head to feet, / but, sister, I'll break you most dearly / with sweet words"—the descent to bathos becomes a headlong plunge. The problem is not Komunyakaa's easygoing prose, studded with the ampersands all the hepcats use (he's more comfortable in a register less rhetorical than the governor's soap-boxing), but his failure to realize that the poem's virtue comes from underplaying the monstrousness, rather than inventing a sneering villain no more believable than Snidely Whiplash.

Komunyakaa presents himself as a divided soul, a Vietnam vet torn between Donne and boogie-woogie, a man who has never forgotten his Louisiana roots but is unashamed of throwing Kant, or Hegel, or Kierkegaard into a poem. Yet beneath that surface lies the complacent pride that forces him to say, "Led Zeppelin is still in my nogginbox." (Actually, a character says that, but the reader understands.) He's a sixties survivor who feels obliged to mention that he survived tear gas and billy clubs. Then he mentions it again.

Komunyakaa recognizes the power of his broken heritage, presented without the primping self-regard that has long marred the work of Walcott. Alas, Komunyakaa can't resist the lure of political poems that say nothing beyond the drearily predictable, whether he visits Auschwitz in the guise of Orpheus, or conjures revolution in Iran, or sees up close the poverty of India. The reader might be forgiven for feeling that wherever evil lurks, there goes Komunyakaa—like Green Lantern or the Shadow.

Now in his midsixties, Komunyakaa is drawn to moral bullying, complete with gouts of mushiness ("I remembered the scent of loneliness / in my coat left draped over the chair"), needy longing ("Anything for a hug or kiss, / anything to be healed"), and histrionic pleas ("Why can't they stop / trying to find lost selves / & outlaw galaxies?"), with William Carlos Williams plumminess added to taste ("Just bite into this one, & your tongue will remember / foreverness"). Not every poet can get teary-eyed over the silk worm:

> *A flounce of light is the only praise*
> *it ever receives. I need to trust*
> *this old way of teaching a man*
> *to cry, & I want to believe in*
> *what's left of the mulberry leaves.*
> *Humans crave immortality, but oh,*
> *yes, to think worms wove this*
> *as a way to stay alive in our world.*

If a poet like this works very hard, and is very lucky, he might one day become a flabby sentimentalist like Gerald Stern.

Komunyakaa knows what a different poet he might be. He hears some sort of commotion outside his room in Shanghai but is reluctant to interfere. The next morning, he's told that the baby of the couple down the hall had choked to death after swallowing a lead bird. (The poem's ending is mawkish, but until then he channels C. K. Williams, that bard of guilty conscience, to stirring effect.) A prose poem reveals that the poet keeps the voice of a former lover, long dead, on his answering machine—the lines are far more telling in their mournful restraint than the poem on Auschwitz. The elegy gains in force from its discretion, for he never mentions that the woman, the poet Reetika Vazirani, murdered their baby before committing suicide.

Carl Phillips

Carl Phillips writes in a woozy, disembodied shorthand, his voice hovering over the page in lyrical meditation that seems to start before the poem begins and continue into Neverland after it ends. *Double*

Shadow is the latest installment of this talking cure, the poems imitating the shortcuts and half-comprehensions of speech, or the drifts of memory:

> *Like any other kingdom built of wickedness and*
> *joy—cracked, anchorless, bit of ghost in the making,*
> *only here for now. Blue for once not just as in*
> *forgive, but blue as blue . . . As affection was never*
>
> *twilight, but a light of its own, blindness not at all*
> *a gift to be held close to the chest, stubborn horse*
> *meanwhile beating wild beneath it, stubborn heart,*
> *a dark, where was a brightness, a bright where dark.*

The slippage of syntax, the frequent negations and diminutions, the pushy abstractions, the showy antithesis—the intelligence is partly in the style, but also partly buried by style.

The poems offer experience both half-lit and melodramatic, like lost paintings by de la Tour. Phillips's world, the world that syntax creates, is impoverished in connection and action—the poems can gasp out awe or chew on a gobbet of disappointment (most end on a note of affirmation or resignation—it's either *Yes! Yes!* or *Rats!*), but they never argue or develop a thing. Phillips is an avatar to college students who write in fragments because they don't know how to compose a complete sentence.

The freaks of syntax might work better if Phillips seemed in control, but the lines are frequently haunting and hapless at once: "Guttering in its stone urn from a century, by now, / too far away, the candle made of the room / a cavernousness." Why were those errant commas after "century" and "now" allowed to stand? Was there no way to avoid a mouthful of Styrofoam like "cavernousness"? Such a style is intriguing, then frustrating, and at last irritating—or at worst insulting.

> *How the birches sway, for example. How they*
> *tilt, on occasion, their made-to-tilt-by-the-wind*
> *crowns. How by then he had turned his head*
> *away, as if a little in fear; or shy, maybe . . . Also*
> *the leaves having stopped their falling. Or there*

were no leaves left—left to fall. Which to call
more true? Love
                    or mercy?

Many of Phillips's poems float along in the sublime and return to earth
with a bump. If bathos is always a sinking, there must be a word for
the updraft of pretension or profundity here, the sudden hot-air rise to
blather. *Love or mercy?* Call that *blathos.*

Phillips is hardly the only contemporary addicted to *blathos*—there
are poets much worse, *blathos* specialists like Li Young Lee and Mary
Oliver. This seems a flaw more crippling, however, in a poet with a
keen mind and quirky poetic gifts—despite his bundle of rhetorical
tricks and knife-thin range, Phillips has an enviable interest in language, in the internal dialogue of hesitation and regret that fuels our
self-deceptions (as Jorie Graham possesses, less fruitfully). The sentiment he lapses into is just sugarcoating, but in poetry sugarcoating is
worse than arsenic. Phillips has published seven books of verse in the
past eleven years (as well as a selected poems), books so similar they
might be clones. Perhaps it's time for him to take such serious gifts
more seriously.

Rae Armantrout

Rae Armantrout's poems are micro-dreams of sly vanity, their brute
coyness typical of much late-generation avant-garde poetry. *Money
Shot* lives in stark juxtapositions—sometimes there's a snippet of science ("each // stinging jelly / is a colony"), sometimes a scrap of old-
fashioned suburban imagism ("Stillness of gauzy curtains // and the
sound / of distant vacuums"), sometimes a touch of cut-rate surrealism
("Give a meme / a hair-do").

The "money shot" is a porn-factory term for filmed ejaculation,
the *eruptus* of *coitus interruptus*. The dust jacket demurely shows the
Duchess of Alba's hand from Goya's famous portrait—the connection
is scarcely less mystifying than a few of the poems, though it could al-
lude to her alleged affair with the painter, her supposed appearance as
The Naked Maja, the price of Goya's commissions, or any number of
things. It's a tease, as much of Armantrout's work is a tease.

Most of her poems offer little resistance to the conscientious reader (the book could be read on a lunch break), but now and then they revel in the iffiness to which experimental poetry is dedicated:

IndyMac:

Able to exploit pre-
existing.

Tain.

Per. In. Con.
Cyst.

IndyMac was one of the big failed banks, the Independent National Mortgage Corporation. Armantrout commented on this passage in an interview with *Chicago Weekly Online*: "'Mac' . . . suggests McDonald's, but also now 'Mac'ing down' on something, or 'PAC-man'—suggests a greedy franchise. And it's paired with the word Indy, which suggests independent boutiques. . . . Then 'Able to exploit pre-/ existing'—that's a phrase that I got from a newspaper article about banking. . . . You know, the banking system was able to exploit the pre-existing blah-blah-blah. And then the poem breaks into single syllables: 'Tain. // Per. In. Con. / Cyst.' All those syllables . . . occur in words like maintain, retain, persist, insist, consist, and then there's just the word—cyst. I guess the words that are just syllables are a kind of cyst, free floating references to acquisition and attainment."

This is not nearly as helpful as it is hilarious—I don't know which is better, the loopy free-association or the *blah-blah-blah.* Yet how private these associations are, and how hopeless the road map to them. (There are free-floating cysts in the iris; but how a reader could get from IndyMac to Pac-Man is a mystery—as explanation this is the Higher Ditziness of the Humpty Dumpty School.) If the Mac in IndyMac can mean McDonald's, then Indy can mean Indiana Jones, independent film, Indianapolis, or any number of irrelevant things. As for that jumbled wordplay, sure—*persist, insist, consist,* as well as *pertain* and *contain* (though not *intain*). As for *maintain* and *retain,* it's as if she hasn't read her own poem.

Armantrout relies on a cloud of knowing to organize this unknowing, but you have to be Armantrout to live in the cloud. The temptation to make meaning by juxtaposition can be overwhelming, but it's a temptation that should sometimes be resisted:

> *The pressure*
> *in my lower back*
> *rising to be recognized*
> *as pain.*
>
> *The blue triangles*
> *on the rug*
> *repeating.*
>
> *Coming up,*
> *a discussion*
> *on the uses*
> *of torture.*

This is funny, then not funny at all. Though she's likely referring to the real pain suffered from her bout with adrenal cancer, even a more direct reference would seem like self-absorption at the expense of those who have suffered torture. The lines come too close to the sin of confessional poetry, that my pain is always more interesting than yours.

The defense of a poetry of splinter and shard, of tessera and ostrakon, has long been that our fragmentary, disconnected modern lives are best reflected in fragmentary, disconnected forms (no wonder that after a dollop of post-postmodernism a reader would kill for a little story). But why should art always imitate life—and why should its form somehow be imitative, too? (I doubt that life seems more fragmentary and disconnected now than during the Wars of the Roses.)

> *But they're lying,*
> *which degrades them.*
>
> *An immigrant*
> *sells scorpions*

> *of twisted electrical wire*
> *in front of the Rite Aid.*
>
> *I look away before.*

You can say various things about this poem, which seems perfectly easy to interpret. Ah, but I confess I just opened the book at random and picked out a stanza here or a line there—we have long needed a postmodern *sors Vergiliana*, and Armantrout is just the woman to provide it.

This Pulitzer Prize–winning poet is a museum exhibit of how unexperimental experimental poems have become. Armantrout relies on a very small bag of tricks, many of them old when free verse was young: the short, breathless lines; the smirking *ars poetica* ("'Why don't you just *say* / what you mean?' // Why don't I?"); the bodice-heaving antithesis ("The fear / that all *this* / will end. // The fear / that it won't"), with enjambments like stop signs—or, worse, bottomless abysses. Does she end a poem on "the"? Of course she ends a poem on "the"! Wallace Stevens once ended a poem on "the," but he used it as a noun—and the poem was a much better poem. It wasn't trying to imitate some fall into the emptiness of unmeaning.

I love Armantrout's idea for a film genre called "diversity noir" ("a shape-shifter / and a vampire // run rival / drinking establishments"). She has a gift for the sneaky phrase ("Money is talking / to itself again"), but like a lot of experimental poets she can't resist bossing the reader about. Poems that tease are appealing, but not ones that are teasing and bullying at once, that have a come-hither look and a go-thither command. The best poems here don't try so hard to force the reader to go where the poet wants.

Far too much experimental verse comes out of two phrases William Carlos Williams wrote in haste and perhaps regretted at leisure, phrases for which anthologists have been grateful ever since: "So much depends upon" and "This is just to say." You could staple one or the other to the beginning of most avant-garde poems, and the poems would be no worse. They might even be better.

Les Murray

When Odysseus told his tales, he was compared to a bardic singer; but Homer did not make him sing. Still, perhaps he should be considered the oldest poet-traveler known to us. Like Byron and Shelley, he saw the world, a world much smaller to the Greeks. The "poet-traveler" (a term we owe to Alphonse de Lamartine) became the model for the poet-jet-setter who has lunch in Abu Dhabi before a reading in SoHo, who picks up the check in one place and is handed a check in another.

Les Murray is our latest passport poet—like Walcott, and Brodsky, and Heaney before him, his poems bear the stray anecdotes of life in exotic places, places that would have been beyond the means or stamina of a poor gypsy poet.

> *In a precinct of liver stone, high*
> *on its dais, the Taj seems bloc hail.*

> *We came to Agra over honking roads*
> *being built under us, past baby wheat*
> *and undoomed beasts and walking people.*
> *Lorries shouldered white marble loads.*

Murray's muddled, lumpen imagery, half dry-wit and half misdirected-energy, is an acquired taste—the whitish Taj like a bloc of hail (is that *block* or *bloc*, like the Eastern bloc?), the roads of honking cars, the "undoomed beasts" that must be sacred cattle. However indelible, in their galumphing wording such images seem like outsider art, paintings scrawled with an elbow dipped in motor oil.

For a poet-traveler, however, Murray is an awful stay-at-home. Most of the poems in *Taller When Prone* are outback poems—apart from giving readings abroad, from which he earns half his income, he hardly stirs from the family farm in New South Wales. Murray is a willful poet, as full of fussy and peculiar phrases as a marsupial is stuffed with fussy and peculiar DNA. I appreciate the baroque conviction of his eye, but frequently the junk puns and contrived metaphors stop the poems cold—"these laws in Isaac Neurone," "heir-splitting," "horse-penis helicopters," "ute-dancing dope-eye dogs," "black cockatoos . . . / unflapping as Blériot monoplanes."

At worst, the poems are compiled in a bizarre telegraphic shorthand:

> *Stone statues of ancient waves*
> *tongue like dingoes on shore*
> *in time with wave-glitter on the harbour*
> *but the shake-a-leg chants of the Eora*
>
> *are rarely heard there any more.*

It's not that you can't disentangle this (the Eora aboriginals lived near Sydney), it's that it's hardly worth the effort. Elsewhere the crack-jawed puns diminish the delicate and moving language of which Murray is capable. When he describes the "muscles and torsoes of cloud" or writes that "bees summarise the garden," when he compares the galaxy to "sugarbag / in a char branch / fronted by chinning bees" ("sugarbag" is honey) or sees "ocean cliffs / stacked high as a British address" (presumably an address like: The Rev'd Goodspeed ffolkes / Poodlescarp / Fondthorp / nr. Six Mile Bottom / Cambs), you think, "Good old Murray, he's hit it for six." Then you think, "I hope he didn't mean 'summer-ize.'"

English poetry hasn't had a poet as blundering since Hardy, nor one as lovable since Larkin—but Murray's like a man trapped in an elevator, raging against the universe and throwing his fists about. In his ramshackle way, using phrases cobbled from unlikely parts, he can make his elegy for Isaac Nathan, which begins so unpromisingly with the stone statues above, into something both comic and disconcerting, not denying the absurdity of death, but not neglecting its sorrows. Nathan, who wrote the music that inspired Byron's *Hebrew Melodies*, became the first man in Australia killed by a trolley.

Killing the Black Dog, published in Australia in 1997 and now reprinted with an afterword, is a memoir of the paralyzing depressions Murray suffered after moving back to the farm in 1985. With a fair amount of pharmaceuticals, sharp doses of kindness, some steely will, and of course that universal elixir and cure-all, poetry, he eventually recovered from his phobias and panic attacks, though as the afterword relates he found that no recovery could be permanent. The workman-like prose, despite touches of grandiosity ("shredded mental kelp marinaded in pure pain"), is often dull; but the misery of these memories is heartrending. Murray's wretched childhood has left him with a persecution complex all too apparent as he recounts the slights and disappointments of sixty years ago—but perhaps after such a childhood, as Dickens knew, there is never a way past the past.

The poems appended to the memoir, which Murray calls the Black Dog Poems, are more agonized and emotionally befuddled than his recent work, sometimes depending far too much on knowledge of his adolescence: "Higher Studies were critique / but my mind was a groover / and a fiver a week / postponed me as a lover." There's a revised version of these lines in *Taller When Prone*, but the poem is just as indecipherable if you haven't read the memoir.

Murray's poems are often meditations on almost nothing (if you forget to read the title you sometimes have no idea what the poem is about). He's a poet of sensibility who trusts far too much in sensibility—the poems are whimsically organized, almost always out at elbows and knees, bizarre where they might be plainspoken, full of odd angles, and at times about as close to the doggerel of William McGonagall as a good poet has ever dared:

> *Where humans can't leave and mustn't complain*
> *there some will emerge who enjoy giving pain.*
>
> *Snide universal testing leads them to each one*
> *who will shrivel reliably, whom the rest will then shun.*

If you can merely snigger quietly and turn the page, Murray remains one of the oddest and truest poets we have.

Geoffrey Hill

Geoffrey Hill's austere, crabbed, confounding new book wrestles with a shadow, the shadow of identity. The oral tradition, as Lord Raglan pointed out most of a century ago, rarely lasts with any accuracy beyond two generations. Hill has lately discovered that one of his great-grandfathers was Welsh—family rumor mentioned a Roma ancestor, but Hill has had to settle for a Welsh iron puddler who worked in the Black Country. The poems in *Oraclau | Oracles* are Hill's border ballads for the misty marchlands beyond Offa's dike, partly the invocation of brute pastoral, partly self-inquisition over certainties long unquestioned. These 144 stanzas, cast into the crippling rhyme scheme of Donne's "The Canonization" and "A Nocturnal upon Saint Lucy's Day," are devoted to the "world much fabled to be what it is— / Radiant mica'd creatures drawn through stress."

Hill's abiding status as an outsider has been shored up by this lately discovered identity, but the nature of his engagement with his newfound land remains elusive. (Not many Englishmen going on eighty have longed to discover Welsh ancestors.) The recalcitrant stanzas stretch out, hammered into place like so many lengths of iron rail— the poems make obeisance to some of the knotty personalities of Welsh politics and art, but the bond stands unfulfilled. Hill is no more than his arguments, not least his arguments with himself (he's a man who lives "in theme- / Possessed Britannia / Stuck with her tacky amalgam of blame. / I yield to none in confessional mania"). There is some intimation that this gain of identity is also a loss, that a man who learns he is not what he believed suffers, not just a crisis of faith, but an erasure. Perhaps that is the secret argument of Keats's "Ode on a Grecian Urn"—if beauty is truth, and truth beauty, there's not much left to say, at least by those untrue or unbeautiful.

Though Hill allows himself some variation in rhyme scheme or shift in line length, the stanza normally ends with a triplet rhyme spliced to a couplet, an exaction difficult even over the short length of Donne's poems. At length, the triplets seem noisy and frantic, Hill's usual contortions of syntax and thought rendered that much more exhibitionistic:

> *Salute the bards—the prized effoliate*
> *Atavisms—who yet recite*
> *Pieties through contentious sleep:*
> *Choosing not to despise*
> *Your graft that sullenly revivifies*
> *Expired encomia to exequies:*
> *Standing your call, re-opening your vein;*
> *Wanting some better grace to entertain.*

Hill's late oracular mood, his bardic yawp, has sometimes required a syntax that would give Milton the d.t.'s.

If you have to discover your Welshness with the help of a genealogist (Hill discussed the revelation at length in *Poetry Wales* last summer), there can't be much left in you, unless you believe in the one-drop rule. Hill's romantic gesture to lost blood must fulfill some unmet yearning, the outsider's wish to continue outside, long after he has been gathered into the fold; yet even a shallow gesture may be profound, given longings deep enough. Hill's flaunting of the foreign in him is not limited to the smattering of Welsh words (*foel, cwm, hebog, hiraeth, llyn*—or hill, valley, hawk, longing, and lake) and Welsh worthies (Nye Bevan, Dylan Thomas, Lloyd George, Aneurin Fardd), but the exemplary monsters and ludic figures who appear in this fever dream seem merely a passing slide-show.

Hill is our greatest religious poet since Eliot (as well as the most mortally funny), however suspect his faith, however uncertain his fidelity—he has a "wishful thinking towards grace." Indeed, his born-again Welshness is often cast in terms of the Passion—in signs and symbols of alchemical transfiguration ("Hermeneutics dark with alchemic soot"), of suffering ("Christ descended into our suffering / But not into crippling sad age"), of the miracle of the Resurrection ("The great stone threatens. / Has it moved?"). These are not beyond the poet's mockery ("The Day of Judgement will do its flame-thing"), yet all point toward a man conscious of mortality. If what has been lacking has been a sense of belonging, it is not without a keen sense of absurdity that Hill seizes a tradition and a language that can never be his own.

The poem lives, then, in self-discovery that may be self-annihilation; and some of the bristling energies with which the poet carves out lines upon that benighted country suggests some darker estrangement of the soul. Hill has long been a difficult and rewarding poet, but the rewards are often those of hard labor. The most radiant, painterly, and untrustworthy moments of *Oraclau | Oracles* come in Hill's rendering of landscape, untrustworthy because one of his gifts is to catch the land in half-light, to make permanent the momentary glow:

Again dusk-fallen snow ghosts its own twilight
Where the red dragon spat fire to the chapels,

From the dark forge-heart wrought apostles,
While in oak woods worlds fell too quiet.

He has performed such metamorphoses so often for England that Wales (whose flag bears the red dragon passant) seems the recipient of a gift without a scrap of Wales to it—the genius might be reflex only. Yet in some paroxysm of desire and disgust, Hill has been possessed by, not merely this alien country (a country within a country), but the Welsh notion of *hwyl,* a word wrapped in both ecstatic passion and the deep intuition of belonging that might be called Welshness.

Oraclau | Oracles is one of five short books Hill has recently completed, a few to be issued separately until all are included in his *Collected Poems, 1952–2012.* If the bardic strain in late Hill has been amplified and made grotesque here, grotesqueness can be a thing embraced, and even finally loved.

World War II Poetry, Reloaded

Above all I am not concerned with Poetry.
My subject is War, and the pity of War.
The Poetry is in the pity.
—Wilfred Owen, "Preface"

War makes strange bedfellows, as beds make strange warfellows. During the Phony War—the eight months of chest- and tub-thumping following the formal declaration on September 3, 1939— British journals and newspapers found time to ask, "Where are the war poets?"

The question proved difficult to answer. Two years later, not long after the end of the Blitz, the journal *Horizon* issued a manifesto, "Why Not War Writers?" The house organ of progressive culture lamented the lack of contributions from poets to the war effort, noting that *"The Times* and other papers asked why this war produced no poets. The poets wrote essays on why they couldn't write poetry." Poets on the left had shied from the subject while the Soviets and Nazis were allies, but with the German invasion of Russia in the summer of 1941 there was no longer any excuse. The manifesto, signed by Cyril Connolly, the magazine's editor, as well as George Orwell, Stephen Spender, and Arthur Koestler, proposed an "official group of war writers":

The Government . . . is discovering that it is making a mistake in reserving the occupation of journalism but not of creative writing. During the Spanish War writers of international reputation such as Hemingway, Malraux and Silone exerted a deeper influence than journalists. Their propaganda was deeper, more humanly appealing and more imaginative than newspaper men had space or time for.

Such appeals to authority seem peculiar now, though for Britain the danger of invasion had barely passed, and it was feared that the United States might never join the Allies. (In June 1940, an MP had asked if the government would deprive Auden and Isherwood, safe in America, of their nationality.)

Though discontent crystallized around the missing war poets, the form of the question is less interesting than why the question was asked. It could not have been posed in America, not in that way. America had entered the Great War too late for war poetry to develop—there was no history of it, yet British poets had created an example, if not a tradition. The idea that armed combatants would spend their off hours writing poetry was a novel one. Poems on a passing war, even poems by civilians, were rarely remembered when the war was over. If you except Whitman's Civil War poems, which evaded the usual sentimental gestures, not a single decent poem emerged from the most costly war America had fought—and Whitman was not a soldier. (There have been many arguments defending the war poetry of Melville, another noncombatant, but never a convincing one.) Where were the memorable poems of the Mexican War, the War of 1812, or the American Revolution?

In Britain, however, poetry had been central to the Great War. During years of ruinous losses, the poems of soldiers paying tribute to soldiers came to embody the national spirit and commemorate the sacrifice. (On Remembrance Day, still more solemnly observed in Britain than Memorial Day in the United States, people wear a poppy badge because of "In Flanders Fields.") World War I poetry, whether drummingly patriotic or pickled-in-acid cynical, derived from the Boer War, and almost entirely from poems written by non-soldiers: the most notable, or only the most notorious, were Kipling's "If —," Hardy's "Embarcation" and "Drummer Hodge," Swinburne's "The Transvaal" ("Strike, England, and strike home"), Housman's "Astronomy," and Henry Newbolt's "Vitaï Lampada" ("The Gatling's jammed and the Colonel dead . . . / 'Play up! play up! and play the game!'").

Before that ("Gunga Din" and "The Charge of the Light Brigade" are scarcely poetry), you'd have to go back to the English Civil War to find poems of any merit, and even the sonnet by Milton ("Captain or colonel, or knight in arms") is interesting only because it is Milton's. The oddity is, not that there have been a few extraordinary war poems, but that war poems exist at all. Between virulent hostility and the whitewash of patriotism, there is little middle ground.

Later wars have produced poems enough, though few worth writing and fewer worth reading—and even those almost always antiwar. Just as armies prepare to fight the war just past, Britain looked back to Great War poets like John McCrae and Rupert Brooke, Wilfred Owen and Siegfried Sassoon. Why, the journals declared, had there been no "In Flanders Fields" or "The Soldier"? (The choices marked their place as secular hymns.) Why, when the country was again in danger, had no new voices risen to stiffen the backbone and the upper lip? At the end of 1939, the *TLS* had addressed the "Poets of 1940," noting that the "first shock of the war produced a paralysis of the poetical intelligence." It warned that should poets "fall into resignation or despair, . . . the Dark Age is assured. . . . It is for the poets to sound the trumpet call."

The Great War had ended so recently that boys born not long after the Armistice were just old enough to serve, some perhaps under the same sergeant-majors who had ordered their fathers over the top. The poets themselves soon had had enough. In 1940, amid dedicatory stanzas to his translation of the *Georgics*, C. Day-Lewis wrote some slyly Marxist lines that began "Where are the war poets? the fools inquire." Later that year, he produced a lyric even more mordant under the title "Where Are the War Poets?":

> *They who in folly or mere greed*
> *Enslaved religion, markets, laws,*
> *Borrow our language now and bid*
> *Us to speak up in freedom's cause.*
>
> *It is the logic of our times,*
> *No subject for immortal verse—*
> *That we who lived by honest dreams*
> *Defend the bad against the worse.*

Day-Lewis wrote in the shadow of Yeats's magisterial "On Being Asked for a War Poem," but his concern with the bureaucracy of language anticipates Orwell. Rhetoric that stirred the imagination two decades before had become no better than empty words. It is a measure of distance that to a more cynical day patriotic poetry appears almost anachronistic. Indeed, reading the poems of the Great War almost a century after Ypres and the Somme can be hard going.

"In Flanders Fields" seems insufferable now—"Take up our quarrel with the foe: / To you from failing hands we throw / The torch" sounds like a paean to the Olympic Games. (McCrae was Canadian, but Canada was a dominion of the Empire.) The ruined pastoral of "The larks, still bravely singing, fly / Scarce heard amid the guns below" might work better if the moral weren't so bullying, but "We are the Dead" is bombast dressed up with pathos and "If ye break faith with us who die / We shall not sleep" a pulpit manner trying to be both uplifting and threatening. The use of "ye" had long been sign of threadbare antiquarianism. (In Hardy's "Channel Firing," which employs a similar trope to comic effect, not even God uses such diction.)

The sonorities of "The Soldier," memorized by generations, have come to sound more fatuous than noble. Brooke's sonnet starts with the shock of mortality, and those are the lines usually quoted:

> If I should die, think only this of me:
>   That there's some corner of a foreign field
> That is for ever England. There shall be
>   In that rich earth a richer dust concealed.

The jingoism of that last line is rarely remarked—presumably it would be the Britishness of the dust that enriched the earth, not the Brookeishness. By the time the poem straggles to an end, it is mired in Little England nationalism more fit for a holiday camp:

> And think, this heart, all evil shed away,
>   A pulse in the eternal mind, no less
>   Gives somewhere back the thoughts by England
>   given;
> Her sights and sounds; dreams happy as her day;

> *And laughter, learnt of friends; and gentleness,*
> *In hearts at peace, under an English heaven.*

These postcard sentiments and Anglican theology—or is that just nostalgic meteorology?—are scarcely better than the smug chauvinism of Brooke's other anthology piece, "The Old Vicarage, Grantchester" (though the intricate sidling of "no less / Gives somewhere back the thoughts" was masterfully developed by Larkin). People can often quote the final lines of that prewar longing for England, set in Berlin; but those who grow misty at the burden of "And is there honey still for tea?" rarely bother to read the whole thing. This weedy bit of pub advertising starts with doggerel ("Just now the lilac is in bloom, / All before my little room; / And in my flower-beds, I think, / Smile the carnation and the pink") and jingles along toward lines that look increasingly suspect now ("there the shadowed waters fresh / Lean up to embrace the naked flesh. / *Temperamentvoll* German Jews / Drink beer around"). Byron would have laughed the perennial schoolboy out of Grantchester.

The journalists of 1939 may have been itching for poems of this sort, but their reputation has long been slightly disreputable. In Jon Silkin's *The Penguin Book of First World War Poetry* (1979), "In Flanders Fields" was marked with an asterisk to show where the anthologist "dissented from the implied judgements of taste." Other poems to suffer the scarlet asterisk included Julian Grenfell's "Into Battle," Alan Seeger's "Rendevous," and Wilfred Owen's "Anthem for Doomed Youth." (Brooke's sonnet went unmarked, the editor admitting that it was present "for a variety of reasons," none stated, which looks suspiciously like a confession of embarrassment.)

Too many poems from the Great War were encrusted with a Georgian diction that moved toward tears what should have moved toward horror. The better poems were the work of soldiers who fought and suffered but were gruesome about it. These were not the poems for which the newspapers were clamoring. Siegfried Sassoon's "The General" stands for many poems more bitter:

> *"Good-morning; good-morning!" the General said*
> *When we met him last week on our way to the line.*

Now the soldiers he smiled at are most of 'em dead,
And we're cursing his staff for incompetent swine.
"He's a cheery old card," grunted Harry to Jack
As they slogged up to Arras with rifle and pack.

.   .   .   .

But he did for them both by his plan of attack.

This owes something to Kipling's Three Musketeers; but including the working-class remark isn't condescending, at least not entirely—the lines bear equally toward misplaced trust and the cynicism that is the particular relief of soldiers. (It's difficult to measure how deep the irony goes in that grunted observation, if there is irony at all.) The men of the line seem almost charmed by the general—after the battle (Arras was very costly to the British), it's his staff who catch the curses. If the final line suggests that the wayward faith is the soldiers' and the cynicism the poet's, of course he was a soldier, too. There is added pleasure in the general's empty-headed greeting (the repetition is part of its hollow cheer), as if he were out on his estate of a morning and merely acknowledging the gardeners.

That bitterness is transformed in the brute specifics of Ivor Gurney, who came very close to the world-weary mockeries of Auden while Auden was still a schoolboy. In lines like "others argued of army ways, and wrenched / What little soul they had still further from shape, / And died off one by one, or became officers," or "Where are they now, on state-doles, or showing shop-patterns / Or walking town to town sore in borrowed tatterns / Or begged," he began to shape a forensics of war, and war's aftermath. If his poems often seem mere gestures, notes that never became more than notions, he sounds more modern a century later than perhaps he did at the time.

Wilfred Owen is too often gauzy and plummy, turning literary at the wrong moments; yet, despite the fumbling that limits his best work, he has an extraordinary talent for endings, a talent almost as great as Larkin's. In the final lines of "Anthem for Doomed Youth" ("The pallor of girls' brows shall be their pall; / Their flowers the tenderness of patient minds, / And each slow dusk a drawing-down of blinds") or "Arms and the Boy" ("And God will grow no talons at his heels, / Nor antlers through the thickness of his curls"), you forget the Grand Guignol for something human sized and human shaped, even if he's talking of God. Many poets love endings that spiral off into the aether; Owen commemorated the war most tellingly when the poem was all but done.

Edward Thomas at his best is a pastoral poet like Frost, but quieter, less ridged with opinion, less brusque and self-confident.

> *This ploughman dead in battle slept out of doors*
> *Many a frozen night, and merrily*
> *Answered staid drinkers, good bedmen, and all bores:*
> *"At Mrs. Greenland's Hawthorn Bush," said he,*
> *"I slept." None knew which bush. Above the town,*
> *Beyond "The Drover," a hundred spot the down*
> *In Wiltshire. And where now at last he sleeps*
> *More sound in France—that, too, he secret keeps.*

The last lines of "A Private" are easy to misread. "A hundred *spot* the down" doesn't mean that townsmen could spy, from some overlook, the down in Wiltshire where the ploughman camped. ("Downs" are rolling upland country, "The Drover" the local pub, "Greenland" a joke—and perhaps a compacted allusion to Blake's "green and pleasant land.") Rather, hawthorn bushes *speckle* the country above town— so he might have slept in any of a hundred places. "And where now at last he sleeps" is a nice piece of wrong-footing—before the enjambment, it might have referred to another hawthorn bush, had his body been carted home; but he sleeps in the grave in France that remains as unknown as his bush hotel.

The Unknown Soldier for whom tombs were built at least left a corpse, but soldiers like the ploughman simply vanished, their graves unmarked, their bodies never recovered. They did not rate even a cenotaph. (The bodies of such ploughmen were sometimes ploughed up in peacetime.) The poet's quiet observation, worthy of similar observations by Frost, is that a man private in life can remain private in death, that such privacy is the last refuge of personality—it marks him out among the thousands in a way death cannot, because death is an individual tragedy but en masse mechanized, dull, anonymous. His rank is merely a caustic footnote, or an epitaph—even the army labeled him private.

How pastoral the poems of soldiers are! There is a desire fulfilled in being denied, a longing for peace (soldiers often remarked on the birdsong in the silence after battle, or, like McCrae, even during battle) that becomes an intimation of death—the wish goes back to Falstaff's babbling of green fields, or further to the Elysium of the honorable dead, which Dante made his Limbo. (McCrae deserves credit for not mentioning that the field poppies were blood red, but perhaps he didn't have to).

The natural grievance toward officers was more subtly turned by Edgell Rickword:

> Colonel Cold strode up the Line
>   (tabs of rime and spurs of ice);
> stiffened all that met his glare:
>   horses, men, and lice.
>
> Visited a forward post,
>   left them burning, ear to foot;
> fingers stuck to biting steel,
>   toes to frozen boot.

A colonel might well burn the ears of his troops in anger, but in "Winter Warfare" this is the special burning of frostbite, a fire without the comfort of heat. (The "tabs of rime" are cunning. Officers could be identified by the red tabs or gorget patches on their uniforms—in trench slang, officers were called "tabs.") Colonel Cold shows a bravery few officers could muster, striding through No Man's Land—but amid the barbed wire, with his alter ego Hauptmann Kälte, he delivers the coup de grâce to the wounded. The weather serves as the displaced object of hatred; however killing the winter, the cold is not just death personified, but the embodiment of the behavior of officers. (In Joseph Heller's World War II novel, *Catch-22*, the secret of war is that the officers, no less than the enemy, are trying to kill their men.) Yet when such soldiers could not be rescued, the cold offered a gentle death—freezing is an anesthetic.

Perhaps it's only an accidental grace when Rickword mentions the colonel's spurs—the cavalry officer was an archaic figure in a war where the horse charge had come to grief against the machine gun, a war soon mired in the trenches. The cavalry officer was a ghost of honored service from wars past. Sometimes the despair of such poems lies, not just in the tone, but in the trivial details—here, the effect of the cold on even the lice, an effect that might otherwise have been accounted a benefit. The best of the Great War poems are grim in a jaunty way, as if Kipling's soldier tales were beneath them all—the poets could hardly escape him, if they read like most young men. That light touch must have seemed out of reach to the poets of the next war—the humor, where there is humor, dares the reader not to examine the violence and terror beneath.

The poems of the First World War are good all too often in the extremity of their subject, because of the mass graves surrounding the art, good because they are the work of amateur soldiers acting like professionals. They are good in all the ways poems can be without being good enough to trouble later readers, except as period pieces. To honor them is to honor the soldiers, and where they died to honor their deaths. The poems of those who saw the war at a distance can seem mere trifles (like Yeats's "An Irish Airman Foresees His Death")—yet the trifles were often better poems.

A generation later, the prolonged clamor for war poets did not stop even after there were a few poets around. *Poetry* published a special war-poetry issue in August 1943, when the outcome of the war was still in doubt. The editor noted that the question "What of poets and the war?" might "be betraying thereby a rather sentimental view not only of poets, which is not so bad, but of war, which is disconcerting. As though war were the signal for a sudden outburst of noble or patriotic emotions." Those unhappy that the poet was not writing about the war, he remarked, had been equally unhappy when he did write of the Depression—though that was called propaganda. (The suspicion of poems occasional or didactic has been long-standing and often self-serving—perhaps only elegies escape the taint.)

Poetry is affected not merely by events, but by the culture surrounding events and the styles available to the poet. (Had Whitman been a conventional poet of 1861, we would not remember his verse.) The culture of poetry in World War II was different from that of the previous war, and what made it different was in part the responsibilities imposed by those earlier poems. The styles, too, were more brutely divided; but style is only a medium. The history of poetry in the second war, like the first, is partly that of style failing subject, not merely subject absent style.

If poets like Brooke had created a poetry tuned to the national spirit, poets of World War II were confounded by their predecessors. The lack of war poets provoked the usual armchair analysis—the war was a different war, the horrors more horrible. The *TLS* in 1939 thought the second war had followed so hard on the first it lacked "novelty to awaken the creative spirit." Ronald Blythe, in his anthology *Components of the Scene* (1966), suggested that "perhaps the uniquely barbarous way in which World War Two ended—Belsen and the atom bomb—suddenly drove the whole subject beyond what were believed to be . . . the barrierless limits of the artist's comment." The failure to speak during the war was compounded by a failure to speak afterward, especially about the Holocaust. The poet's silence, which at the beginning seemed merely a lack of patriotism, after the surrender appeared—to some at least—acquiescence in the extermination of the Jews. This was the subject of Theodor Adorno's notorious remark, "*Nach Auschwitz ein Gedicht zu schreiben, ist barbarisch, und das frißt auch die Erkenntnis an, die ausspricht, warum es unmöglich ward, heute Gedichte zu schreiben* [To write a poem after Auschwitz is barbaric and even corrodes the knowledge that explains why it has become impossible to write poetry today]."

This desire for a certain kind of poetry, and the ensuing bluster over the failure of poets to provide it, proved the foundation of a commonplace, that the poets of the First World War were better than those of the Second. The judgment has been so pervasive that objections have gone unheard. In his anthology *Poets of World War II* (2003), Harvey Shapiro admits that "common wisdom has it that the poets of World War I . . . left us a monument and the poets of World War II did not." Shapiro, who had flown thirty-five missions as a radio gunner over Europe, compiled the anthology in part to make the case against received opinion. More than a quarter century after the last shot was fired, Stanley Kunitz could say that "no poet—American or British—was to achieve superlative distinction or special identity from a distillation of his World War II experiences." Even the *Oxford Handbook of British and Irish War Poetry*, published within the last decade, takes for granted the failure of the later poets, one of the contributors arguing that "during and after the Second World War, the poets did not make enough political and poetic connections." (Ronald Blythe thought the Great War had perhaps "set a precedent of poetry during battle and fiction afterwards.") When Kingsley Amis proposed, half a century after Pearl Harbor, one answer to the "old question, 'Why were the Great War poets better than the Second War lot?'" it was an old question because it had never properly been answered, and perhaps never properly asked. (His anemic answer was "Because a good half of the Second lot managed to stay out of it.")

World War II eventually produced gouts of poems—a small industry developed to rush verse from the front into print. Gouts of poems, but few that entered the popular imagination. The only two war poems still commonly anthologized are Randall Jarrell's "The Death of the Ball Turret Gunner" and Henry Reed's "Naming of Parts."

Were they better, the Great War poets? The poems of the Second World War were often bad, as most poetry is bad, with the added burden of sometimes assuming a naive idealism out of tune with the times, and if not with the times then with the soldiers. American and British poets did not simply adopt the manner of World War I poets, though there were poems enough in that vein (we should speak of manners, not manner). Few soldiers were happy with a war that followed by only two decades the war to end all wars. Almost worse was the reaction of experience to innocence, since many poems raw in their realism were raw as poetry, too.

The poets who received the most attention during the war were soldiers. Karl Shapiro, who won the Pulitzer Prize for *V-Letter* (1944), was a medical-corps clerk on New Guinea. His war poems now seem arch and affected, slightly phony when they try to imitate the soldier's gruffness, too arty when they don't. They show a fatal susceptibility to the lard of allusion.

> *The doctor punched my vein*
> *The captain called me Cain*
> *Upon my belly sat the sow of fear*
> *With coins on either eye*
> *The President came by*
> *And whispered to the braid what none could hear.*

The captain called me Cain! The sow of fear! (The "braid" would be the officers.) This is symbolism driven to delirium: for current events, we have "Great Paris tolled her bell / And China staunched her milk and wept for bread," while off Thessaly the "dynamited mermen washed ashore." By the time "Gog and Magog ate pork / In vertical New York," the poor reader has been reduced to giggles (the lines sound like Auden after touching a third rail—or Crane on a second quart of gin). Shapiro couldn't help reaching for the overegged metaphors that make his poems nearly unreadable now.

John Ciardi, a B-29 gunner on raids over Japan, was a stolid and stiff-necked poet, his work sometimes leavened with the crude comedy that left him a gallumphing Roethke of the front line. Like a lot of war poets, he tried too hard to make poems into poetry:

> *Tibia, tarsal, skull, and shin:*
> *Bones come out where the guns go in.*
> *Hermit crabs like fleas in armor*
> *Crawl the coral-pock, a tremor*
> *Moves the sea, and surf falls cold*
> *On caves where glutton rats grow bold.*

The lines from "Elegy for a Cave Full of Bones" grub painfully after poeticisms, especially lurid poeticisms. Not happy enough with seeing a "jelly on the stones," the speaker soon threatens to "spill the jellies of a man." The clumsy tetrameter couplets rise in pitch to "In the ammoniac caves of death / I am choked for living breath." This is as good as chemistry (ammonia is a choking gas) as it is bad as poetry. Ciardi seems to have read too much early Eliot without mastering his tone — or his modesty, or his weariness, or his cynicism.

Ciardi's manly vulgarity is the raw comedy of what Sweeney might have written, had he written "Elegy Just in Case": "Here lie Ciardi's pearly bones / In their ripe organic mess. / Jungle blown, his chromosomes / Breed to a new address." The internal triple-rhyme of the third line is cheerfully anarchic; but the pun on a soldier's "mess" seems unfortunate, and the last line has a hard time going from syntax to meaning. Such poems failed to provide the visceral shock of *Life* magazine photographs or the immediacy of radio or newsprint. The war was by some measure a photographer's war, even more than the Civil War or the Great War. (The most disturbing pictures of the Great War were not widely seen at the time.)

A poetry similarly rhetorical could be far more successful—style was not entirely at fault. Richard Eberhart was rather old for the navy, but he served in Virginia as an aerial free-gunnery instructor. "The Fury of Aerial Bombardment" begins with lines only slightly better than Shapiro or Ciardi:

> *You would think the fury of aerial bombardment*
> *Would rouse God to relent; the infinite spaces*
> *Are still silent. He looks on shock-pried faces.*
> *History, even, does not know what is meant.*

Eberhart knows how to buffer the grandness, however; he catches the muddle of war, the inability of God or history to make meaning of it. The dead sound of the exact rhyme on "meant" seems unusually apt for a meaning that is unmeaning—"meant" must be read back, not merely heard back, into "bombardment" (surely "Channel Firing" lies somewhere in the background). Yet the poet knows that grandiloquence cannot stand on its own; and his ending, without sacrificing the high-flown manner with which he began, brings the private part of combat home:

> *Of Van Wettering I speak, and Averill,*
> *Names on a list, whose faces I do not recall*
> *But they are gone to early death, who late in school*
> *Distinguished the belt feed lever from the belt holding pawl.*

It's something of a tour de force to end on a "pall" that is not a shroud. (The belt holding pawl and the belt feed pawl, as it was usually called, lay close together on the Browning .50 caliber machine gun—if you didn't know the difference, you couldn't load the gun or clear a jam.) The haphazard meter, at base iambic but varying from tetrameter to hexameter, is crowded with substitutions. Such irregularity in so highly fashioned a poem creates a struggle within the lines that here reads as a struggle against emotion. The mention of gunnery school reminds us how recently these anonymous boys had been schoolboys, some perhaps still in high school when they enlisted. The poem is more devastating when you realize that these dead aircraft gunners

were the boys Eberhart had taught, and he taught them on the same
.50 caliber Brownings used by the ball-turret gunner in Jarrell's poem.

Such muscular rhetoric was more specific to Robert Lowell's early
style. Lowell, who served five months in prison as a conscientious objector, is rarely considered a war poet; yet his early poems were intimate with war, even when the details came second- or third-hand.
In "The Exile's Return," he rudely updated Thomas Mann's novella
Tonio Kröger, written a decade before the Great War:

> *There mounts in squalls a sort of rusty mire,*
> *Not ice, not snow, to leaguer the Hôtel*
> *De Ville, where braced pig-iron dragons grip*
> *The blizzard to their rigor mortis. A bell*
> *Grumbles when the reverberations strip*
> *The thatching from its spire,*
> *The search-guns click and spit and split up timber*
> *And nick the slate roofs on the Holstenwall*
> *Where torn-up tilestones crown the victor.*

Lowell's bristling iambs—"thud metre," as Berryman wittily called
it—shoulder the lines along, thundering like those guns, resounding
like that church bell. (It's not clear what "search-guns" are—probably
German 88 flak artillery.) You could not say that Lowell found his
style in the war; but the stark necessities of his early poems, their attempt to recast English verse by bringing back the fever of Donne
and Webster, suggest that he found war in his style. Mann's Kröger,
who thought (in Bayard Morgan's translation) it might be "necessary
to be at home in some sort of a penal institution in order to become
a poet," returned to his home town only to be mistaken for a swindler
on the run. This unhappy homecoming must have been resonant to a
poet recently released from prison. Kröger believed that artists had to
be removed from feeling: "We artists all share a little the fate of those
eunuchs that used to sing for the Pope. . . . Our singing is touchingly
beautiful. And yet—"

Allen Tate's "Ode to Our Young Pro-consuls of the Air," by contrast,
strains so for effects ("Sad day at Oahu / When the Jap beetle hit!"),
it's hard to take seriously. The subjects are dark enough—the little
that poetry can do in war, the absurdity of most war poetry—but Tate's

heavy-handed ironies are made worse by the claustrophiliac stanza of Drayton's ode "To the Virginian Voyage." Often the lines are close to knockabout farce:

> Boys hide in lunging cubes
> Crouching to explode,
>   Beyond Atlantic skies,
>   With cheerful cries
> Their barking tubes
> Upon the German toad.

What is a war poem, after all? War poetry has often been defined as poems by soldiers, as in Ian Hamilton's anthology *Poetry of War, 1939–1945* (1972) and Vernon Scannell's study *Not Without Glory: Poets of the Second World War* (1976). Scannell even distinguishes between the soldier-poets who fought and those who did not, though he oddly believes that Randall Jarrell saw combat. Indeed, what does one do about Jarrell, who wrote some of the most affecting poems of the war but washed out of flight school and never left the bases in the States? (He spent some of the war sorting mail.) His poems might have been just as good had he been a bartender, picking up tales from returning airmen. What of Shapiro, the medical-corps clerk who was bombed and strafed but almost never saw the front lines? He was usually charged with manning a typewriter. Or Lowell, who spent his parole mopping floors in a hospital? Or Stanley Kunitz, a conscientious objector who served the Air Transport Command stateside and became a staff sergeant? And what of veterans who wrote three or four decades later? Some who at first could say little wrote later with the weight of long grief or long guilt.

The anthologies of soldier poems mean to honor sacrifice, but separating soldiers from the civilians they had been treats them partly as freaks—as if there were something by nature extraordinary in a soldier writing verse. Such men slide too easily toward sainthood, for saints are just exemplary freaks. But should war poems be the sole provenance of men in combat? (The newspapers that asked, "Where are the war poets?" when there was scarcely a soldier on the line must not have thought so. If war poems were restricted only to men who saw combat, the history of war poetry, apart from a few strays, would not start until

World War I.) Shouldn't the war poet also be the woman on the home front or the child who grew up during the Blitz? Eliot saw the distinction long ago:

> When we ask for "war poetry," we may be asking for one or the other of two different things. We may mean patriotic poetry. . . . Or we may be asking for poets to write poetry arising out of their experience of war. . . . The bigger experiences need time, perhaps a long time, before we can make poetry of them.

Shouldn't the poet be any soldier or civilian who simply lived through the war, whether within sound of the fighting or a continent away, writing in the passion of the moment or the ruptured tranquillity long after? The very term "home front" recognizes the part played and the losses endured. (The latest revised edition of *The Penguin Book of First World War Poetry* [1996] was expanded in part to include more poems by noncombatants.)

It is past time to recognize the brooding necessities and mixed affinities of World War II poetry, and to establish a canon more conscientious. A proper anthology might open with the firebombing of London in the second part of "Little Gidding." Eliot's jittery stanzas on destruction ("Dust inbreathed was a house— / The wall, the wainscot and the mouse") fall toward the imitation terza rima that alludes to Dante's meeting with Ser Brunetto in the *Inferno*.

> After the dark dove with the flickering tongue
> 　　　Had passed below the horizon of his homing
> 　　　While the dead leaves still rattled on like tin
> Over the asphalt where no other sound was
> 　　　Between three districts whence the smoke arose
> 　　　I met one walking, loitering and hurried
> As if blown towards me like the metal leaves
> 　　　Before the urban dawn wind unresisting.
> 　　　And as I fixed upon the down-turned face
> That pointed scrutiny with which we challenge
> 　　　The first-met stranger in the waning dusk
> 　　　I caught the sudden look of some dead master.

The dark dove (the German bomber, presumably) becomes a homing pigeon—and the home it returns to will soon suffer greater destruction than the home it destroys. "Dead leaves still rattled on like tin" may be only a small touch, though in Eliot the small touches can be everything; yet how persistent and therefore insistent "rattled on" is compared to "rattled." A few lines later, the windblown simile hardens into "metal leaves," as if mere thought had forged them—the passage otherwise takes place in deathly silence. The poet was a fire warden during the Blitz.

Eliot's "A Note on War Poetry," written on commission in 1942, reads like a footnote on method: "Where is the point at which the merely individual / Explosion breaks // In the path of an action merely typical / To create the universal, originate a symbol / Out of the impact?" Such abstraction has none of the crispness of his prose; but, however dreadful the poem, it shows that the preeminent literary man of the day took the problem seriously. Like "To the Indians Who Died in Africa" and "Defense of the Islands," such an occasional poem seems a rearguard defense against the question posed by journalists, the passion as parched and theoretical as the language. Written as if to be engraved on the chalk cliffs, "Defense" almost comes to life when it echoes *The Waste Land* (sailors "contributing their share to the ages' pavement of British bone on the sea floor") or the Spartan epitaph by Simonides ("say, to the past and future generations of our kin and of our speech, that we took up our positions, in obedience to instructions")—*almost*, but the distance from either is deadening.

The Pisan Cantos form an extraordinary portrait of a mind that has come through war and been damaged, Pound's classical world shattered and fragmented, desperately grasped at from his outdoor cage (at first one of the death cells) in an internment camp at Pisa. We have no better record of a first-class intelligence brought almost to madness by defeat—railing, bitter, self-justifying, unforgiving, yet capable of black humor, bantering with his captors while locked up like the "nigger murderer" and the rapist.

> *What thou lovest well remains,*
> > *the rest is dross*
> *What thou lov'st well shall not be reft from thee*

> *What thou lov'st well is thy true heritage*
> *Whose world, or mine or theirs*
> > > *or is it of none?*
> *First came the seen, then thus the palpable*
> > *Elysium, though it were in the halls of hell,*
> *What thou lovest well is thy true heritage*
> *What thou lov'st well shall not be reft from thee.*

These are some of the most moving lines in *The Cantos*, moving because of where Pound was, moving because of what he had lost through his own . . . *stupidity* would be too incomprehending, *hubris* too grand. The poems are those of a man of books kept from books (he was at first allowed only Confucius, the Bible, and a Chinese dictionary)—they read like an attempt to recreate his library *ab ovo*.

The modernists were not equally successful. There was nothing to prevent Marianne Moore from writing war poems that would have done honor to her career, nothing except her inability to use the oblique touch that skewed the best of her poems toward genius. Patriotism was a dead weight on many poems written during the war—but then so was cynicism. (A sentimental cynic is worse than a sentimental patriot.) You don't have to read much of "'Keeping Their World Large'" to wish she had never touched the subject. Her poems about animals were usually dryly free of sentiment, but after Pearl Harbor she became a conflicted flag-waver, appalled at the price of victory:

> *that forest of white crosses; the*
> *vision makes us faint. My eyes won't close to it. While*

> *the knife was lifted, Isaac the offering*
> *lay mute.*
> > *These, laid like animals for sacrifice,*
> *like Isaac on the mount, were their own substitute.*

The ideas are deviously layered, as so often in Moore (the soldiers are self-sacrificing Isaacs); and the second line has Whitman's boldness, his refusal to look away. Still, grandiosity overtakes these deaths. (Later she thinned the passage out without making it better.) What God demanded of Abraham was a test of obedience, a test that if not good for the father was disastrous for the son. Is war only the perverse test of a god who requires submission, no matter the cost? No angel intervened for the Tommies or GIs. Moore ends, "They fought the enemy, we fight / fat living and self-pity. Shine, O shine / unfalsifying sun, on this sick scene." Those who inveighed against war profiteers and bellyaching on the home front were as irrelevant as any *Ladies' Home Journal* editorial (the cities of America faced none of the dangers of cities in Britain). Moore knows this, and despises this; but in such heartfelt breast-beating the poem collapses in on itself.

If "'Keeping Their World Large'" is bad, "In Distrust of Merits" is worse: "Some // in snow, some on crags, some in quicksands, / little by little, much by much, they / are fighting fighting fighting that where / there was death there may / be life." Moore was weakest in the cris de coeur that littered her later work. These high-flown lines have some of the complicated imagination of her best poems, but too often they seem mealy and earnest. The Keatsian flourish that ends the poem ("Beauty is everlasting / and dust is for a time") drops with the clink of a counterfeit nickel—such words would have been cold comfort to those who became dust. This curiously belligerent poem seems a reply, nearly a century late, to "Onward, Christian Soldiers," sung at the signing of the Atlantic Charter in 1941. (Moore wrote a friend, "I readily concur with those who tell me that 'In Distrust of Merits' is not poetry—mere sincerity.")

Wallace Stevens was little better. His "Examination of the Hero in a Time of War" begins, as so rarely in his work, with a sense of the weight of fact, of surroundings, of the physical rather than the metaphysical.

> *Force is my lot and not pink-clustered*
> *Roma ni Avignon ni Leyden,*
> *And cold, my element. Death is my*
> *Master and, without light, I dwell. There*
> *The snow hangs heavily on the rocks, brought*
> *By a wind that seeks out shelter from snow. Thus*
> *Each man spoke in winter. Yet each man spoke of*
> *The brightness of arms, said Roma wasted*
> *In its own dirt, said Avignon was*
> *Peace in a time of peace, said Leyden*
> *Was always the other mind. The brightness*

Of arms, the will opposed to cold, fate
In its cavern, wings subtler than any mercy,
These were the psalter of their sybils.

Stevens on the war is like Henry James on cast-iron architecture—the style overwhelms the subject. Toward the end, the passage winds off into the Stevensian aether (the *psalters of their sybils,* indeed), but not before suggesting what sort of war poetry Stevens might have written, had he not been Stevens.

The self-regarding coda to "Notes toward a Supreme Fiction," on the other hand, is best forgotten: "The soldier is poor without the poet's lines, // His petty syllabi, the sounds that stick, / Inevitably modulating, in the blood. / And war for war, each has its gallant kind." Despite mention of blood, this is as bloodless, as denatured, and as dull as war poetry gets—worse, the lines propose that each war boasts brave poets as well as brave soldiers, which rather overrates the poet's courage. Still, Stevens's remarks elsewhere about war poetry, though stilted and fussy, strike at the central impasse:

The poetry of a work of the imagination constantly illustrates the fundamental and endless struggle with fact. It goes on everywhere, even in the periods that we call peace. But in war, the desire to move in the direction of fact as we want it to be and to move quickly is overwhelming.

Nothing will ever appease this desire except a consciousness of fact as everyone is at least satisfied to have it be.

Often, however, it isn't fact that makes the war poem, but the sensibility of fact, or the illusion of fact—or the knowledge that violent death lies just beneath the surface of words.

Jarrell's "The Death of the Ball Turret Gunner" must be included, not because it is the most famous poem to emerge from a terrible war, but because it has a brutality worthy of Dante.

From my mother's sleep I fell into the State,
And I hunched in its belly till my wet fur froze.
Six miles from earth, loosed from its dream of life,

I woke to black flak and the nightmare fighters.
When I died they washed me out of the turret with a hose.

Jarrell was overfond of personae (often women or children), and here
the infant airman is like a character from one of the *Märchen*—he has
gone straight from the womb to death, with only snatches of life between (he's a version of Bede's bird flying through the mead hall). It's
easy to forget, when you've read the poem a hundred times, that the
shock comes the first time from the gunner relating his own death (it's
a narrative trick Jarrell used more than once), as well as the efficient,
brutal way the military cleans up his remains.

Jarrell's use of "State" bothers some readers—like a lot of young
men, he was Marxist at the time. (Probably under the influence of
Auden, Jarrell uses the word again in "A Lullaby" and "The State.")
"State" seems wrong for this gunner, this newly born animal in "wet
fur" (fur would have lined the collar of his M-422 flight jacket); but
it removes him from patriotism or sentiment. His death reads like
an abortion (in a note, Jarrell says he "looked like the foetus in the
womb"). This must have been a night bombing run—the flak would
have been nearly invisible, the "nightmare fighters" probably Messer-
schmitts painted black or using the mottled night camouflage. Many
of Jarrell's bomber poems seem to describe the air war before late 1943,
when the Merlin-equipped P-51 Mustangs were able to accompany
bomber groups deep into Germany. Jarrell's note claims that the gunner was "hunched upside-down"—this is an odd misunderstanding.
It's not clear whether he ever saw the Sperry ball turret in operation.
One recent scholar, though Jarrell explained that the turret was "set
into the belly" of the plane, decided that the dead crewman was a tail
gunner.

Jarrell often forced his poems to a weepy close, but long before the
close a poem like "In the Camp There Was One Alive" falls apart in
cheesy melodrama (the fall might start with the title). Still, like "A
Camp in the Prussian Forest," it's an early poem about concentration
camps, memorable as an attempt to grasp the horror. He must have
realized its inadequacies, because "In the Camp" was one of only two
poems from *Losses* (1948) he failed to include in *Selected Poems* (1955).
Jarrell had a sentimental streak wider than a four-lane highway, and

his war poems are not immune to it—the best don't keep asking about existence. "A Camp in the Prussian Forest," "The State," "A Lullaby," and "Protocols," though not as powerful as "The Death of the Ball Turret Gunner," are awful in the old sense. "Protocols" *is* sentimental, but the deaths in it are not.

Auden's "September 1, 1939" (the date of the German invasion of Poland) is not always considered a war poem, in part because it's not explicitly about war—without the title, it might seem another example of a genre he perfected in the thirties, the poem of collective foreboding. Its most striking line, "We must love one another or die," so quickly became famous it was used after the war in *The Secret People* (1952), a movie that explored a London shadow world of assassins and conspiracies. (Auden grew to loathe the line, revised it to "and die," then dropped the stanza and finally the whole poem.) Roundly despised at home for not returning when hostilities broke out, he had written about the war before it *was* the war—"Epitaph on a Tyrant" and the sonnets of "In Time of War," later revised as "Sonnets from China" (Auden went to China the year after the Nanking Massacre) are among the most compelling poems written under the coming war's shadow—but they are not conventional war poems.

One of the difficulties facing World War II poetry is that many of the best poems were written after the war, even long after. Anthony Hecht and Richard Wilbur both served in the infantry in Europe. Though even his early work was attracted to violence (there's a lot of violence when you sift the foppery out), Hecht's most striking war poems appeared much later. "'More Light! More Light!'" (Goethe's alleged deathbed words) begins with an English heretic burning at the stake ("the death was horrible, / The sack of gunpowder failing to ignite. / His legs were blistered sticks on which the black sap / Bubbled and burst as he howled for the Kindly Light"). The victim is at least allowed a "pitiful dignity," dying to the sounds of prayer. All this is preamble to a scene near a German forest (Hecht often proceeds by indirection), where two Jews and a Pole are forced to dig a grave, and the Pole at gunpoint is ordered to bury them alive. When he refuses, he's placed in the open grave himself and buried up to his neck by the Jews. Then he obeys. Hecht's point is that at neither execution did the Kindly Light appear (the reader can't fail to note that Christ's death was more prolonged than the heretic's, and equally terrifying).

Hecht, who was a Jew, saw the liberation of Flossenbürg concentration camp and interviewed survivors. For years afterward, he recalled, he "would wake shrieking"; but he eventually wrote two poems nearly unbearable, "Persistences" and the late sestina "The Book of Yolek." "Persistences" begins with the frilly elegance of Hecht's early poems; but the language is crisper, more deadly, and more capable:

> The leafless trees are feathery,
>   A foxed, Victorian lace,
> Against a sky of milk-glass blue,
>   Blank, washed-out, commonplace.
>
> Between them and my window
>   Huge helices of snow
> Perform their savage, churning rites
>   At seventeen below.

In that extreme cold, the speaker sees shapes forming and reforming until they become apparitions—of friends, enemies, or simply those coming for justice.

> Those throngs disdain to answer,
>   Though numberless as flakes;
> Mine is the task to find out words
>   For their memorial sakes
>
> Who press in dense approaches,
>   Blue numeral tattoos
> Writ crosswise on their arteries,
>   The burning, voiceless Jews.

"Burning" returns us to the death ovens, as the poem in a quiet way returns to the cold of those terrible winters in which the suffering in the camps and on the line was severe. The speaker imagines the ghostly figures as "Ancestral deputations / Wound in the whited air, / To whom some sentry flings a slight, / Prescriptive, 'Who goes there?'" The voiceless Jews become the naked visions imagination imposes on the random fall of snow, as if Hecht were on sentry duty again, a revenant from his own past. (The cold of the Ninth Circle in the *Inferno* seems unrelated, unless Hecht is suggesting that the Jews were treated like traitors by those good German Lutherans.) These and other poems, some almost as good ("Still Life" and "The Cost," the latter only obliquely about the war), some lesser ("'It Out-Herods Herod. Pray You, Avoid It.'"), frame the darkest vision of the war while seeming very much postwar, poems scoured out of memory, poems of what could not be forgiven.

Richard Wilbur served in an infantry signal-company in Italy and Germany. "First Snow in Alsace" is on the surface a poem about the cleansing erasures of snow:

> The snow came down last night like moths
> Burned on the moon; it fell till dawn,
> Covered the town with simple cloths.
>
> Absolute snow lies rumpled on
> What shellbursts scattered and deranged,
> Entangled railings, crevassed lawn.
>
> As if it did not know they'd changed,
> Snow smoothly clasps the roofs of homes
> Fear-gutted, trustless and estranged.
>
> The ration stacks are milky domes;
> Across the ammunition pile
> The snow has climbed in sparkling combs.
>
> You think: beyond the town a mile
> Or two, this snowfall fills the eyes
> Of soldiers dead a little while.

Wilbur's early work was archly poetic; the decorative language, like the snow, conceals and almost prettifies the abandoned or bombed-out houses "fear-gutted, trustless and estranged" (rather than, say, "fire-scarred, windowless, and decayed"). The ameliorating abstraction, uttered in that calm, forbearing tone, gradually becomes part of the self-deception—snow disguises the evidence of war, but in days or months the snow will be gone.

The visions remained with Wilbur long after the dead had been buried and the ruins cleared. "Terza Rima" was published in 2008, more than six decades after the end of the war:

> *In this great form, as Dante proved in Hell,*
> *There is no dreadful thing that can't be said*
> *In passing. Here, for instance, one could tell*
>
> *How our jeep skidded sideways toward the dead*
> *Enemy soldier with the staring eyes,*
> *Bumping a little as it struck his head,*
>
> *And then flew on, as if toward Paradise.*

Both poems are cast in terza rima; but in the first, shortened to tetrameter, the intricate rhyming comes to seem passive, almost passionless. (There is much to say about the relation between war poetry and the *Inferno*, of which Ciardi later produced a passable translation.) The latter poem, however, contains the horror hidden in "First Snow"—nearing ninety, Wilbur at last achieved the moral darkness and brutal humor missing in his earlier work. This may be the last war poem of significance written by a veteran. As Auden saw in 1942, "As a rule war experiences are like any others; poets cannot use them until they have become thoroughly digested memories."

To the anthology of World War II poetry would be added Lowell's "The Quaker Graveyard in Nantucket" and "Memories of West Street and Lepke," as well as a few lesser pieces. The poems of basic training would include W. D. Snodgrass's "'After Experience Taught Me . . .'" and Henry Reed's "Lessons of the War" (all three sections, not just "The Naming of Parts"). The training was apt to the mechanization of war, breaking down personality into machine parts. Eliot's observations of the Blitz would be accompanied by Dylan Thomas's "A Refusal to Mourn the Death, by Fire, of a Child in London." Howard Nemerov's "Grand Central, with Soldiers, in Early Morning," and Edgar Bowers's "Aix-la-Chappelle, 1945," are poems by soldiers about subjects far from the front lines. (Nemerov was a pilot, and Bowers served in Army Counter Intelligence.) There would be room for John Berryman's "1 September 1939," Adrienne Rich's "(Newsreel)," Philip

Larkin's "Conscript" (heavily indebted to Auden), and Jane Cooper's "The Faithful"—all see the war from a distance, and all were written by noncombatants.

The work of many soldiers often the mainstay of Second World War anthologies would be reduced or discarded. It's shameful to find almost nothing in Keith Douglas or Sidney Keyes or Louis Simpson or Lincoln Kirstein worth reading now, shameful to omit William Meredith, Stanley Kunitz, James Dickey, Alun Lewis, Alan Ross, and many others. (I have ignored war poetry not in English, since it did not affect the tradition or form part of it—that doesn't mean it was negligible.) The anthologies of the war have paid too much attention to the second-rate, to poems interesting largely because of what they say, or how near battle the poets were. The license of such poets is that they were there, but merit cannot be based on proximity or immediacy—to ask otherwise is merely maudlin.

Poets who lived through the war as children proved more sensitive than many soldiers—this imaginary anthology would include Geoffrey Hill's "Ovid in the Third Reich," "September Song," his sequence "De Jure Belli ac Pacis," and the Coventry passage from *The Triumph of Love,* though perhaps not slighter poems like Charles Simic's "Prodigy" and "Cameo Appearance" (his prose on the war is more affecting). The reach of World War II poetry might not extend to Sylvia Plath's "Daddy" or James Fenton's "A German Requiem"—there is a moment when the war moves from presence to reference, as in Plath's poem, and when, for a generation too young (Fenton had not been born when the war ended), it becomes a matter of pure imagination. (The poems indirectly affected may nonetheless be important—the Great War lies in the background of *The Waste Land.*) The youngest contributor to the poetry of the war would be James Tate, born in 1943. "The Lost Pilot" was written for the father he never met, a bomber co-pilot killed in action. When you add to these the many poems where the war lurks in the background, like Elizabeth Bishop's "Roosters," and poems of retrospection like Thom Gunn's "Claus von Stauffenberg" and Donald Justice's "The Voice of Col. von Stauffenberg Ascending Through the Smoke and Dull Flames of Purgatory," you have the outline of an anthology that surpasses the poetry of the Great War in vividness, in the authority of suffering, in the austerities of grace.

Frank O'Hara's Shopping Bag

Death is often a good career move in poetry. No sooner are the obsequies finished and the baked meats eaten than the publisher warms up the presses for a definitive edition of the collected poems, solemnly proofread down to the last querulous comma. Yet not all poets are well served by such an exhaustive volume, which may seal up a reputation forever—indeed, such a book has sometimes been called a tombstone. A collected poems may be cruelest to a poet whose genius shone as intermittently as a firefly.

At forty, Frank O'Hara was struck one night by a Jeep on a Fire Island beach. He died scarcely two years after the publication of *Lunch Poems* (1964), the volume that introduced him to most readers. As a poet he wrote so much—so wildly and unevenly much—it has been difficult to reach a just estimate of his wayward, influential talent. O'Hara was born in Baltimore and schooled at Harvard, a roommate of Edward Gorey and a friend of John Ashbery. He soon went to work at the Museum of Modern Art, where he rose to become an associate curator. As he had fallen in with a crowd of painters and poets that included Willem and Elaine de Kooning, Franz Kline, Larry Rivers, Helen Frankenthaler, Jackson Pollock, James Schuyler, and Kenneth Koch, it was perhaps natural to make poems out of their parties, feuds, love affairs, and drunken gossip.

By the poetic fashion of the day, it was not natural at all. In the heady atmosphere of postwar Manhattan, however, young poets hostile to the philistines surrounding them (even coddled artists believe their society philistine) envied the technical bravado and rebellious invention of the abstract expressionists. The poets of the New York School, as they were eventually known, were long on spontaneity and short on traditional literary effect. O'Hara later recollected, according to Brad Gooch's biography, *City Poet*, that he and other young poets "divided our time between the literary bar, the San Remo, and the artists' bar, the Cedar Tavern. In the San Remo we argued and gossipped: in the Cedar we often wrote poems while listening to the painters argue and gossip. So far as I know nobody painted in the San Remo while they listened to the writers argue."

O'Hara's earliest poems, the work of Harvard and just after, sound like Wallace Stevens at the soda fountain ("Oh! kangaroos, sequins, chocolate sodas! / You really are beautiful! Pearls, / harmonicas, jujubes, aspirins!"). Jazzy, elated as an eel, a talent giddily in search of a manner, the poet scatters exclamation marks like penny candy. Posing as a wide-eyed innocent, O'Hara was drawn to illogic and absurdity, to modes of presence and display far from poets like Yeats and Eliot and Lowell. When Auden chose Ashbery's first volume for the Yale Series of Younger Poets, he wrote O'Hara a thoughtful rejection, saying, "I think you (and John, too, for that matter) must watch what is always the great danger with any 'surrealistic' style, namely of confusing authentic non-logical relations which arouse wonder with accidental ones which arouse mere surprise and in the end fatigue."

The peculiar thing about O'Hara's "surrealistic" style is that it sounds not like early Ashbery but like late Ashbery:

> *How many trees and frying pans*
> *I loved and lost! Guernica hollered look out!*
> *but we were all busy hoping our eyes were talking*
> *to Paul Klee. My mother and father asked me and*
> *I told them from my tight blue pants we should*
> *love only the stones, the sea, and heroic figures.*
> *Wasted child! I'll club you on the shins!*

Ashbery developed such insouciant nonsense into a charming anti-literary manner, but O'Hara soon grew bored with it. He was always looking for some vivid stimulus, preferably one a little outlandish—not a bad thing for a curator of modern painting, perhaps, but not necessarily a good one for a poet (O'Hara treated contemporary art with far more deliberation than he treated poetry). He began to make poetry from whatever happened around him—today he might just write a blog. At the time, however, this preoccupation with the trivial, with the nothing of life that is nothing, seemed to jettison everything—meter, the calculated symbol, the grave poetic tone—associated with the manners of the art. However much one loves *Four Quartets* or *Lord Weary's Castle*, it's refreshing to open O'Hara and read,

> *Leroi comes in*
> *and tells me Miles Davis was clubbed 12*
> *times last night outside BIRDLAND by a cop*
> *a lady asks us for a nickel for a terrible*
> *disease but we don't give her one we*
> *don't like terrible diseases, then*
> *we go eat some fish and some ale it's*
> *cool but crowded we don't like Lionel Trilling*
> *we decide, we like Don Allen we don't like*
> *Henry James so much we like Herman Melville*
> *we don't want to be in the poets' walk in*
> *San Francisco even we just want to be rich.*

The headlong style, the lines broken like bread sticks, the punctuation limping along or missing entirely, captures the city's rush and welter, though O'Hara's physical world is curiously impoverished. Every poem seems to start from scratch. The back cover of *Lunch Poems* claimed that frequently O'Hara, "strolling through the noisy splintered glare of a Manhattan noon, has paused at a sample Olivetti to type up thirty or forty lines of ruminations." This was most unlikely (even more so the notion that he had "withdrawn to a darkened ware- or firehouse to limn his computed misunderstandings of the eternal questions of life"); but the lie was as close to an *ars poetica* as the poet ever made.

O'Hara's instincts may have been anti-Romantic, but Wordsworth would have noticed that walking around Manhattan wasn't all that different from walking around some Lake District fell or other. You noticed one thing, then another, and perhaps you composed a few lines as you went. What O'Hara most objected to about poetry, however, was the hard work. A poet like Yeats turned his first thoughts, often in prose, into verse that disguised the labor of its passage ("A line will take us hours maybe; / Yet if it does not seem a moment's thought, / Our stitching and unstitching has been naught"). The labor was never meant to look laborious. O'Hara wanted his poems to look easy as a sewing machine, but to take no work at all.

The poet's genius in these "I do this I do that" poems, as he called them, was to stop trying to have a point—the off-course thinking that was normally the means to a poem became the heady, helter-skelter end. He wrote compulsively about what moved him—his lovers, and avant-garde painting, and ballet, and of course the movies (few poets have invoked Googie Withers and meant it fondly). Wilde might have said that such things were too important not to write trivially about them; but O'Hara almost never faces up to the emptiness beneath this high life and low desire—if there's a subconscious revealed, it's very hard to detect. The poems describe an urban pastoral where no one has a real job, where martinis flow like nectar, and where the days of Elysium are marked by the arrival of a new issue of *New World Writing*. Whitman's search for the democracy of the American demotic— what he called *slang*—a century later had become the hilarious musings of a vain young man about town (O'Hara wrote about homosexual life with a cheerful nonchalance rarely matched since—Allen Ginsberg by contrast was slightly lugubrious about sex). It's hard to know whether Whitman, who took poetry seriously, would have laughed or wept.

Still, it's hard not to smile in appreciation at a poet who can write that he was lying abed when the sun woke him up to say,

> *"Frankly I wanted to tell you*
> *I like your poetry. I see a lot*
> *on my rounds and you're okay. You may*
> *not be the greatest thing on earth, but*
> *you're different. Now, I've heard some*
> *say you're crazy, they being excessively*
> *calm themselves to my mind, and other*
> *crazy poets think that you're a boring*
> *reactionary. Not me."*

The poem borrows from Mayakovsky, from whom O'Hara also took his governing notion that the poem should wrap itself around the poet. Poetry needs to be taken down a peg, once in a while; and O'Hara never condescended to the reader, unlike some slapstick poets now.

He refused to apologize for his narcissism, his comic pretensions, his sometimes insufferable archness. These were the effects mastered and the price paid.

In the early sixties, there was a distinct falling-off in the verse—what had been effervescent as champagne turned flat and stale, as sometimes happens in poets who begin with a lot of élan and little of anything else. O'Hara finished fewer and fewer poems, as if exhausted by the very scenes that once provoked him (two-thirds of this new edition of *Selected Poems* was written between 1954 and 1960). Still, some of the best poems of lunatic happenstance came in these years, including what is arguably his most famous, which ends

> *and I was in such a hurry*
> *to meet you but the traffic*
> *was acting exactly like the sky*
> *and suddenly I see a headline*
> *LANA TURNER HAS COLLAPSED!*
> *there is no snow in Hollywood*
> *there is no rain in California*
> *I have been to lots of parties*
> *and acted perfectly disgraceful*
> *but I never actually collapsed*
> *oh Lana Turner we love you get up.*

O'Hara's wonderful poems are all too easily drowned out by the vivid mediocrity of the rest. At times the banalities pile up and overwhelm the poems—but then the banalities *were* the poems. Rarely has an American poet so influential (two generations of urban poets have come out of O'Hara's shopping bag) written so many poems dull to anyone except his genial fanatics—his very idea of the aesthetic courted failure as a method. With a Goldsmith or a Gray, the mediocre results from a lack of gift, the good from lucky accident. When O'Hara was lucky, he was very lucky, because his method could not help but fail most of the time.

This long-needed new selection of O'Hara's poems, replacing Donald Allen's standard work of more than thirty years ago, has been thoughtfully edited by Mark Ford. He has kept about two-thirds of the old selection, adding fifty or so poems and a small sheaf of the poet's rambling prose statements and reminiscences, some of which sound more like Ernie Kovacs or Lenny Bruce than the author of these insouciantly unserious poems (O'Hara loathed academic hauteur, though he needn't have sounded so oafish about it). The selection is not perfect; Ford has included a grindingly self-conscious play as well as two long poems almost unreadable now, full of campy nonsense like "whoops-musicale (sei tu m'ami) ahhahahahaha / loppy di looploop" and "le bateleur! how wonderful / I'm so so so so so so so so so so happy," which sounds like Ezra Pound on happy pills. The long poems are weakest, not because the manner was difficult to sustain—O'Hara could have gone on forever—but because the manner became so irritating when sustained. There may be serious intentions lodged in trivial things, but the poems often remain blissfully trivial. Still, among the shorter poems Ford has missed little of permanent value, while remaining admirably fair-minded to O'Hara's variety—of the poems discarded, I would have kept only "Poem ('I ran through the snow like a young Czarevitch!')" and "Mary Desti's Ass."

It's hard to care about a lot of O'Hara's poems, but he doesn't want you to care. To accept the present as a fallen realm risks making it insignificant, while other poets of the period, especially Elizabeth Bishop, wrote deeply without loss of a lightness of bearing. In his best poems—"Thinking of James Dean," "Why I Am Not a Painter," "On Seeing Larry Rivers' *Washington Crossing the Delaware* . . . ," "Ode: Salute to the French Negro Poets," "The Day Lady Died," "Les Luths," "Poem ['Lana Turner has collapsed!']," and half a dozen others—O'Hara found something beyond that terrible vacancy he was trying so hard to fill. (His best poems are rarely his most characteristic or frenzied.) The style, though at times foolish and self-parodic, remains fresh fifty years later. However much these poems live in the world of Lowell's "tranquillized *Fifties*," their giddiness in the face of despair, their animal pleasure in gossip, their false bravado, their frantic posturing and guilelessness and petty snobberies—and these were O'Hara's virtues—give us as much of a life as poetry can.

The Village of Louise Glück

Even before the unknown versifier of Isaiah, poets probably looked at a lush meadow and saw a graveyard. Louise Glück's wary, pinch-mouthed poems have long represented the logical outcome of a certain strain of confessional verse. Starved of adjectives, thinned to a nervous set of verbs, intense almost past bearing, her poems have been dark, damaged, and difficult to avert your gaze from.

Poets, those creatures of routine, tend to settle into a style sometime in their thirties and plough those acres as if they'd been cleared by their fathers' fathers' fathers. Read a poet's second or third book and you will see the style of his dotage. Poets restless in their forms, unwilling to take yesterday's truth as gospel, are as rare as a blue rose; and rarer still are poets like Eliot, Lowell, and Geoffrey Hill, who have convincingly changed their style mid-career.

A *Village Life* is a subversive departure for a poet used to meaning more than she can say. All these years that Glück has been writing her stark, emaciated verse, there has been an inner short-story writer itching to break out. (The publicity optimistically refers to the new style as "novelistic"; but there is no novel here, only patches of long-windedness.) The lines are long, the poems sputtering on, sometimes for pages, until they finally run out of gas, as if they were the first drafts of a torpid afternoon. Even so, there's a faith in speech, as well as a generosity of instinct, apparent in these laggardly lines, though the reader may be forgiven for thinking that some charities are impositions.

As in *Spoon River Anthology*, Glück uses the village as a convenient lens to examine the lives within, which counterpoint the memories of her life without. Unlike Masters, she writes without moralizing, though with the same steady knowledge that our destination is the grave ("To get born, your body makes a pact with death, / and from that moment, all it tries to do is cheat"). Unfortunately, the quickest way to the mortuary is apparently marriage:

> He has found someone else—not another person exactly,
> but a self who despises intimacy, as though the privacy of marriage
> is a door that two people shut together
> and no one can get out alone, not the wife, not the husband,
> so the heat gets trapped there until they suffocate,
> as though they were living in a phone booth.

Perhaps I'm not the only reader who finds Glück hilarious, in a ghoulish way—like a stand-up vampire.

The tales that unfold piecemeal from this country town (what is gossip but a part of the whole?) bear the scars of everyday life—childhood fraught with unspoken secrets, adulthood always on the verge of adultery, lives of resentment and suppressed rage, lives missing passion or self-knowledge. The world of this village seems so repressed, you're surprised the inhabitants don't kill each other just to have something to do—or something to talk about. The unchanging fields stretch beyond, overseen by their animal familiars, the bat and earthworm (both given poems *in propria persona*), creatures by nature blind and ravenous. The flourishing olive trees suggest that this site of municipal suffering lies somewhere in Italy or Greece, countries burdened with the myths of the ancient world.

This is a fantasy village, of course, this village of Glück's. (If she's recalling Cesare Pavese, she's no match for him.) There are cars and movies and television, so it isn't medieval, however timeless the attitudes; but the world of cell phones, iPods, and computers has passed it by. Indeed, it's not clear whether the poet has projected certain scenes from an American childhood onto this fictional screen (the poet's voice is particularly hard to distinguish from her inventions here). What she has created is an HO-gauge model of sterility and futility, a place stultified in its antique habits and the passage of despair from adult to child, a Kafkaesque landscape marked by the autumn burning of leaves, an annual holocaust. Here the dead seem almost living, and the living already half dead—"Nothing proves I'm alive. / There is only the rain, the rain is endless." Even the view, with all the passive and frozen beauty of a Japanese scroll, is too much to bear ("as though this beauty were gagging you so you couldn't breathe").

The poet has long resisted giving her interior world any richness of description—a poem may contain rain, sea, clouds, sheep, a mountain, yet you learn little beyond the naked nouns. When a simile comes along, it's as if she had declared a public holiday (I'd max out my credit card for a few adjectives). What she chooses to reveal of this static pastoral lies in the predations or evasions of her verbs: *flood, escape, shudder, vanish, scuffle, prowl, stalk*. This mimesis denied creates a terrible hunger in the reader—Glück's intensity is often a form of starvation. It's like watching a black-and-white movie—the landscape is drawn in chiaroscuro (perhaps the poet is a closet Manichaean). For a poetic world to be this narrow, the poet's desires must be powerfully austere. The real world, in other words, is so overwhelming it must be edited.

Every desire in Glück is cautious, every pleasure suspect. She's almost a feral poet, beadily watching her prey before making a devastating remark—her favorite form of greeting is the ambush. Yet such wariness betrays a terrible sensual longing, sustained despite inevitable disappointment. Even eating a tomato is antic with danger:

> They're beautiful still on the outside,
> some perfectly round and red, the rare varieties
> misshapen, individual, like human brains covered in red oilcloth—
>
> Inside, they're gone. Black, moldy—
> you can't take a bite without anxiety.

Like human brains! After reading such lines, not only do you not want to eat bad tomatoes, you no longer want to eat good ones. I'm not sure such poetry betrays a healthy diet.

Glück's world is as close to Darwinian savagery as any poet has invented (her psyche red in tooth and claw), but it would be a mistake not to see how vulnerable she is beneath her brutal observations. A poem about a mother trying to tell her daughter the facts of life is full of mortifying embarrassment—mother gives daughter one of those insufferable books that make sex harder to follow than instructions for assembling a bicycle.

> *Whatever holds human beings together*
> *could hardly resemble those cool black-and-white diagrams,*
>   *which suggested,*
> *among other things, that you could only achieve pleasure*
> *with a person of the opposite sex,*
> *so you didn't get two sockets, say, and no plug.*

The terrible need not to lie to herself ("Nothing remains of love," Glück says darkly, "only estrangement and hatred") forces the poet to rehearse the old tales to see where the disaster began.

Glück is perhaps the most popular literary poet in America. She doesn't have the audience of Mary Oliver or Billy Collins, whose books rise to the top of the poetry best-seller list (even poets are surprised to learn there is one) and stay there, as if they had taken out a long-term lease. Glück is too private and cunning a poet ever to win too many friends—indeed, part of her cachet is that her poems are like secret messages for the initiated.

Her early poems were all elbows and knees, Plathian with a rakish edge, full of wordplay and tight jazzy rhythms. Glück became a minimalist's minimalist, moody, anxious to her fingertips—a nailbiter's nailbiter. Since the early days of modernism, there has been an argument about how little a poem could contain before too many of the burdens of meaning passed from writer to reader. The one-word poems briefly the rage in the sixties (one of the more famous was Aram Saroyan's "oxygen," just the element such a poem lacked) established that an ironic gesture needs no more than a single word to make its case—it's unfortunate that the argument proved so small and uninteresting. Yet Glück has forced a whole world into a snow globe, and her phrases have been especially rich in their betrayals.

Returning after some decades to a less styptic mode of speech takes courage, or desperation—sometimes finding a new rhythm, however, is like finding a new life. It's good to see a poet old enough to draw Social Security making new contracts with the language. Unfortunately, Glück doesn't yet have control of these long measures—the lines are slack, the fictions drowsy, and the moments of heightened attention like oases in a broad desert (the poems don't argue, they merely accumulate). Without the energies of her short lines and sharply drawn moods, she turns out to have an imagination almost as conventional as anyone else's.

Glück is still a poet of sensibility more than sense, which means that the mortal pressure of her verse exceeds her ability to make memorable phrases. She offers the gratifications of what she calls, dryly, "normal shame and anxiety," even when the content remains slightly vacant. A *Village Life*, though far from her most interesting or most characteristic book, is oddly personal in its distracted way, like an interminable stage whisper (there are odd echoes of M. Night Shyamalan's Walt Disney dystopia of five years ago, *The Village*). Glück learned much from Plath about how to make a case of nerves central to poetry (both poets owe a shadowy debt to Eliot); but finally Plath is a poet for whom the world was too full, and Glück a poet for whom the world is not safe until absolutely empty.

Glück remains our great poet of annihilation and disgust, our demigoddess of depression. At her discomforting best, she reminds me of no poet more than Rilke, who was also a case of nerves and who also lived close to the old myths. Though her comments about him have been hedged, of all the Americans now writing Glück is the closest to being his secret mythographer. Her silences fall at times like moral resistance, and the most striking lines of her chatter are as haunting as an elegy for herself.

Verse Chronicle: Civil Wars

Michael Dickman

Michael Dickman's scrawny, twitchy new poems look undernourished, but they have mean little ambitions. Cast in short clipped lines
(with the occasional long line thrown in as ballast), his second collection, *Flies*, is full of fever dreams of childhood, the haunting presence
of his dead older brother, and flies, flies, flies. There are other animals
as well:

> *My feet did not touch the floor*
>
> *My heart raced*
>
> *I counted my breath like small white sheep and pinned my*
> *eyes open and stared at the door*
>
> *Any second now*
> *Any second*
> *now.*

It's hard to write from a child's point of view without fatally compro-
mising the illusion or seeming cheerfully stupid. Elizabeth Bishop,
in "Manners" and "Sestina," managed it brilliantly by simplifying the
perceptions but not the intelligence. Dickman's child, or man-child,
is full of sentimental clichés and false notes (surely "breaths" would
have made more sense)—at times the poems read more like cartoon

strips. The passage above, where the boy awaits the dead brother's appearance as a superhero, could have been written in thought balloons.

Dickman represents the third, possibly the fourth, generation of
American surrealism, a style (or perhaps a sect) that has always seemed
rather mush-headed in a hardboiled, go-ahead country addicted to
facts, facts, facts. With its whiff of anti-religious sentiment, Surrealism may look revolutionary in France or eastern Europe—what better
threat to Christians than visions that aren't Christian? In America, it's
more like middle-class self-indulgence.

Dickman has little to add to the droopy watches of Surrealists gone
before; but, now that the movement has grown ever more attenuated,
he sees its possibility as a manner without a lick of necessity. If he says,
"I was just whispering // into my glass // pillow" or "I've been standing
in front of a mirror for a hundred years // My glass clothes tossed across
the bed," you don't think, "Oh, the young Apollinaire!" You think,
"Cinderella!"

With his rabbity enjambment and insistent double-spacing, the
poet tries a little too hard to be outrageous. It's almost sweet when he
writes, "There's nothing better / than shaving your father's face / except
maybe / shaving // your mother's legs" (I could have done without
the rimshot spacing), but I suspect the world has not been holding its
breath for his speculations on the private life of Emily Dickinson:

> Standing in her house today all I could think of was
>   whether she took a shit every morning
>
> or ever fucked anybody
> or ever fucked
> herself.

This seems a touch more impolite than Swift's Strephon, emerging
from a lady's dressing room ("Disgusted Strephon stole away / Repeat-
ing in his amorous Fits, / Oh! Celia, Celia, Celia shits!"). Swift took
romantic longing down a peg. Dickman is just some guy with creepy
fantasies.

The poet is best, perhaps, in his take on the Old Testament. He recognizes the absurdity (even the majesty) of religious practice borrowed

from desert tribes three millennia back and still used as a PowerPoint guide to faith: "We invented a chimney let's feed it lambs // Feed it hooves // Holly // Choke it down // Leave piles of ash wherever we walk." His obsession with flies, however, is all too reminiscent of the most famous novel of arrested development after *The Catcher in the Rye*—who knew that keeping William Golding on the eighth-grade reading list would lead to "The flies need to be killed as soon as we're done eating this delicious meal they made // They serve us anything we want / in toxic tuxedos / and // shitwings"?

I confess I cannot see the "incipient violence" or "manic overflow of powerful feeling" (how far Wordsworth has fallen) previous readers have noticed in such poems. What has been called a calculated clumsiness seems just, well, clumsy. Dickman's childishness provides, not access to the world of innocence by a man of experience, just a reason to prolong post-adolescence a few more years. When he stops acting like a gent with a red rubber nose, when he ignores the yen for a gee-whiz flourish ("At the end of one of the billion light-years of loneliness . . ."—but a light-year measures distance, not time), he lets in the bleakness from which these poems might have been composed.

The morbid pacing of his poems (they're jazzy line by line but dull in the stretch) and their difficulty accommodating both giddy surrealism and tract-house blues keep them from pursuing their version of pity and terror with more than a gauzy affectlessness. Dickman's like one of those damaged boys off in the corner drawing burning houses and pulling the wings off insects. You worry about him, this demon kid whose poems are scrawled in fingerpaints or fiddled on an Etch A Sketch.

Henri Cole

Henri Cole's wounded new book, *Touch*, lives in a world where every glance, every embrace, every kiss is a transaction worthy of Ricardo or Keynes. The poems have been written under the sign of the mother, a mother who though dead remains one of the few living presences in the poet's world. The rare traces of his military father suggest that Mom was an exemplary monster ("'Remember you got a father,' he used to say. / 'You weren't born by yourself' ").

The emotional genealogy of Cole's recent books seems airless at times—most of the poems are unrhymed, unmetered "sonnets" more and more constricted by the form (Laocoön would have felt his situation roomy by comparison). They have a brute, even brutish honesty; and even moments that start in beauty end in tooth and claw:

> How brightly you whistle, pushing the long, soft
>
> feathers on your rump down across the branch,
>
> like the apron of a butcher, as you impale a cricket
>
> on a meat hook deep inside my rhododendron.

The image of the apron seems merely decorative, until you realize it's there to introduce the butchery. (Cole is another fan of double-spacing, but where does the escalation stop? One line to a page?)

The mother's death lies at the center of this savage, ravishing book, like the Minotaur in the middle of the maze. There's nothing so intimate the poet won't expose it, whether death itself ("All of life was there—love, death, memory— // as the eyes rolled back into the wrinkled sleeve // of the head") or the body on the mortuary slab:

> its mouth sewn shut, with posed lips,
>
> its limbs massaged, its arteries drained, its stomach and
>   intestines emptied;
>
> a pale blue sweater, artificial pearls, lipstick, and rouge.

Death, like life, is a series of beautiful humiliations—the "posed lips" are a particularly convincing and dispiriting touch. Cole often sees his mother as Rembrandt saw his sitters—gluey with age, mottled by half-forgotten sins, still burning somewhere with the banked spirit of youth, and the face worked over by the fists of a professional. Perhaps the tour de force of the book is the mother's report of her own funeral—it must be disappointing, you imagine, to notice that "white satin covered me to the waist // and was crudely stapled // around the edges of the coffin." Only a perfectionist would see that—and only someone heartless feel obliged to tell you. Once the body is charged with form-aldehyde, flies cannot do their work—when she says that the "white maggots wriggled" after the burial, the poem suffers its one lapse from verisimilitude.

Cole is one of the great contemporary poets of shame (linking him to a very different poet, C. K. Williams). He revisits the mortifications of childhood, condemned always to live in the stranglehold of family history. Loneliness permeates these poems, the terror of longing exceeded only by the horror of togetherness. Something of the speaker's isolation is suggested by a drug-addled lover hilariously addicted to texting: "'Loser old man u r a cheap cunt,' // he wrote, 'I need coke. Unless ur buying, // answer is no.'" Recording it is one way the speaker, so debased by his needs, can betray the lover in turn. The poems witness a degrading world where manners and the grace of language have been eroded by technology.

For a book so intimate with the failings of the body, almost porno-graphic in its rendition of pain, it's curious that the grim mechanics of sex lie always in shadow. Cole becomes a stronger poet with his pain at a remove, instead of broadcast with a megaphone. It can be difficult for a poet so scathingly honest to accept that not all honesties are equal—the sharpest moments appear when he's the least personal.

> *Each night they come back, chasing one another*
>
> *among the fronds after gorging on papayas,*
>
> *to drink from the swimming pool. With my sleep-*
>
> *stiffened bones, I like to watch them, careening*
>
> *into the bright pool lights, spattering the walls with pulp*
>
> *and guano, like graffiti artists.*

"I can hardly stand it and put my face in my hands," the poem ends, "as they dive to-and-fro through all their happiness." The bats, of course, are social beasts.

In *The Visible Man* (1998) and *Middle Earth* (2003), Cole wrote two of the most devastating books of the last two decades. I was not so much a fan of the talking animals in *Blackbird and Wolf* (2007) — half the time the poet seemed to be channeling a milk-and-water version of Ted Hughes. *Touch* finds in the bestial world an adequate mirror to human affairs, while keeping Dr. Doolittle at bay.

The poet's control is not always so sure. There are lines embarrassingly over the top (when the mother gives birth, "Tears ran out of her eyes like animals. // Fragrant convolutions from her insides / filled the room with the strife of love") and too many poems that end on a little pneumatic — or perhaps Plathetic — urgency ("I feel happiness. I feel I am not alone," "Earth was drawing me into existence," "the body whose tissue // once dissolved to create breast milk for me"). Such moments subtract only a little from these mortal poems both reverential and ashamed.

Katherine Larson

Katherine Larson is a field ecologist whose relation to nature lies somewhere between the scientist's and the poet's — in *Radial Symmetry*, she's drawn to the mystery of things, and also to the ways mystery can be mastered. Like a lot of scientists (Loren Eiseley comes to mind), she goes all mushy when she tries to render the world outside the lab:

> *The late cranes throwing*
> *their necks to the wind stay*
> *somewhere between*
> *the place that rain begins*
> *and the place that it ends*
> *they seem to exist just there*
> *above the horizon at least*
> *I only see them that way*
> *tossed up*
> *against the gray October*
> *light.*

There are many poets writing now in what might be called the New Breathlessness. Perhaps Merwin and O'Hara are distant precursors of the style, though these students of students don't have the former's phrasing or the latter's wit. Reading such poems, you think that this is what would happen if the Dutch boy had pulled his finger from the dike—or read too much Jorie Graham.

Larson is capable of images of disturbing beauty, half familiar, half strange (a "Seri woman in sepia, / bare-breasted in a skirt of sewn-together pelican wings"); but her poems are loosely organized, unfocused, and frequently bloated with a grandiose phrase or two:

> I know I'm still alive because I love
> to eat. On the table's a gift
> from fishermen: pink gills embroidered
> blood, the eyes—two mirrors snapped over
> with iron. This shark that I will cut and soak
> in lime has a mouth made for eating darkness—
> an architecture built without a need for dawn.

That sounds like the voiceover to a bad documentary—you can almost hear the strings swell as the credits start to roll.

If Larson were willing to settle for striking images, willing to let them do their work without lardy generalizations like the "sea always asks for more" or "how certain small truths disappear against / a larger truth," she could make better use of that acute, Marianne Moore–ish eye. Moore knew how to tease the moral out of the mussels, as it were; but Larson is tempted to slap headlines on things, whether it's the "rotting sea lion carcass with the plastic Coke bottle / lodged inside its throat" or simply an outing to the beach:

> The day you sawed off the head of the dead dolphin
> with your mother,
>   you were trying to get past the abstraction of death
>
> to the singularity of dying.

Freud may have to be rewritten.

As for the science, Larson doesn't quite know what to do with it. When she writes, "The tide seeps in with its pewter description, / simple and flat under halophytic grasses," the first image is so riveting I'm sorry she had to drag in the five-dollar word (it means that the grasses flourish in salty soil). The science isn't quite poetry and the poetry is a light-year or two from science.

Too often Larson brings her dreamlike style up short with some ga-lumphing observation ("Green grubs dropping from palm fronds to the porch, the sour-sweet / of cheap lemonade. // And always the dia-lectic of inside/outside")—or, worse, pitches headlong into the style of romance novels:

> All the stars are cowards:
> they lie to us about their time of death
> and do nothing but dangle
> like a huge chandelier
> over nights when our mangled sobs
> make the dead reach for their guns.

If that were an allusion to Goering's alleged remark, "When I hear the word 'culture,' I reach for my Browning," it would be funny. Perhaps the days are long gone when a poet like Donne could use science as if it were second nature, when metaphysics translated easily into art.

Billy Collins

"Billy Collins is widely acknowledged as a prominent player at the table of modern American poetry," according to the flap copy of *Horo-scopes for the Dead*. I hadn't gotten the memo! American poetry is now apparently just like the World Series of Poker, with a ten-grand buy-in and the prospect of Internet fame forever. Actually, that sounds like a Billy Collins poem, but it's the kind Collins rarely writes any more. He still has clever ideas, but he no longer knows what to do with them. There's a poem called "Hell," for instance:

> I have a feeling that it is much worse
> than shopping for a mattress at a mall,

of greater duration without question,
and there is no random pitchforking here,
no licking flames to fear,
only this cavernous store with its maze of bedding.

The nattering salesman won't shut up and let you remember the lines from the *Inferno* you're trying to think of; you try this mattress, then that one, then that other one—you try them, well, forever. That's the way the ending might have gone, but telling you at the start that Hell is much worse doesn't do much for the mild traumas that follow. Instead of leaving his couple testing mattresses for eternity (my idea of perdition, right after trying on new pants until Hell's an ice-skating rink), the poem has them

        lying down side by side,
arms rigid, figures on a tomb,
powerless to imagine what it would be like

to sleep or love this way
under the punishing rows of fluorescent lights,
which Dante might have included
had he been able to lie on his back between us here today.

This is a very gentle version of damnation; and it doesn't help by reminding the reader of Larkin's "An Arundel Tomb," a poem far more terrifying and far more loving.

The trouble with Collins's recent work is that, even when the premise is droll as ever (there's a man visiting his parents' grave who asks if they like his new glasses, and a squirrel that breaks into an aria; there are meditations on the chairs no one sits in, and on the secret life of mirrors), even when the idea screams out for the Billy Collins treatment, all he can manage are a few smirks. No one ever went to Collins for good poems. You went for the whimsical premise, the pang of *ubi sunt* regret, the genteel absent-mindedness. Now you get a poem that looks like a bird house slapped together in the back of someone's garage. When there's sorrow, it's buffered sorrow; when there's happiness, it's discount happiness. You're grateful for the whiff of despair, the faint breath of joy, but you miss all the highs and lows.

Like a stand-up comic, Collins has routines rather than arguments; but he used to riff with a kind of breakneck delight. Someone at dinner asks if Zeno's paradox could be employed in the martyrdom of St. Sebastian. Soon the imaginary arrows are flying over the menu of Cornish game hen and trout amandine—always getting closer to the poor saint-to-be, but never quite finishing the job. (The poet suggests that Sebastian would have been dead of a heart attack long before the arrows struck home.) The poem doesn't come to much—it's as if Collins no longer cares. He doesn't even bother to recall that St. Sebastian didn't die from arrows. He survived, a little worse for wear (no thanks to Zeno), and was unromantically clubbed to death.

Collins takes nothing too seriously, but he lacks the genius of the great comedians—whether Swift or Chaplin, Auden or Keaton—who could suggest the vast abysses comedy keeps out of sight. When he tries to be sober-minded, he's not like the boy who cried, "Wolf!" He's like the boy who cried, "Pie fight! Pie fight! Pie fight!" and now wants to tell you the Mongol hordes are here. The new poems all too often end with a little quiet sobbing and the wringing of handkerchiefs. But what high hopes they have at the start!

> I would have to say that the crown
> resting on the head of my first acid trip
> was the moment I went down on one knee
> backstage at the Top Hat Lounge
> and proposed marriage to all three of the Ikettes.

What would life have been like with three gorgeous wives who each evening greeted the poet, home from his labors at the rock face of poetry—three hot women swaying in their red sequin dresses as they whipped up his evening meal, all the while singing in harmony! I feel another Billy Collins poem coming on. It's a shame he didn't write it.

Michael Longley

Michael Longley has lived in the shadow of Seamus Heaney, who for the last half-century has cast an Everest-sized darkness over the poets of Ireland. You can't blame Longley's generation for making fun of

Famous Seamus—it's not that a prophet is without honor in own country, it's that his country doesn't want him to forget where he came from. Decades ago, Longley turned to poems in miniature, like a diamond cutter with a loupe and the determination to pursue elegance on a smaller scale.

Longley has the devotion to Irish landscape of a slightly deranged plant hunter. Many of the poems in *A Hundred Doors* are a nose-down crawl through meadows "covered in lady's smock and ragged / Robin." There's the twayblade,

> *inconspicuous*
> *With greeny petals in long grass,*
> *Lips forked like a man, two leaves*
> *Some call sweethearts, our plant today,*
> *Fed on snowmelt and wood shadows,*

or the shepherd's purse, with its "seed pods—little hearts— / Spoon-shaped petals on spikes." At times he seems to have reinvented himself as one of those nineteenth-century parsons Darwin dreamed of becoming—the sort with a secret life as an amateur naturalist (Clark Kent on Sunday, Super Bird-Twitcher the rest of the week).

Too much of Longley's new work suffers from a tweedy innocence—there are thumbed-over memories, elegies for the recent dead, and a sentimental poem for each of his grandchildren (you're glad he has only half a dozen). I wish the poet were more reckless in old age—he settles too easily for a string of observations, as showily rendered as a painting in a book of hours, but ending in some softhearted remark, stuck in the mawkish like a wasp in amber. These fragments of rural life are like outtakes from Frost, but without the Yankee cunning that made American pastoral so unpredictable.

Longley's father won the Military Cross in World War I (a medal equivalent to the Silver Star). The immediacy and aggression of the poems about the war are like a jolt of electricity:

> *Squatting—a sniper's target—*
> *Nothing to wipe your arse with*
> *Except letters from home—*

Love letters—ink and skidmarks—
Radiant blue and shit—
And there was no grass either.

The grass would have been something else to wipe with. The sacrifice of those intimate words, the soldier's utilitarian calculation of comfort, the details as pungent as "skidmarks"—there have been few poems about the Great War as steel-eyed and unforgiving, while recognizing that even the call of nature is part of war, too.

There are no atheists in foxholes—so the religious would like to believe. Longley sees something in the trenches more rueful:

> *Christ is washing the feet of his Company.*
> *He has an endless supply of talcum*
> *And old newspapers for lining their boots.*
> *He is promoted after Passchendaele.*

Such a poem lives in the balance between savage irony and honest regard—the Christ who was a servant to servants is not part of the church militant; but dutiful soldiers get promoted, too, and even loved.

It has been hard for Irish poets to place themselves in relation to Heaney, just as it was once hard for them to live anywhere near the vast estates of Yeats—a poet can take up too much room (for many poets, Yeats and Eliot used up all the air in the parlor). It's no surprise that the boldest Irish poet after Heaney, Paul Muldoon, had to purge his style (unhappily, in my view) of almost all traces of the older poet. I wish Heaney's peers wouldn't cede quite so much ground or prove so content with lesser ambitions. Longley writes of a passage in the *Metamorphoses* where Achilles faces one of the Trojans:

> *He pummels chin and temples—knock-out punches—and*
> *Trips him up and kneels on ribcage and adam's apple*
> *And thrapples Cygnus's windpipe with his helmet-thongs.*

"Thrapple" is the good old dialect word for strangle. You want to tell Longley, however noble the discipline of observation, to get his face out of the flowers and grab a bloody spear.

Geoffrey Hill

Geoffrey Hill's jarring, discordant new sequence is an elegy for the composer William Lawes. A musician in ordinary to the court of Charles I, during the Civil War Lawes was posted to the King's Life Guards, supposedly a safe troop; but he was killed at Rowton Heath during the siege of Chester. *Clavics* takes its title from the "science or alchemy of keys," so the poet says, but here the keys are musical ("clavichord" derives from the Latin for key). You will hunt in vain for the word—Hill's droll citation is to the "*OED*, 2012." Not yet!

The thirty-two poems have been cast in peculiar form: a twenty-line stanza, varying from dimeter to pentameter, followed by one half as long and shaped like the winglike stanza of Herbert's "Easter Wings." The rhyme scheme is like a briar patch (with so many short lines, the rhymes give these poems the jim-jams, and the rough meter fails to make them the least musical). The formal discipline Hill has set himself—call it willed masochism—makes it harder for his talent to thrive. There are the usual whispers and grunts, the hints and glimmers of meaning, but also stretches no more enlivening than the answers to a Finnish crossword.

It takes some adjustment to read these crabbed hyperborean lyrics. Seventeenth-century lyrics could be no less crabbed; the difficulties entertained, the shackles made to measure, are the grateful if ungraceful homage of one artist to another, dead before his time.

> *So he survives*
> *Demi-famous*
> *The rakish hat*
> *Musicianship that moves*
> *Oddly in state.*
> *Why do you so plug wit and drollery?*
> *Clop-clip-clop, ups with his troop to Chester*
> *Unmerrily*
> *To register,*
> *To be felled,* slain,
> *Etcetera.*

"Lawes," Hill writes, "makes his way in grinding the textures / Of harmony." The musician died at forty-three, not young but youngish—an artist killed in war, followed down the centuries by a long list: Byron, Gaudier-Brzeska, Rupert Brooke, Wilfred Owen, Edward Thomas, Alain-Fournier.

No elegy is a simple matter—it becomes a negotiation between the living and the dead, a relation made no easier when three and a half centuries have passed. Hill writes of the musician's death, "punched semibreve / Like fatal bullet through the fine slashed coat"—the coat might have been slashed by sword, if slashes were not part of Caroline and Jacobean fashion. The semibreve (a whole note) serves as a bullet hole, as if there were musics to death—the puns are obituaries of an abbreviated life. Hill's insistent, layered wordplay has long been an acquired taste, a taste even familiar readers have had to reacquire as his books have grown more peculiar and arcane. His more prickly devices (reader-unfriendly, if you like)—bullying stress marks; intrusive, hectoring voices—are not employed here, or in the case of the voices much toned down.

The poet that Hill has come most to resemble is, a little bizarrely, Walt Whitman. English poetry has rarely had a poet who makes no distinction between the elevated diction of a don whose hobby is reading seventeenth-century theology and the slang of a chav happy with tea and chips—Whitman's "blab of the pave" finds a late convert in a poet who would seem hostile to such a democrat. Hill's juxtaposed registers produce such oddities as *Are you conning me simple rhyme? I am, /* Bro. Ease this screw of paper from my fist." Now "sovran maims," "Mathematicall Roses," "Judith of Bethulia"; now "Supremo," "unburned CDs," "bling," and "taking the piss." He contains multitudes, and they don't get along.

Hill wants the reader never to forget that, though the past lives into the present, the present must shoulder its way into the past. The rhymes force the poet to manic play that makes the syntax skitter four ways at once, without any consequent gain in depth. The tangled music is often difficult to bear—in the smoke and mirrors of syntax, Hill's late mysticism seems to battle its way into form. And what of the angel wings? In the lower stanza, the typographer has sometimes stretched the letter spacing to keep the wings suitably angelic or airworthy. The visual effect is unconvincing. (Hill makes jokes about them — "upright an hour-glass / Better if egg-timer.")

The poetic language here is uneven, but perhaps evenness is not required — his valedictory works, elastic in length and sometimes repetitive in form, ending not in resolution but exhaustion, have been a series of self-provocations. The elegy's opening sections seem to prick the poet to speech — the reader might think *composing* yet another pun that slashes two ways in the music of these figures ("I shall be lucky to twitch / Creative fire," "Confess / Melancholy / A touch too much my thing"). There are lines of breathtaking elegance —

> Making of mere brightness the air to tremble
> *So the sun's aurora in deep winter*
> *Spiders' bramble*
> *Blazing white floss —*

and lines that seem sheer gobbledegook: "Statute's oxymoron / Impassionate lost thistle-rhomb / No intercept from zero friskly drawn." Though the brilliant passages are rare (it would not be hard to call this juddering mass the clangor of the battlefield), the elegiac purpose and command are more deeply driven. Lawes's music was expended in service to the "king-martyr" Charles I, a "double-dealer," a man who "betrayed friends." Can art serve the tyrant and still be art? Can the morally bad patronize the moral good? The questions lie close to the heart of a poet who has rejected his time — Hill's use of the demotic is edged with contempt, just as his long-vanished phrases are an act more of submission than subjection.

Clavics is the second of five Daybooks to be published in advance of Hill's *Collected Poems, 1952–2012*, where the others will be gathered. These are poems easy to dismiss — and yet, and yet. However much Hill has lately been writing against his gifts, the gifts are there, smoldering like an underground coal fire, impossible to put out.

Verse Chronicle: Guys and Dove

Mark Strand

Mark Strand's easygoing charm and labored whimsy have a seventies feel, as if the Bee Gees had never retired. The prose poems in *Almost Invisible* tilt toward contrived fables and dopey meditations, at worst self-indulgent musings after the imagination has shut down for the day and at best Kafka lite. Strand has always been a misfit in American poetry, his sleight-of-hand surrealism only half embraced, his strongest emotion subject to puckish doubt. He's a master of the throwaway line (and also the throwaway poem, but I've already used that joke about Ashbery). A banker walks into a brothel of blind women and claims he is a shepherd:

> *"I can tell by the way you talk," said one of the women, "that you are a banker only pretending to be a shepherd and that you want us to pity you, which we do because you have stooped so low as to try to make fools of us." "My dear," said the banker to the same woman, "I can tell that you are a rich widow looking for a little excitement and are not blind at all." "This observation suggests," said the woman, "that you may be a shepherd after all, for what kind of rich widow would find excitement being a whore only to end up with a banker?" "Exactly," said the banker.*

There's a darkness to such drollery—the self-delusions of sex, the come-hither playacting (with a little slap at Arcadian fantasies, like those of Marie Antoinette), the comeuppance of love. That the whore might indeed be a rich widow is nicely understated, yet the poem remains utterly trivial.

Strand's lightly worn panache, like the cocked fedora on the head of Alain Delon, has a certain retro appeal; but even in a short collection his feline complacence can prove too much of a good thing—or, rather, too little. One of the unhappy results of the reaction against modernism has been how self-conscious poets have become. Too often they feel it necessary to give the reader a nudge of the elbow, as if to say, "See! It's only poetry!" Such gestures are gratifying mostly to the author—it's not just that the suspension of disbelief has been suspended, but that the author has played the reader for a dope.

Strand succumbs so eagerly and so often to sugar-plum guff, his bonhomie seems slightly suspect—you know he's manipulating you, and you know he knows you know. When he ends a poem, "I might have come to the aid of an echo and made the stars shiver in sunlight," or "what happened after the home of the troubled heart broke in two would also begin," you think he can't be serious; but of course he's serious—he's serious about being sentimental.

If the only choices are to believe the poet a callous cynic or a tear-jerked jerk, it's difficult for the reader to trust his tone. Strand's early books *Reasons for Moving* (1968) and *Darker* (1970) had a pitch-perfect sense of the difference between irritating drollery and dry humor (though even the humor seems a bit dated now). The poetry of his old age has wallowed in plush romanticism, elegiac and nostalgic and sometimes even moving. These new poems have the show-offy intelligence and devil-may-care graces of his early work but are hapless besides, with empty-headed titles ("Futility in Key West," "Mystery and Solitude in Topeka," "In the Grand Ballroom of the New Eternity") purchased in a job lot from John Ashbery—Stevens no doubt deserves to have the stuffing knocked out of him, but in his day such titles took romanticism down a notch.

Strand's roguish ideas start with pursed lips and a lifted eyebrow, yet even Pangloss couldn't be satisfied with a poet so self-satisfied. A man takes a taxi with a prince he wishes to interview:

> "I have no hobbies," he explained. "My one interest is sex. It can
> be with a man or a woman, old or young, so long as it produces the

desired result, which is to remind me of the odor of white truffles or
the taste of candied violets in a floating island. Here, let me show
you something." When I saw it, saw how big it was, and what he'd
done to it, I screamed and leaped from the moving cab.

Shades of Huysmans! Despite the slapstick ending, that Proustian perfume takes a long while to dissipate.

Too often Strand, such a natural flaneur, seems so confident in his
indolent craft he can't be bothered to give the poems an actual pulse.
You wonder what might have happened had he found his gifts more
resistant. Beneath the mugging sub-philosophy, the Zen koans for
dummies, often with a dollop of schmaltz laid on, there's a brooding,
a detachment, a nascent melancholy just beyond the poems' reach.

Geoffrey Hill

The brutish labors of Geoffrey Hill's later books recall, not King Si-
syphus condemned to working-class servitude, like Wilde at oakum-
picking, but Giles Corey pressed to death during the witch trials, his
last words "More weight! More weight!" *Odi Barbare* (Barbaric Odes)
is a crabbed sequence of outbursts and meditations, fifty-two sections
cast in Sapphic quatrains. These valedictions have the earned grace
and over-earnest gravity of a poet long used to the edge of darkness.

> *It is not our*
> *Grief devalues clamant eternals. I am*
> *Sick of this dying*
>
> *Time that bends so beautifully around things;*
> *Justice named sum total of ev'ry virtue.*
> *Mia cara, how well you held account of*
> *Seabird and shadow.*

Sidney's Sapphics are nimble and darting, Hill's club-footed and
leaden—and yet how lovely these sutured lines are, with their winking
enjambment on "dying // Time." To announce at the outset that you

are driven to "Measure loss re-cadencing Sidney's sapphics / Not as words fall but as they rise to meaning" suggests a problem of choreography—unless loss of grace is part of the punishment.

Hill has tortured his line to meet the meter ("ev'ry" is not the last concession), but the result is a syntax in which words seem to have been mislaid or marched off the premises.

> *Recognition turning upon cognition,*
> *Fictive played-out ghosts of the Leonati,*
> *Passive agon gravity's apatheia*
> *Held by momentum.*
>
> *Bifold lamentation embarked on lamely.*
> *This is some doing, soul of late embarking.*

The Leonati appear briefly and mutely in *Cymbeline*. It isn't that the passage makes no sense; it's that the sense requires a fair amount of spackling and make-work. Faced with this poet's more mulish allusions, a reader used to strolling through the stacks might once have felt prepared. Knowledge is no longer enough. What are we to make of the sentence "Nonsense too deep meaning a derogation"? Is the verb missing? Should there be a hyphen after "deep"—or a semicolon? (Very Coleridgian, then.) Or should you just throw commas at the thing until you get "Nonsense, too deep, meaning a derogation"? Hill's willful obscurity long ago became a niggardly revenge upon readers.

The poet's recent books, those palimpsests of Masonic learning and arcane grievance (a palimpsest is twice lost), are like the carbonized scrolls of Herculaneum. You hope for a lost play by Aeschylus, but you're more likely to get some minor rhetorician's treatise on prepositions. To ask the reader to pore over words that yield so little is a convenient way to separate the sheepish from the goatish; but it beckons to Hill's religiose masochism, his howls of pain, and the occult theocracy he seems to bar at the front door only to smuggle in through the back. God, so Hill says, "Worries his self-satisfied bulk, the indis- / Criminate vengeance of the Flood, and blithely / Switches the Rainbow"—yet there's more than a little of the bullying Jehovah in the poet.

Even to begin the long course of learning required here, the reader must be prepared to work up Carducci (the Italian poet who provides the title), Aula Regis, Abram Chaldee, hymns to Mathesis, clarimote, *Rattus rattus, Quaderni*, Igboland, Poggio, *Didone trionfante*, Ghelderode, Ensor, Shantineketan, spieltrieb, illth, Gwalia, Hendre Fechan, dyscracy, Nitro Glisserinski, and much else. ("Clarimote" so far defeats definition.) The poems make most headway against the barbaric, however, when most simple.

> *Mirrors fading where the bright-brutish roses*
> *Held themselves royally akin their nature.*
> *Berkeley could have granted us our existence*
> > *Had we but known him.*

> *Still suffices language its constitution;*
> *Solipsist somehow must acknowledge this. Not*
> *Quite enough said when what was said is nothing*
> > *Granted recital.*

> *Here is my good voice; you may well remember*
> *Making up these things. It is what I do. Hark,*
> *Love, how cross-rhythms are at stake to purpose*
> > *From the beginning.*

The language here takes its cue from cadence, pulling the sapphics through the line, supporting but enticing, eliding but forgiving. Passages freed from adamantine obduracy—that is, Hill's Patent Cement—are rare. Meaning in this poem is fiercely guarded; but the text is not entirely resistant, and with patience some of the fog begins to clear. (You feel that Hill's long ambition has been a poem that on first reading is perfectly impenetrable, a mirror of ignorance.) There is a difficulty in literature that is enlivening and ennobling—that of *Moby-Dick* or *The Waste Land*—and a difficulty that suffocates. Though Hill too often now succumbs to the latter, somehow, by fits and starts, his verse struggles toward clarity, freeing his words despite himself.

Hill makes the familiar obeisance to familiar themes, jawing on about our barbaric day, the old wounds of World Wars I ("Passchendaele's chill mud at a gulp engorging / Men and redhot rashers of sizzling metal") and II ("I recall those fifty / Spavined destroyers"), as well as the artists ruined by time ("Blazoned EP also sent in credentials") or the survivors of time's humiliations ("so maybe Rembrandt's *The Polish Rider* / Probably not Polish, not Rembrandt even"). This frustrating, bedeviling book, its lines too often hobbled, has the rare graces that make even a few lines by Hill a specific in a time bad for verse. If this is not a *Paradiso*, it is a *Purgatorio* in sight of an ending.

Vladimir Nabokov

Vladimir Nabokov was a poet before he became a novelist. As with Joyce and Faulkner, the vices of his poetry became the virtues of prose. How fortunate the exile from poetry was: had their reputations rested on verse, three of the great novelists of the twentieth century would have remained unknown. Nabokov was a young man when his family fled the Russian Revolution, and his poems often look back on the heritage and patrimony stolen from him. He was winningly modest about his verse, but his art was both conscious and compelled. Nabokov's own selection, published in *Poems and Problems* (1970), has been supplemented in *Selected Poems* by two dozen or so poems from Russian previously untranslated and some uncollected poems in English. "Pale Fire" and other poems in his fiction have been excluded on unconvincing grounds.

The Russian poems have been rendered into a kind of mock Victorian by the novelist's late son, Dmitri. What are we to make of stanzas like "Undisturbed the dragonflies hover, / like diamonds sparkle their wings, / encircled by snowy-white roses / that follow the font as it sings" or "Across the basin's water / the magic flame will float; / accoasts in rapid order / the little nutshell boat"? *Accoast*, so far as I can discover, has not been much used since the day of Spenser. When the father writes a panegyric to Shakespeare (about whose identity Nabokov seems to have had doubts), the son can do no more than turn the lines into monstrosities like "Thus was enfolded / your godlike thunder in a succinct cape" and "Reveal yourself, god of iambic thunder, / you hundred-mouthed, unthinkably great bard!" The subject might be some *Mitteleuropa* dictator, the translation done by his worst enemy.

It's no use suggesting that the sins of the son have been visited upon the father. Nabokov's own translations are not much better. A man may have many gifts, yet not the gift for poetry:

> *What bliss it is, in this world full of song,*
> *to brush against the chalk of walls, what bliss*
> *to be a Russian poet lost among*
> *cicadas trilling with a Latin lisp!*

The introduction by the Nabokov scholar Thomas Karshan makes heavy weather of Nabokov's verse, which is just the wrong weather to make. The poems have a few virtues, but almost everything the novelist did in verse he could do far better in prose. The infant Nabokov read English before he read Russian (he was famously trilingual from childhood, speaking French as well); but if he had an English ear for prose, more or less, he had only a Russian ear for verse. His contributions to the *New Yorker* seem to have been written with clenched teeth (a bumbling, unfunny "ballad"; an ode to a model; a portrait of a literary dinner that turns into a cannibal feast) and were perhaps mistaken for being congruent with the then celebrated *New Yorker* wit.

The poems have aged badly, like the attitudes in them. A man finds himself in what he thinks must be heaven, where he meets a beautiful, naked little girl. The nymphet seems willing:

> *With a wild*
> *lunge of my loins I penetrated*
> *into an unforgotten child.*
> *Snake within snake, vessel in vessel,*
> *smooth-fitting part, I moved in her,*
> *through the ascending itch forefeeling*
> *unutterable pleasure stir.*

Ah, those days when pedophilia was innocent. (The man's in hell, of course.) This might be called porn for Victorian translators—it's the sort of thing that used to be left in footnotes, and in Latin. I have forgotten to mention that in the middle of the vision the girl vanishes and the man complains that "obscenely bleating youngsters / were staring at my pommeled lust." *Pommeled lust!* You can't get phrases like that at Walmart.

I have never been a great fan of Nabokov's fiction, which reads as if composed by an eighteenth-century automaton with only a flywheel for a heart. I make a partial exception for *Lolita*, but only partial—its set pieces are outrageous and surprisingly sad, but the deserts of prose between defeat me. (That the tale can no longer be read so blithely will remain as much of a problem as the use of "nigger" in *Huckleberry Finn*. We are no longer in a century when sex with twelve-year-olds is considered amusing. That does not mean that we stop reading, merely that there is resistance to overcome.) Nabokov was often afflicted with a hyper-aestheticism that makes his verse at times cold meats from Ronald Firbank's table (the verse reveals the underbelly of Nabokov's prose): the poems are fatty with words like "semi-pavonian," "lyriform," "macules," "marron," "cacodemons" and such, with lines like "she took me by my emberhead" or "They burn the likes of me for wizard wiles / and as of poison in a hollow smaragd / of my art die." The problem is not that Nabokov the poet doesn't write half so well as Nabokov the novelist; the problem is that he doesn't write half so well as *Lolita*.

Many of the poems look back on that lost youth and childhood in Russia, where Nabokov's family was wealthy and where at seventeen he inherited a riverside mansion and its estate. There's an ode to the dead country, and a striking dream (not lost but spoiled in translation) in which the speaker is taken out to be executed but finds himself rapturous over flowers blooming in the death ravine. O Russia! The pains of exile come through, no less painful if sometimes ridiculed. Subjects make a personality—other poems consider Jesus; Joan of Arc; appearing in someone else's snapshot; the discovery of a new butterfly (Nabokov's papers on lepidoptera are now recognized as groundbreaking); and what becomes of an amateur naturalist in heaven, where there are no animals to describe, just angels.

It's hard to be fair to Nabokov's poetry, just as it would be hard to be fair to Marx's, or Shirley Temple's. They would be out of their depth— that is to say, into their shallowness. Nabokov worried that after death his books would vanish. In all the wretched verse dragged forth here from Russian emigré magazines of the twenties and rotting files of the *New Yorker*, there's a single stanza that suggests the odd, cloistered magic of this author. A class of college students asks a visiting Russian poet, "Is your prosody like ours?" He answers:

> *The rhyme is the line's birthday, as you know,*
> *and there are certain customary twins*
> *in Russian as in other tongues. For instance,*

love automatically rhymes with blood,
nature with liberty, sadness with distance,
humane with everlasting, prince with mud,
moon with a multitude of words, but sun
and song and wind and life and death with none.

Though the English is no doubt a muffled version of the Russian, you hear the intelligence of aspect, the dark love of language, that Nabokov brought into exile. *Selected Poems* otherwise succeeds in a Nabokovian irony—by destroying the poet's reputation completely. You can learn from Nabokov a hundred ways to write poetry badly, but not a single way of writing it well.

Rita Dove

The critical reaction to *The Penguin Anthology of Twentieth-Century American Poetry*, edited by Rita Dove, has been violent, silly, depressing, and symptomatic—and it hasn't gone nearly far enough. A long head-shaking, well-mannered evisceration by Helen Vendler in the *New York Review of Books* was followed by Dove's cri de coeur in a letter to the editor. (Vendler had been chair of the jury that nominated Dove for the Pulitzer Prize a quarter-century ago.) This bewildering and myopic book is not an adequate portrait of American poetry of the late century. It might instead be called an expression of contemporary anxieties about poetry.

All anthologies suffer the prejudices of their making, just as period films filter past mores and manners through the bias of the present. In one recent blockbuster, World War II fighter pilots never smoked a cigarette—it was like watching a western where all the cowboys politely refuse a shot of whiskey. An editor afraid to challenge the hidebound notions of the day is not of much use.

Dove's anthology superficially resembles many others in this crowded field. It starts with Edgar Lee Masters, continuing through the great modernists into the varied generations after, down to poets who have just turned forty. Yet how ghostly this vision of the great poets seems! Robert Frost is represented by five short poems and one longer; Stevens by the same number, none of any great length; Williams by four poems and an excerpt; Pound by "Mauberly," three short poems, and a fragment from one Canto; Eliot by *The Waste Land*, "Prufrock," and "Preludes"; and poor Marianne Moore only by "The Fish" and two of the many versions of "Poetry." A college student would have little idea why these half-dozen poets have been the subject of continual study since they revolutionized American verse almost a century ago. Gwendolyn Brooks gets three times as much space as Moore; Melvin B. Tolson more space than Frost, Williams, or Pound; Robert Pinsky more than Stevens, Moore, Cummings, Crane, Auden, Roethke, Bishop, Berryman, Jarrell, or Lowell.

It would seem almost inarguable that an anthology ought to gather the best poems of the period, even if you have to include fifty poems by Frost before you even think of Angelina Weld Grimké. That's the radical and austere aesthetic position; but even a mild version would separate more clearly the great from the not so great, and the not so great from the actively dull. Dove's anthology is so inclusive you're surprised everyone's second cousin isn't here. Yet among the poets missing from the first half of the century are Vachel Lindsay, Eleanor Wylie, John Crowe Ransom, Allen Tate, Yvor Winters, Ogden Nash, Lorine Niedecker, Richard Eberhart, Robert Penn Warren, George Oppen, and J. V. Cunningham—and, later, Donald Justice, Louise Glück, and Gjertrud Schnackenberg. I might have dumped a few of these myself; but it's painful to find these poets missing and yet a horde of mediocre poets crowding the pages at the end of the book.

Dove's rule is that poets had to live in America and write in English. She doesn't set a term for residence, but presumably it had to be longer than a two-week vacation. Auden is in, meagerly, but not Joseph Brodsky; Paul Muldoon, but not Anne Carson. It's to Dove's credit that she presents poets often ignored because of race or gender—she's far more generous to black poets than most anthologists, and among younger poets the minorities have almost become a majority (helped by the apparent die-off of white male poets some years ago). Even here Dove is not without editorial judgment—among the poets she leaves out are W. E. B. Du Bois, Sterling A. Brown, and Richard Wright. Younger black poets write so well, however (four Pulitzers in the past two dozen years), that they do not need condescending favors; and white poets do not write so badly that they can be roundly ignored.

If some of this is due to "representation," representation can be a very sharp knife. When sociology masquerades as aesthetics, your fairness seems immediately unfair to everyone left out (there's a point where "balance" is prejudice by another name). The blogs have been alight with rage over the absence of Appalachian poets, disabled poets, cyberpoets, performance poets, avant-gardists of every stripe, and many other groups implicitly maligned. Once you establish "representation" as a shibboleth, there's no stopping. Pity the poets of Hoboken, who get nary a look-in here. Where are the transgender poets? Where have the fetishists gone? Is there even a single pre-pubertal poet? *Ubi sunt* the poets of the VFW, the AFL-CIO, and the Daughters of the American Revolution? No art is an equal-opportunity art. Talent is always asymmetrically distributed. It's an injustice, to be sure, that most of the great modernists went to Harvard or the University of Pennsylvania, just as it's an injustice that more presidents were born in Virginia than in any other state.

The anthology has learned little from the sins of anthologies past— it's bottom heavy with the poetry of our moment (ninety-nine poets born from 1868 to 1939; seventy-seven from 1940 to 1971). No anthology can dispassionately represent the present: the sensible anthologist would choose a dozen poets born from 1940 to 1955, half a dozen thereafter, and call it a day. Those would be his bet on the future— Dove has cast a massive seine and caught a lot of flotsam and jetsam. She has made matters worse by adding four poems by herself, when most of her contemporaries are limited to one or two. To think yourself twice as good as almost every poet of your generation suggests a species of self-delusion common in poets but rare in anthologists, because an anthologist without modesty can't be taken seriously.

Dove's problems were compounded by a quarrel over permissions. As the production deadline neared, negotiations between her publisher and HarperCollins broke down. Allen Ginsberg, Sylvia Plath, and other poets were removed. Though somewhat coy in her introduction about this disaster, Dove has been more forthcoming in interviews. Given the absence of a statement to the contrary, it seems that HarperCollins demanded permissions fees so out of line with those of other publishers that agreement became impossible (under the common "most favored nations" clause, if one publisher receives a higher fee, so must the others). Penguin chose to go forward without two poets crucial to any sense of the late century. There has been a howl over *Howl*, and accusations that Dove secretly loathes Sylvia Plath. Defending her decision not to abandon the project, Dove claims that these poets "are widely available . . . in your local public library"—but then why bother with the anthology at all? Just hammer a list to your front door and be done with it. Though Dove does not mention which contemporary poets were affected, the disagreement probably accounts for the absence of Louise Glück, among others.

To give an overview of the century's American verse would have been a difficult task for a poet of critical sophistication, much less one who thinks in platitudes and writes in clichés. Dove's introduction (which she also calls a foreword, apparently not knowing the difference) must have a place in any future anthology of stuffed-owl prose. She views American poetry as a pop-up book:

> Open to the first page, and up would pop a forest: a triangle of birches labeled Robert Frost, a solitary Great Oak for Wallace Stevens, a patch of quirky sycamores tagged William Carlos Williams, and a Dutch Elm for Hart Crane, with a double lane of poplars for Elizabeth Bishop.

I understand the birches, but Stevens wrote no poem about a great oak (I know, I know—she's being "metaphorical"). I'm sure the editor doesn't mean to suggest that homosexuality is like Dutch Elm disease, but she might have chosen her symbols more carefully. We're fortunate Williams isn't represented by a heap of old wheelbarrows and Bishop by a barrel of dead fish.

Dove gushes with fresh-minted platitudes ("Every soup gets cold") as well as fatuous bromides (the "past is never more truly the past than now"), her images rising from the charmingly wacky (the "brittle glee of Edna St. Vincent Millay's flaring candle") to the slightly deranged ("Berryman . . . could no longer resist the Grim Reaper he had carried inside for so long"). There are metaphors clumsy ("inserting special clumpings into the chronological mix"), and gruesome (the "last living witnesses were buried under the poet's allegorical earth"), and sweetly surreal (an "attempt to corral poets into historical arenas"). Or just goofy drivel ("Terrance Hayes latched onto the thick coiled tubers of Gwendolyn Brooks and Robert Lowell").

Then there are the literary judgments: Frost "produced a cadre of pieces geared toward dispensing wisdom." Cummings "treated language as a malleable, evolving ectoplasm"; and Wallace Stevens's poems, it's important to know, "were unlike anyone else's." (Dove apparently believes he was married before he entered Harvard.) The woman in an Amy Lowell poem is a "dichotomy that presented a volatile package." Does the editor really think that Pound's "immersion in many traditions . . . perhaps later contributed to his mounting irrationalism, anti-Semitism, and anti-American rants"? Can it be that "his argument, essentially, was that nothing—no thing—is absolute"? (If any poet believed in verities, it was Pound.) And was Eliot just a "sourpuss retreating behind the weathered marble of the Church"? (Eliot was the only true wit among the moderns, as his letters will eventually show.) These smug, idiotically phrased judgments—with their evolving ectoplasms, volatile-package-wielding dichotomies, Grim Reapers like a prize in a Cracker Jack box, and all the rest—wouldn't pass muster in a freshman lit course.

What can you say when one of the most honored contemporary poets can't write a sentence that sounds literate? All you can do is quote until you cry.

> *Artists shake off complacency to tackle the dreaded monster of mortality with an exalted sense of purpose and doom.*

> *Emily Dickinson and Walt Whitman are generally regarded as the double-yolked egg from which hatched a brood of distinctly American prosodies.*

> *One could explain away the phenomenon of Robert Frost with the adage "He who dies with the most toys wins," but that would be unfair.*

> *Elizabeth Bishop . . . somehow managed to chisel the universe into pixilated uncertainties.*

> *"The Death of the Hired Man" takes the pith and immediacy of Shakespearean drama and places it squarely in the poetic arena.*

A pity that never occurred to Shakespeare. After we're told that "several women breached the ramparts of male power and self-importance," that "The Death of the Ball Turret Gunner" is a "take on haiku," that Ginsberg's "'I' opened the floodgates to a host of literary spin-offs," that Kenneth Koch "led generations to the pools of creativity and bid them drink," it's hard not to get a little dizzy. Here, "introspective black poets . . . were swept under the steamroller"; there, the civil rights movement and the Vietnam War "precipitated a social and interpretive sea change"; somewhere else, "America was licking its self-inflicted Vietnam War wounds."

This cliché-addled, *Time* magazine–style rush to literary judgment is dispiriting but hilarious. Matters are made no better by an alarming number of textual errors and the complete lack of notes in what seems meant as a college textbook. Dove has built a Temple of Mediocrity, scarcely glancing at the century's best poets while lavishing space on the harmless, the hackneyed, the humdrum. The chance to provide an original and convincing vision of the last century has been squandered.

Nobody's Perfect: The Letters of
Elizabeth Bishop and Robert Lowell

A poet should never fall in love with another poet—love is already too much like gambling on oil futures. Two poets in love must succumb to the same *folie à deux* as the actor and the actress, the magician and the fellow magician, because each knows already the flaws beneath the greasepaint, the pigeons hidden in top hats, all the pockmarked truth beneath illusion. Real lovers, Shakespeare long ago reminded us, have reeking breath and hair like a scouring pad.

Lovers may be permitted an exception to this ironclad rule, if they never achieve the bliss of consummation—and therefore never have to wake to the beloved's morning breath the morning after. Many would-be lovers have been divided by family, law, or plain bad luck; before the days of long-distance phone calls or e-mail, the sublimated affair was conducted by postage stamp. The letters of Nietzsche and Lou Andreas-Salomé, Pirandello and Marta Abba, Gautier and Carlotta Grisi show that, though literature has always been good for love (think how many seductions can be blamed on Shakespeare's sonnets), love was even better for literature, if there was a mail box nearby.

Words in Air collects the letters between Robert Lowell and Elizabeth Bishop, from a few months after they met at a dinner party in 1947 to a few weeks before his death of a heart attack thirty years later, a correspondence conducted across continents and oceans as their poetry drove them together and their lives kept them apart. As poets, Lowell and Bishop could not have been more different. His heavy-handed youthful verse, solemnly influenced by Allen Tate, laid down a metrical line like iron rail. (If Lowell's early poems seem stultified now, they were boiled in brine and preserved in a carload of salt.) Her whimsical eye and wry, worried poems condemned her to be treated like a minor disciple of Marianne Moore. Bishop for much of her life was a poet's poet, which means a poet without an audience.

Lowell and Bishop felt drawn to each other's poetry from the start. Though wary of being seduced by an alien style (Bishop, after reading one of Lowell's poems: "It took me an hour or so to get back into my own metre"), they were soon exchanging their work and, sometimes by return mail, sending back fond but exacting criticism. Lowell was a poet trying to get out of his own skin—he changed styles the way some men change socks—while Bishop was desperate to vanish into her words. (The two poets went from not being quite sure who they were to grousing mildly over what they had become.) It doesn't take a Viennese doctor to suggest that the artist's relation to art reveals something about childhood—Lowell's poems were often an act of vengeance upon his parents, while Bishop's concealed her anguish over a childhood best forgotten (she described herself as "naturally born guilty").

Poetry can be a surprisingly lonely art—you end up wishing that Emily Dickinson had discovered someone livelier than Colonel Higginson, someone who showed a little more rapport. It's so rare for a writer to find the perfect sympathetic intelligence, we think sadly of Melville and Hawthorne, Coleridge and Wordsworth, whose hothouse friendships came to grief, in part due to the fatal attunement of their imaginations—not all harmonies survive the wear and tear of character. Bishop and Lowell passed almost immediately from awkward introduction to rapturous intimacy. Though they were delighted by that most valuable specie of literary life, gossip, it was soon apparent what necessary company these brittle, gifted intelligences were.

Their surviving 459 letters, some surprisingly long (Bishop might elaborate hers over weeks, at times swearing she had written Lowell in her imagination), give us the closest view of these wounded creatures—his muscular, bull-in-a-china-shop intellect; her pained shyness and abject modesty, her gaze like the gleam off a knife. She brought out the boyishness in him. They worked out in verse the terms of their fragility—its character, its allowance, its burden. It is not, not just, that their sympathies were nearly absolute (letters, however adoring, begin with an affinity of prejudices), but that each poet proved a nearly ideal audience. "I think I must write entirely for you," Lowell told her.

Sometimes falling in love is as much an act of criticism as criticism is an act of love. Before, during, and after his marriages, Lowell took lovers, from students to a society matron (his poems were charged with an intensity no earthbound lover could match). At the outset of his "enthusiasms," as he called his shadowy attacks of manic depression, he often fixed his attention on some starry-eyed young woman. Bishop was not starry eyed. Lowell was so much in love with her poems, however, it must have seemed logical to fall in love with her. After a near disastrous visit in 1957 (their meetings, long planned and longed for, did not always go well), he wrote her that asking her to marry him was the great might-have-been of his life.

Bishop, who comes across as the more sensible and insightful of the pair, placidly ignored this revelation (she remained somewhat coquettish, from a distance); and their friendship proceeded as before—they continued to address each other as "Dearest," and once Lowell called her "Dear Heart." It is to the advantage of these letters that this love was impossible, as he must have known. Bishop was half a dozen years older and an alcoholic, which might have made no difference; but she was also a lesbian. We owe the brilliance of their letters, not to the love that dared not speak its name, but to the love whose name—except once—Lowell dared not speak. A decade before he died, he wrote, "I seem to spend my life missing you!"

By 1951, Bishop had moved to Brazil, more or less by accident, or the accident of love. She fell in love during a stopover on a long freighter cruise, while being nursed through an allergic reaction to a cashew fruit. She adored the frankness of Brazilians—they took no notice of her shyness. Bishop was charmed by the exotic (perhaps one day, when she has ceased to be their darling, academic critics will accuse her of imperialist fantasies). Through coup and counter-coup, through the yearly snarl of Brazilian politics, she wrote lighthearted poems that kept their darkness buried in the interior. She was always good at concealing what she felt.

Lowell became her lifeline to the literary world left behind. They discussed the books they read, their motley illnesses, how many poems they were writing (Lowell) or not writing (Bishop), their hopes of seeing each other (half a century ago, almost every visit was preceded by protracted negotiation by letter). If they shook their heads over the antics of Richard Eberhart or the later poems of Marianne Moore, we're amused, because we shake our own heads over Eberhart and the later poems of Marianne Moore. Their peers—John Berryman, Randall

Jarrell, Theodore Roethke, Delmore Schwartz—were not exactly dismissed, but only coolly embraced (Bishop and Lowell admired Jarrell, but were not so fond of his poems). Younger poets, if mentioned at all, were mentioned for their faults.

Yet in this avid chatter there is nothing like braggadocio, nothing as bold as Keats's quiet remark to his brother, "I think I shall be among the English Poets after my death." At one point Bishop says, more in sorrow than pride, "I feel profoundly *bored* with all the contemporary poetry except yours,—and mine that I haven't written yet." Their mutual praise is as affecting as the way they would shyly enclose some stray poem like "The Armadillo" or "Skunk Hour," described as trifling, and now an indispensable citizen of our anthologies.

Their admiration even made them light fingered—they borrowed ideas or images the way a neighbor might steal a cup of sugar. Lowell was especially tempted by this lure of the forbidden, using one of Bishop's dreams in a heartbreaking poem about their might-have-been affair, or rewriting in verse one of her short stories. They were literary friends in all the usual ways, providing practical advice (the forever dithery and procrastinating Bishop proved surprisingly pragmatic), trading blurbs, logrolling as shamelessly as pork-bellied senators (Lowell was adept at dropping the quiet word on her behalf). There was a refined lack of jealousy between them—that particular vice never found purchase, though in letters to friends they could afford the occasional peevish remark about each other. The only time Bishop took exception to Lowell's poems was when, in *The Dolphin* (1973), he incorporated angry letters from his ex-wife Elizabeth Hardwick— "*Art just isn't worth that much,*" Bishop exclaimed. She flinched when poets revealed in their poems too much of themselves, once claiming that she wished she "could start writing poetry all over again on another planet."

These poets, in short, inspired each other. Lowell always seems to be stuffing her newest poem into his billfold, so he can take it out later like a hundred-dollar bill. Bishop saw immediately how strange and shocking *Life Studies* (1959) was (its confessional style caused as violent an earthquake in American poetry as *The Waste Land*); but he noticed something more subtle, that she rarely repeated herself. Each time she wrote a poem, it was as if she were reinventing what she did with words, while he tended to repeat his forms until he had driven them into the ground, or driven everyone crazy with them. Bishop was loyal enough to admire, or pretend to, even Lowell's mediocre poems.

If Lowell and Bishop often seem to love no poems more than each other's, as critics perhaps they were right. A hundred years from now, they may prove the twentieth century's Whitman and Dickinson, an odd couple whose poems look quizzically at each other, half in understanding, half in consternation, each poet the counter-psyche of the other. Their poems are as different as gravy from groundhogs, their letters so alike—so delightfully in concord—the reader at times can't guess the author without glancing at the salutation.

These lives were marked by terrible sadness. Bishop's Brazilian lover committed suicide; the poet continued drinking until she started falling down and injuring herself. Lowell's degrading seizures of manic depression, during which he often behaved contemptibly, left him in a permanent state of semi-apology. His three marriages, each time to a novelist, ended badly. Though sometimes blocked or depressed, as a poet Lowell would suddenly bulldoze his way forward; Bishop, timid as a turtle, often terribly lonely, slowly produced small masterpieces, finishing only one or two poems a year (she said, "I've always felt that I've written poetry more by *not* writing it"). The interstices of their lives were remade as art; but that is not enough, if you have to live the life afterward. Even in their forties, they sound worn out.

The pleasures of this remarkable correspondence lie in the untiring way these poets entertained each other with the comic inadequacies of the world. Letters offer the biographical hour—though in some phrase you may see the germ of a poem, you possess all the brilliant phrases that didn't make their way into poems, whether it's Lowell saying that he, his wife, and his mother were all "fuming inside like the burning stuffings of an overstuffed Dutch chair" or Bishop describing the baptism of some babies: "The god-parents holding them shook them up & down just like cocktail shakers." Their remarks about writing have, in his case, a self-amused detachment ("I like being off the high stilts of meter"); in hers, deadpan modesty ("I have only two poetic spigots, marked *H & C*"). He: "Psycho-therapy is rather amazing—something like stirring up the bottom of an aquarium." She: "I bought a small wood Benedito, the crudest kind of whittling and painting. . . . He's holding out the baby, who is stuck on a small nail, exactly like an hors d'oeuvres." In her mid-thirties, Bishop, who called herself a "poet by default," had not read Chaucer; in his late forties, Lowell had to look up the words *gesso, echolalia,* and *roadstead.*

Admittedly, in this concrete block of a volume there are long stretches of nattering, antique gossip, ideas that come to nothing (Bishop habitually started things she could never finish). The late letters often confine themselves to worries over age, money, and dentistry. As the poets grow older, there come the premature revelations of death: Dylan Thomas, then Roethke, Jarrell, Schwartz, Berryman—many of their generation died too young. Comically, Lowell and Bishop more or less adopt the younger poet Frank Bidart, who catered to Lowell during his endless revisions (or perhaps encouraged his manic over-revision—"spoiling by polishing," Lowell called it) and proved Johnny-on-the-spot after Bishop moved to Boston. If at times the poets treated him as a mere factotum, Bidart served as the surrogate son they could gossip about and fuss over.

The editing of this immense volume, in many ways so genially meticulous, reveals that Robert Giroux, in his selection of Bishop's correspondence in *One Art* (1994), grossly altered her punctuation. Nonetheless, *Words in Air* is marred by a raft of typos and a sketchy, inadequate glossary of names. The editors confidently announce that the poets' spelling has been corrected—all a reader can say is, would that they had corrected more of it.

This long, leisurely correspondence seems now of another world, a fading reminder of the golden age of letter writing. For some two decades, Bishop and Lowell have divided postwar American poetry between them, a shared dominion the more remarkable because their manners, their styles, and their philosophies of imagination are so different. Though Bishop was not always highly rated in a generation of poets given to Sturm und Drang, she was worshiped by Lowell; and his is the taste we share now. Their devotion was crucial to their literary life, perhaps more than any of their love affairs. These star-crossed lovers found the muse in each other.

Elizabeth Bishop at the *New Yorker*

In the decades since her death in 1979, Elizabeth Bishop has been recognized as an American original, as much ours and not ours as Whitman, Dickinson, and that transplanted Yankee Robert Frost. A reader's appetite for the lives of beloved poets can be hard to satisfy. Their mortgages are subject to scholarly study, their medical records sold in shadowy alleys, their childhood friends dunned to offer up nuggets of gossip. We would read their shopping lists if we could—such things make them more human, and therefore slightly inhuman, since how is it possible that the authors of *Leaves of Grass* or "Because I could not stop for Death" or *North of Boston* could have needed new stockings, and hair oil, and cornflakes?

The three selections of Bishop's letters already published are now followed by one much quirkier, *Elizabeth Bishop and The New Yorker*, some forty years of exchanges between the editors of that famously secretive magazine and that famously retiring poet. Bishop's personal letters, like her poems, were full of deftly seen detail and mordant self-mockery. A little of that leaked even into these business letters, particularly after her editors became her friends. (It was hard for the editors to remember that when they became her friends they were no longer exactly her editors). A world-class procrastinator and Olympian ditherer, Bishop sometimes didn't finish a poem for decades—she lobbied to be the magazine's poetry critic, but when appointed never turned in a single review. Too much of this overlong book is devoted to the editors' ritual cajolery; apologetic promises by Bishop; promises piled upon promises, like Pelion on Ossa, with excuses added to order; belated submissions; rapid acceptances (or, more rarely, rejections); and the inevitable wrestle over editing.

The difficulties were compounded by distance. For most of two decades, Bishop lived in Brazil, having fallen in love with a Rio aristocrat while recovering from an allergic attack after eating cashew fruit. Her small inheritance went much further there, and living abroad kept her out of the storms of American literary life. Between the perils of airmail and the untrustworthy Brazilian postal system (street mailboxes were apparently never emptied), and the lost letters and wayward proofs that followed, it was a miracle there was any editing at all.

The major theme of these letters is, of all things, punctuation. Though she graduated from Vassar, Bishop was a haphazard and cruelly inventive minder of stops. ("Punctuation is my Waterloo," she wrote glumly.) Tourists hauled in off the Copacabana beach could have given her lessons; but it was up to her editors, chiefly Katharine White and later Howard Moss, to puzzle out her meanings and clarify her unintentional ambiguities. The magazine had a somewhat straitlaced view of grammatical rules (and other things—for years the two women addressed each other as Miss Bishop and Mrs. White). Her forbearing editors, however, dismissed many in-house queries, often allowing Bishop to decide just how far toward sanity she was willing to go. All this is amusing; but the book's editor, Joelle Biele, has crammed in footnotes that record every comma the editors introduced, or failed to introduce, or asked the gods of punctuation for permission to introduce. These footnotes are possibly the dullest ever written.

The New Yorker has been the premier American literary magazine for most of a century. To be published there is a rite of passage for a young writer, though when the magazine was founded in 1925, after a decade in which Ezra Pound, T. S. Eliot, Robert Frost, Marianne Moore, and Wallace Stevens had revolutionized American poetry, it devoted itself to light verse. Later the magazine was spurned by Robert Lowell, who objected to the triviality of *New Yorker* poems. (Pound in his dotage was published for the first and last time, Moss once told me, because the magazine learned that he needed major dental work).

The New Yorker has suffocated at times beneath a mask of wry gentility. For all its glossy reputation, the magazine still turns up its nose at stories and poems that make too many demands on the reader. It's a middlebrow journal for people who would like to be highbrows—and perhaps for highbrows who love a little slumming. The cartoons, as Biele notes, provide an antiphonal chorus to the reckless consumerism of the ads. Just as the literature is for those who want to think themselves literary, the ads are for those who want to think themselves rich. (If you were old money, you'd already own Tiffany by the trunkload.) Bishop's close association with the magazine, almost all her best poems appearing there after 1945, probably contributed to her struggle to be taken seriously. To be a *New Yorker* poet was sometimes a deal with the devil.

Bishop's father died of Bright's disease when she was an infant. Her mother carted the baby home to Canada and back, hither-thither, becoming so distraught she was finally confined to a mental hospital. A quiet tug of war developed between her mother's doting parents in Nova Scotia and her father's wealthier and more conventional parents in Massachusetts. The latter, mortified to find the child being raised barefoot in a muddy village, dragged her back to the States for a proper education. It was a shock at first—Bishop didn't care to be an American and loathed saluting the flag. The girl never saw her mother again.

Bishop suffered from a streak of perfectionism in a personality pricked with self-doubt and almost paralyzed by shyness—for all her mixed feelings about Emily Dickinson, whose letters Bishop found embarrassing, there was more than a little of the Amherst poet in her character. Bishop finished her poems slowly, when she finished them at all (though one of her best, "Visits to St. Elizabeths," was written in twenty-four hours). Among the minor comedies of these letters is Howard Moss pleading, year after year, for a poem he had once caught a glimpse of. Yet the perfectionism oddly made her work spring forth freshly, when it sprang. The melancholy beneath the joy of seeing darkened a style of startling and even uncomfortable vivacity.

These letters offer a rare view into *The New Yorker*'s inner chambers, as well as a workshop in editing, an editor's chief requirement being a talent for diplomacy. At times the politeness of poet and magazine seems that of two countries about to go to war—tactful enough with her editors (though she felt that reading the magazine was like "eating a quilt"), in letters to friends Bishop groused about the revisions proposed. ("They once put 23 commas in a long poem of mine," she groaned.) Every poem was read multiple times by multiple people. The legal department was consulted lest a law be broken, the fact department checked lest a fact go astray; the editors were allowed their way with the poem, and the Proof Room and makeup department their way; and finally the poor poet, at the bottom of this heap of helpfulness, was allowed to protest about commas merrily broadcast or facts too soon made glad. The reader begins to suspect that a dozen other departments, some with no name at all, were lodged in the obscure warrens of that Kafkaesque organization.

Early in the sixties, Bishop gave up her first-reading contract with the magazine, saying that she wanted to write more "experimental" poems; but she submitted her best work anyway and came meekly back to the fold not many years later. She discovered that because of her years away she was ineligible for a *New Yorker* pension, which was apparently almost impossible to understand or calculate. No one could explain any better the cost-of-living-adjustment checks she received, sometimes followed by further checks to adjust the adjustments. There has not been an accounting scheme so Byzantine since Byzantium.

Bishop was fortunate in her editors, who were half in love with her—and what fine and close readers they usually were, niggling but caring. Still, the magazine could go too far. When Bishop referred to a "large aquatic animal," the editor in chief, Harold Ross, who insisted on understanding every poem his magazine published, wanted to know which animal. Bishop eventually grew impatient with the long delays before publication, some poems lingering a year or more in the "bank"—this mysterious repository proved to be merely an office wall with a note card for each unpublished piece, pinned like a dead butterfly. Once she threw a fit when a poem was printed in the back pages. Ruffled feathers were soon smoothed, and things went on as before. And a few times a year, one by one, in came the poems we now know so well; and they were snapped up, one by one.

The book does a serious injustice to Howard Moss, that most conscientious and fastidious of editors. What had been "a creature divided" in the draft of a Bishop poem published weeks after she died was printed as the clunky "contrarily guided." Moss has been blamed, her proof copy having disappeared; but there's no evidence elsewhere in these letters of an editorial change so radical or highhanded. Bishop, on the other hand, once altered "Pajama'd aunts" to "Anandrous aunts" and "dancing eyes" to "avernal eyes." The peculiar revision is more likely hers.

Editions of Bishop's work have proliferated over the decades. *The Complete Poems, 1927–1979* and *The Collected Prose*, both published in the years just after her death, were followed by two volumes of letters and Alice Quinn's captivating edition of the unfinished poems (which introduced readers to the hopeless disorder of Bishop's desk), not to mention a compendious Library of America volume (including yet more letters), and even a book of the poet's crude watercolors. Now come newly edited and much fattened collections called simply *Prose* and *Poems*.

Bishop was first and last a poet, but she was keenly aware that for poets the wages of sin are poverty ("I'm desperate for CASH!" she wrote a friend). The old *Collected Prose*, put together by her publisher Robert Giroux, has more than doubled in size, stories and memoirs and essays now crowded into a miserly format with narrow margins and unpleasantly cheap paper. Edited by Bishop's friend Lloyd Schwartz, who has vacuumed out the archives, *Prose* is a seedy warehouse of goods mostly unwanted and unloved. Bishop's short stories were derivative fantasies out of Kafka and Hawthorne, when not painfully static versions of her unhappy childhood. She had, however, a natural gift for memoir—her moving recollections of the Nova Scotia village, the dislocated months in Worcester, and post-college life in New York possess all the rueful charm of her poems.

Prose has been pieced out, alas, with humdrum reviews and critical essays (when pressed, Bishop tended to hurl quotes at the reader), a mostly unnecessary selection of college juvenilia, a few translations, and the original version of her book *Brazil*, commissioned for the *Life* World Library and ever after regretted by Bishop. She accused the editors of massive rewriting, but that isn't quite true. The *Life* editors were gung-ho about economic development (the phrase "ugly price of progress" was dropped), and like provincial boobs they changed Bishop's description of the Iguaçú Falls from "three or four times greater and more magnificent than Niagara" to "almost as spectacular." Even so, most of her prose was left intact, and what was revised was often just tightened or corrected. Yet how laborious, how dull, the Brazil book is, enlivened only by a colorful anecdote or two. (A Brazilian who did nothing after being insulted was asked if he was a man. He replied, "Yes, I'm a man. But not *fanatically*.")

Of far more value are the poet's confiding letters to Anne Stevenson, then writing the first book on Bishop's work. The poet, who didn't usually discuss her life, revealed that she had always wanted to write pop songs, wished she had gone to med school, and liked children, at least until they were three. She recalled a little proudly that Hemingway had said of her poem "The Fish," "I wish I knew as much about it as she does."

The new editor reproduces the memoirs and stories just as they appeared in *The Collected Prose*. Giroux was a fine publisher; but he was a meddling editor of the old school, and his work with manuscripts cannot be taken on trust. This ungainly book is marred by a lack of notes (without explanation, Stevenson is suddenly addressed as Mrs. Elvin); and it's a pity to find in Bishop's favorite piece of prose, a gallery note for the painter Wesley Wehr, the sentence "Some pictures may remind one of agates, the form called '[illegible].'" A glance at the manuscript, held now at Vassar, shows that the missing words were "thunder egg." The editor might have asked a geologist.

Readers will delight in Bishop's letters and wade through her prose, all for the sake of her odd, whimsical, heartbreaking poems, poems like no one else's. She hated being compared to Marianne Moore, whom she met while still at Vassar; but Moore's sidelong eye and attraction to the exotic were an indelible influence. Bishop saw the world with a willed innocence, which was not, not exactly, that of a miserable adult trying to relive childhood. Yet the pathos of such innocence lies in our knowing that it is experience denied.

From a distance, Bishop's poems are all more obviously, and all more unsettlingly, products of a life and a time. "A Miracle for Breakfast" is now plainly a poem of the Depression and "Sestina" that of an orphan in a house of secrets. Her famous descriptions can be rather severe in their dissociation—the world is freshly grasped, but also desperately transformed. A way of seeing was for her a way of knowing— and it was an unusual eye that could have noticed, in "The Bight," harbor water the "color of the gas flame turned as low as possible," and the local pelicans that "crash / into this peculiar gas unnecessarily hard," then "going off with humorous elbowings." *Poems* includes all the published work, with a generous sampling of the unpublished poems. Though *Poems* and *Prose* look like matched volumes (both have been cast into a type size loved only by accountants), the poems enjoy a finer grade of paper. There are, however, too many sections of uncollected this and uncollected that—this was a lost opportunity to find a more rational organization for her work.

Bishop's lightness of bearing cannot disguise a darkness of being. Gaiety barely conceals the resistant sadness—there is a peculiar infantilism in Bishop, and I fear that is what we love. Yet her warmth and reticence divide her from the confessional poets whose blared secrets she so disliked. She was a displaced person, physically and emotionally; her poems reveal that terrible rootlessness, even when rooted in Nova Scotia, or Florida, or Brazil (she joked that she moved "coastwise"). Even her first book was discreetly fashioned like an itinerary, from childhood in Nova Scotia through New York, Paris, and Key West.

Bishop worried that she had "wasted half one's talent through timidity" and feared that her poems were "precious"; yet her luxuriant vision is tempered and restrained by the anxieties beneath. Her weaker poems ramble prosaically, offering only a scatty attention to the world; and perhaps one day readers will find her portraits of Brazilians affectionate but condescending—drawn to the quaint and naive, she was all too privileged an outsider.

This poet of travel and dream, of lost childhood, of angular moral vision (and a gloomy soul) lived in a twentieth century still at times lost in the nineteenth—indeed, the untouched jungle of the Brazilian poems sometimes harks back to the Americas newly discovered. Though American as apple pie, this three-quarters Canadian, sometime Brazilian could easily be considered the national poet of Canada or Brazil. In "The Man-Moth," "A Miracle for Breakfast," "Cirque d'Hiver," "The Bight," "The Armadillo," "The Burglar of Babylon," "Sestina," "Visits to St. Elizabeths," and a dozen others, she invented countries on a map she had drawn herself.

Elizabeth Bishop at Summer Camp

Elizabeth Bishop at Camp Chequesset.
Source: Courtesy the Esther Merrell Stockton Papers in the Archives
and Special Collections Library of Vassar College.

"I have never been homesick but just at present I feel awfly camp-sick," wrote Elizabeth Bishop, the summer she was fourteen. She had just finished a month at the sailing camp on Cape Cod where she spent her teenage summers, a camp where she found respite from the families engaged in a tug-of-war over her upbringing (it would be too much to say her affections), her father's in Worcester, Massachusetts, and her mother's in Revere and farther away in Great Village, Nova Scotia. For much of her childhood, this shy and sickly girl had been carted from one set of relatives to another like a piece of luggage.

Bishop was born in Worcester in 1911. When she was still a baby, her father, William Bishop, died of Bright's disease (the term a century ago for acute or chronic nephritis). After his death, her mother's grief slowly hardened into suicidal despair, and she tried to take her life by leaping from a hospital window. At last, having for five years dressed in mourning clothes, Gertrude Bishop became delusional, afflicted with imagined illnesses, convinced that she was being "watched as a criminal." In 1916, she was permanently confined to a mental hospital. Her doctors must have felt there was no hope of recovery, because her little daughter was "taught to think of her as dead," according to the poet Frank Bidart. Having been dragged about by her nervous and over-wrought mother, now to Boston, now back to Nova Scotia, Elizabeth found a home with her mother's family in Great Village, where she was enrolled in the village primary school. When her father's parents visited a year and a half later, they were shocked to find the barefoot six-year-old racing wild through the village lanes.

Her Bishop grandparents "kidnapped" her—at least it felt that way, she later said—and carried her off by overnight train. Her father's father was a wealthy New England contractor, the founder of J. W. Bishop Company, which built mills, stores, churches, hospitals, gymnasiums at both Brown and Harvard, the Boston Public Library, the Museum of Fine Arts, and numerous mansions for private clients. The firm, which had been in business since the 1870s, was a nineteenth-century example of vertical integration, owning quarries as well as a woodwork and ornamental-iron mill.

The Bishops were already elderly (her grandfather seventy-one, her grandmother sixty-eight) when Elizabeth was spirited away to Worcester. Most of their nine children were already dead. Her grandparents lived outside the city in a dark, spraddling farmhouse behind a white picket fence, one block before the end of the trolley line, though John W. Bishop Sr. was driven to work each morning by a chauffeur. The Bishops never mingled in Worcester society. Though distant, austere presences to this frail young girl, they were apparently kind and thoughtful. Her grandfather, who showed off numerous gold teeth when he laughed, once carted home, all the way from his company's Providence office, three Golden Bantams—pets for his little granddaughter.

Bishop found life in her home country difficult. Separated from her mother's parents, whom she adored, she "didn't want to be an American." (As she told a critic, "I am 3/4ths Canadian, and one 4th New Englander.") According to her memoir "The Country Mouse," saluting the American flag made her feel "like a traitor"—in the Great Village school, she had been taught to sing "God Save the King" and "The Maple Leaf Forever." Her grandmother in Worcester, whose most violent oaths were "Pshaw" and "Drat," tried to make her memorize "The Star-Spangled Banner," every verse.

Often severely ill with bronchitis, asthma, and eczema, Elizabeth spent nine miserable months with the Bishops. After that disastrous winter, she was dispatched, no doubt by chauffeur, to a drab neighborhood in working-class Revere to live with her mother's eldest sister, Maude (always spelled "Maud" by Bishop). The girl spent the rest of her childhood with Maude and her husband in their dingy second-floor apartment, frequently missing school because of her illnesses. She later said that during those years, "I was always a sort of a guest."

Bishop may have felt close to Aunt Maude at first; later, when she was in prep school, she tried to avoid staying in Revere during the holidays. Her favorite aunt, Grace Boomer, another of her mother's sisters, shared the apartment but moved back to Nova Scotia in 1923, when Bishop was twelve. That same fall, her Bishop grandparents died, first her grandmother and then, five days later, her grandfather. Their son Jack, who became head of the family firm, took charge of her schooling. Whatever Uncle Jack's failings as a businessman (under his management, J. W. Bishop Company soon fell on hard times), as her guardian he sought an education for her beyond that available in public schools—or perhaps he was just shooing her out of the way. Though Bishop felt no fondness for him, he seems to have responded to his young ward. He knew that in Revere she had few friends.

Her cousin Kay claimed that the move to Revere was suggested by Bishop's doctors, who thought her asthma would improve if she lived by the sea, a common prescription of the day. Perhaps the "saltwater camp" on Cape Cod was chosen to get her to the shore, the fees no doubt paid by her guardian—they would have been beyond the means of Maude and her husband. The July after her grandparents died, Bishop was packed off to summer camp for the first time. She returned every summer for the next five years.

Camp Chequesset overlooked the shellfishing fleet in Wellfleet Harbor, in the 1920s still the main source of the town's economy. Across the bay from the town pier, the camp stood on some forty acres of ground once inhabited by Chequesset Indians, whose shell heaps could still be found along the beach. There were two main camp-buildings. Big Chief Hall contained the dining hall, a ward room, and craft shops. On the mantel above its massive open fireplace stood a ship's clock and a pilot wheel, the symbol of the camp. There were more craft shops in the Bungalow, which also had a library of some five hundred books and rooms for visiting former campers—"Old Chequesset girls," as they were called. Though a fair amount of swimming and sailing was required, the camp offered archery, tennis, baseball, dramatics, and dancing, interrupted by walks to the Cape's back shore or a clambake on Jeremy Point. The camp navy consisted of a clutch of sailboats and canoes, a few rowboats and dories, and a forty-foot sedan-cabin cruiser, the *Mouette*, with her famously unreliable engine. The name was French for "seagull."

The campers' "lodges" were scattered in the pines, each with room for three or four girls and a counselor (a "skipper," in the camp's nautical slang). These cabins, screened on all sides, with shutters for bad weather, had been given whimsical names like the Look-Out, the Hopp-Inn, the Kennel, and the Nursery. An early photograph in *Cape Cod Magazine* shows a "cosy dormitory corner" with simple cots covered in what even in black and white look like colorful blankets. The *Mary Louise*, the cabin where Bishop berthed for the summer of 1926, was a forty-seven-foot sloop marooned in a cradle nearby. Forty girls, the youngest twelve years old, spent July and August at this "Nautical Camp for Girls."

Summer camps were once common in the Northeast, many christened with Indian place names or the names of tribes long vanished (among Chequesset's rivals were Cowasset, Wahtonah, Nobcusset, and Winnecowaissa). Such camps have long been in decline, victims of rising staff-salaries, helicopter parents, and, especially on the Cape, the value of the land. Parents now too nervous to let their children walk alone to school would bewilder their grandparents and great-grandparents, who happily shipped off their youngsters for a summer among strangers, with scarcely more than a trunk of clothing and no more proof of life during those months than the occasional scrawled letter.

Bishop must have found it a relief to be out of the stifling summers in Revere and away from her relatives (and the place itself—she once wrote, "Where I live is *so* ugly"). Sometimes she visited her beloved Boomer grandparents in Nova Scotia before school started in September. At fifteen, she wrote a fellow camper from Great Village (the occasional misspellings here and elsewhere in the letters are Bishop's),

> *I haven't any family whatever—excepting a few aunts and uncles who are all trying to bring me up a different way and its glorious not to feel you'll have to turn out well or you'll break someones' heart. One set of uncles and aunts would merely remark, "Her mother's coming out in her," the other "I always knew she'd turn out poorly—look at her father," and they'd peacfully let me slide to my doom!*
>
> *So as soon as I get enough knowledge crammed into me I'm off—to India and Ireland—and oh! wherever its strange and there's a little romance left.*

Camp Chequesset had been founded in 1914, more or less by accident, by William Gould Vinal, a teacher of nature lore at Rhode Island Normal School (now Rhode Island College). Vinal was thirty-two when he came to summer at Wellfleet. The article in *Cape Cod Magazine* two years later reported that "he had no idea of starting a girls' camp. During the season three or four girls were invited to the camp for a few days, and they liked the location so well that they wanted to come again the next year."

Perhaps Vinal started the camp as a teaching laboratory (he also founded a nautical camp for boys down the cape at South Dennis). The college professor who liked to be called Cap'n Bill became one

of the great promoters of teaching children "nature lore," the term
he preferred to the more academic "nature study." (Nature study was
a subject to which much thinking was devoted—a journal by that
name was first issued in 1900, succeeded by the *Nature-Study Review*
in 1905.) Vinal wanted to drag children out of the cities and back into
the woods or onto the beaches. As he put it in the preface to his most
influential work, *Nature Recreation*,

> *The study of nature has been constant, but the objectives of nature*
> *study have been continuously growing and changing. Nature lore*
> *originated with the pioneer who loved his woodsy home. . . . From*
> *rail splitter to horse trader, nature practice met and solved social*
> *needs. It was the way of Thoreau and the training school for Lin-*
> *coln. . . . With the development of industrialism and the concentra-*
> *tion of population in cities, there disappeared both the need and*
> *the place for daily intimacy with the out-of-doors.*

Published in 1940, the book remained in print for decades—he
signed it William "Cap'n Bill" Gould Vinal and came to be known as
the Father of Nature Recreation. To restore that lost love for the minutiae of nature, the curriculum of Camp Chequesset offered the campers "lore" that had not "degenerated into an ambitious accumulation
of facts chained to the pickled and desiccated biology of the past"—
they learned not dry facts but directed observation, or the art of spying
alfresco. Like the Boy Scouts and the Woodcraft Indians, Chequesset
and similar camps otherwise touted the healthy vanities of outdoor life,
providing a sort of *mens sana in corpore sano* for the middle classes.

If Thoreau might be called the philosopher of nature lore, of the
gains in spirit found in contemplation of weeds and warblers (perhaps
the American version of the sublime), then Teddy Roosevelt was the
practical sage of robust outdoor living, convinced he had cured his
asthma by a regimen of vigorous exercise. Thoreau and Roosevelt were
the tutelary figures of the camp movement. Even in the 1920s, summer
camps like Chequesset took advantage of America's lingering suspicion, not just of city ways, but of cities far more diseased and polluted
than now.

What could a new camper at Chequesset expect? According to
the *Camp Chequesset Log*, the small stapled newsletter (and fairly

transparent sales organ) issued quarterly through the winter months, the new girls, after a bath, were sent in search of the "Tree of Life"— probably an improving moral illustration of the sort once found in religious texts. This chart or scroll was found lying atop one of the Chequesset shell heaps, where the girls ate a box supper. Afterward they were led to the outdoor theater for a solemn ceremony of welcome. While some of the seasoned campers held pine branches, others played the forest spirits representing the camp virtues: Health, Happiness, Comradeship, Honor, Loyalty, Service, Consideration.

It was without irony that these virtues were often pursued through competition. The girls were divided into four crews: the White Caps, the Pirates, the Sea Gulls, and the Yohos, Bishop's crew, of which she eventually rose to be cox'n. Each summer the best crew was awarded a model ship, which joined the flotilla of such models in drydock in the dining hall. The Yohos were the top crew in 1924, Bishop's first summer at camp, and 1929, her last. A camp photograph shows the ten Yohos of 1925, each dressed in white middy and dark bloomers (probably forest green, the camp color), gathered around a shadow box holding the model of the Mayflower won by the previous year's crew.

Girls at this saltwater camp were expected to excel in swimming and sailing—the counselors kept detailed records of their progress. One of the swimming charts is preserved at the Wellfleet Historical Society. Probably from the summer of 1929, it lists fifty-eight requirements, from Breathing to 440 Yd. Swim. Bishop (her name misspelled "Biship") had fulfilled all but five, including the essay and that quarter-mile swim. Completing the full roster was considered a formidable accomplishment. A camp log of 1925 congratulated three girls on this feat, which in the history of Camp Chequesset had been achieved by only one girl before.

The *Chequesset Log* did what it could to make mastery of such subjects enticing: "Perhaps, if you were only a Snail this year, you will be a Sea-Arrow next, or perhaps you will change your rank from Landlubber to Captain; and if you can be a Crawler what satisfaction will be yours." The tone of the log, like that perhaps of the staff, was fatiguingly hearty, a mixture of high-mindedness and juvenile humor, with a sales pitch on almost every page, including pleas for the names of potential campers—it once offered a template letter, addressed from Ann Ole Veteran to Willa Tarbe (Will a Tar Be), for girls who wanted to invite

Bishop and the Yoho Crew of 1925 [above, kneeling at
bottom left; below, back row, second from right].
Source: Collection of the author.

their friends aboard. When camp was over, each girl and her parents were sent a copy of her swimming and boating charts. No doubt the hearts of some girls sank at thought of a summer report-card; but the camp log, in its wholesome way, justified this by invoking Melville: "Your daughter's summer at camp is not complete unless you take account of stock," it thundered, with no more than half the righteousness of Ahab. "Moby Dick calls it stowing down and clearing up."

Campers would not have returned summer after summer just for the report cards. Vinal explained some of his didactic method in a 1921 article in the *Nature-Study Review*. The previous summer, before the girls arrived, he had held the first Nature-Lore School for Camp Councilors. This article and a companion piece, "Counsel for Councillors," were illustrated by snapshots of Camp Chequesset girls sketching a sea cliff and studying an ancient tree-trunk uncovered at low tide. Apart from pages of practical information about where to obtain topographic maps, cloud charts, or stereopticon lanterns, Vinal gave homely advice about turning fruit jars into aquaria, framing a piece of linoleum to make a blackboard, and tacking mosquito netting over bird cages to make insect breeding-cages.

Vinal also recommended that campers buy a small loose-leaf "camp notebook" for their field notes, "to be carried in a pocket or attached to a belt." He put some thought into this notebook, which needed to have pages for "accounts, music, and photos," as well as "firm, smooth covers," printed with the camp name, useful as writing desk or drawing board.

Bishop possessed just such a loose-leaf notebook, its lined pages 3 1/2" x 6". She wrote a letter to a camp friend on a pair of torn-out pages, using others to draft some of her earliest poems. (The book itself, which probably met Vinal's other requirements, has disappeared.) Bishop kept it handy even when she wasn't at Wellfleet. "Auntie found my little black notebook hidden under a chair seat," she wrote her friend. "I think she wanted me to show it to her but I wouldn't. . . . It lies hidden behind the fairy tales in the bookcase now."

Vinal's campers were set various tasks: to scout trees by checking a page of tree leaves, or to follow the overgrown King's Highway, using map and compass, wagon ruts, and "hub bruises or blazes on tree trunks." These exercises were often cast as games ("tree cribbage" was one), with prizes for the winning team—old coins discovered on nearby Billingsgate Island, for instance. Vinal emphasized that each girl would respond differently to what she saw and that the campers' notes and essays—after a social call on the town hermit, say—were not to be treated as school lessons. "Let it be emphasized," he wrote, "that nature councilors are not to trespass on this private property with a red eye or a red pencil for spelling, split infinitives, or vertical twists to the penmanship. The number of poets and writers killed off by this method will never be revealed but let us not kill the spirit in camps." The best of the girls' sketches, poems, and stories were tacked to the camp bulletin-board.

William Vinal's notions of nature lore were highly local. Like Thoreau, he believed in studying whatever the nearby fields and beaches had to offer. (The year after Bishop left camp, the girls were taken to visit Thoreau's Cape house, which still stands by Williams Pond between Wellfleet and Truro.) This ethos was quite different from that of the Boy Scouts, which tried to instill a practical body of knowledge about camping that could be used anywhere (thereby perhaps betraying its military origins). The upper Cape offered mute examples of ecological change, so campers could be trained to see that a dark line crossing a sea cliff revealed the shape of the original hill. Glacial deposits, retreating dunes, the shift of a long pond to a round one—all could be read by the practiced eye.

Camp Chequesset was less a camp founded on a grand design than a somewhat makeshift and jury-rigged enterprise using whatever came to hand. The daily plan was a slave to serendipity ("It was very informal," recalled a camper from the 1930s). The girls might sail to Billingsgate Island to dig clams, or take a day trip on the *Mouette* to Plymouth or Provincetown (where at fourteen Bishop discovered a book of George Herbert's poems), or a three-day cruise through the Cape Cod Canal to Buzzards' Bay and Nantucket. On the way, the girls might visit the *Charles W. Morgan*, the old whaleship retired to a cofferdam on the South Dartmouth estate of Colonel Edward R. H. Green—now at Mystic Seaport, she was the last remaining American whaler. The colonel not only renovated her but moved to his grounds an entire shipsmith's shop from New Bedford and built life-sized models of a try-works, a cooperage, and a counting house. Chequesset possessed a certain charming haplessness—if the captain and his crew sailed off to a camp meet with neighboring camps, they might spend a long morning looking for the right cove.

Visits from old salts formed part of the Chequesset curriculum: a Captain Small entertained the girls with yarns of wrecks along the Atlantic shore; and one Captain Kelley, who built the model awarded each year to the best crew, revealed the secrets of his finicky craft. One day the latter brought his friend Captain Sears, who seems to have been admirably taciturn. "We tried to get him to tell of his experiences at sea," reported the camp log, "but he said that Cap'n Kelley was the speechmaker, and he couldn't say anything. One unsuspecting conversationalist asked him how many ships he had sailed on, but was corrected, to her chagrin, when he answered that he didn't go on ships much,—he had usually sailed on schooners and brigs." It is per-

Bishop on the porch of the Bungalow with a fellow camper and an
old sailor, probably Captain Kelley.
Source: Courtesy the Wellfleet Historical Society.

Bishop and the Chantey Team of 1927 (Bishop is second from right)].
Source: Courtesy the Esther Merrell Stockton Papers in the Archives and Special
Collections Library of Vassar College.

haps Captain Kelley in one camp photograph, sitting in a rocker on
the porch of the Bungalow, a model ship in his hands and Elizabeth
Bishop at his feet.

The girls suffered the common camp tithe of physical exercise.
They made the usual moccasins and leather purses and turned the
usual copper sheets into the usual paper knives and bookmarks. They
wove rugs and scarves probably no one wanted or needed. The evenings included sing-a-longs, the songbook heavy on peppy camp-tunes
and old standards clumsily rewritten for Chequesset. More diverting,
perhaps, were the rousing sailor songs and sea chanteys ("Haul the
Bowline," "Paddy Doyle," "Blow the Man Down"), their lyrics enough
to make a temperance meeting blanch. Bishop was good enough to
make the Chantey Team in 1927.

Cap'n Bill and his successors kept the girls occupied with a bois-
terous and extravagant inventiveness. A camp play in 1927 was introduced by "singing, a balloon dance, a fencing exhibition, a poem, and
chanteys sung by the camp." Two summers later, the Kitchen Kabinet

Orchestra played a symphony: "Frying pans, clothes baskets, and stove pipes were turned into violins, cellos and French horns. . . . The touching story of Robin Adair and his Sweet Adeline was told in music. Oh sweet kazoos!" The summer after Bishop left, camp events included the family reunion of "Mr. Chequessetti" (requiring an Italian dinner), a Topsy-Turvy day (with reveille at midnight), and the Rum Runners Rendezvous: "The dining-hall was transformed into a wharf den with a few lanterns, many cork floats, and a net or two. . . . The Cookies [cooks] as the toughest of 'longshoremen' threw slum gully on to our plates or slammed down a bottle by our elbow with as much savoir faire as if it were their life occupation." Out in nature, too, Vinal delighted in keeping the girls off balance: "What one should do on a particular occasion cannot be forecast. It is not preparing prescriptions nor is it dealing out patent medicines. It is furnishing opportunities for the love of the beautiful and timely suggestions for companionship with out door life."

Vinal's writing on nature lore can perhaps be forgiven its whiff of evangelical brimstone. He wanted to show the natural world as a living thing, not something to be dissected in a laboratory. "A resolution was made at Chequesset," he remarked in the *Nature-Study* article, "that no study of plant or animal life should be made except it be alive and in its native haunt."

> *Last June we knew that the barn swallow was feeding her young on the bungalow porch; that the chickaree had rented the mailbox in the pines; that a chippy, a robin, and a pine warbler were within 30 feet of the dining room door; that Bufo the toad was beneath the steps; that the blue-birds were rearing their second families in the boxes; that red perch would be caught at Gull Pond; that the squid, and the skate, and the hermit crab would be seen on the shore; that the swamp azalea would scent the ponds and arethusa dot the meadows.*

Such a philosophy, if that is what it amounted to, explains the extraordinary emphasis at Chequesset, not just on conventional crafts and homemaking arts ("the directors realize that perhaps some day the girls will be married," wrote the reporter for the *Cape Cod Magazine*), but on vivid writing and unruly imagination—and especially on teaching the campers to observe the nature surrounding them.

In that letter from Nova Scotia late in the summer of 1925, there is perhaps a hint that Bishop had already begun to school her eye.

> *I have been swimming several times in the lovely red sandstone rockhole. It is so pretty for little yellow leaves float all over the top and make little brown and gold shadows on the bottom.*

Even when her poems were still mired in a twenties version of the poetic, her literary intelligence had begun to emerge in letters. Bishop's letters at fourteen and fifteen don't linger over description but occasionally create a scene or an atmosphere that rises, often too "poetically," above the details: "The bay turns to moon-silver and across it the lights of Nahant glimmer like a bracelet of worn old jewels," "Its raining now—all dingy colored rain—and the leaves are falling like bits of sodden gilt," "Asthma gives me an unpleasantly *whalish* feeling. I wallow in pillows and puff like an old grampus." It would be tempting to say this is the close *invention* of details, since similes and metaphors are made, not born. The best natural description consists of the particular transformed—the poet's eye is metaphorical, not scientific.

Chequesset girls were, of course, not supposed to memorize the dry terms of biology and anatomy—Vinal wanted the campers to write down only what they saw. Bishop's teenage descriptions are not distant in kind, only in sophistication, from the lines she later wrote in "The End of March" ("The sky was darker than the water / —*it* was the color of mutton-fat jade) or "Love Lies Sleeping" ("Along the street below / the water-wagon comes // throwing its hissing, snowy fan across / peelings and newspapers). When Bishop learned to master her eye, the invention became description.

Through this intense study of the nature at one's feet, Vinal hoped to develop in the girls what he called a "broader intelligence." He seems enlightened in refusing to direct their attention too rigidly, like some martinet of the marsh—if this girl was fascinated by the pine warbler, that one might prefer the barn swallow. In the preface to *Nature Recreation*, he invoked the ghost of Louis Agassiz, who "aroused a new enthusiasm for living material and strove to emphasize the importance of firsthand contact with nature." This was the Agassiz who built a house on a glacier to learn about glaciers, the Agassiz who forced his anatomy students to study a dead fish over and over, without microscope or scalpel, until they learned something about it. Though Vinal sold the camp in 1925 to a former camper and counselor, it's clear from his continued visits and the evidence of the camp logs that the culture of Chequesset endured.

Chequesset also fostered another kind of companionship. "In so small a camp," as the camp handbook put it in 1930, "it is essential that each girl be one whom both campers and parents will welcome as a delightful comrade. Chequesset reserves the right to dismiss any girl who does not fit into the group." Little was known about Bishop's private life during those camp years until a cache of letters to a fellow camper, including the letters already quoted here, was bequeathed in 2004 to Indiana University.

Elizabeth Bishop met Louise Bradley in 1924 at South Station in Boston, where they were waiting for the train to Chequesset. Bishop recalled the moment a couple of years later:

> *Louise, Louise, you're just the same aren't you? You haven't grown up—and left me behind? I remember the first time I saw you—In the dirty station. You were very excited over seeing all the campers again—and when you came to me you said "I don't know you but I'll kiss you, too."*

Though Bradley was three years older, from the beginning their friendship seems to have been one of equals. Bishop at last found in her a confidante and kindred spirit. Louise Bradley has been a missing person in Bishop's life. She appears neither in Brett C. Millier's biography, *Elizabeth Bishop: Life and the Memory of It* (1993), nor in the memories collected from the poet's friends and family by Gary Fountain and Peter Brazeau in *Elizabeth Bishop: An Oral Biography* (1994). Though twice mentioned in the volume of Bishop's selected letters, *One Art* (1994), she's confused with a different Louise.

The earliest letter in *One Art* dates from New Year's Eve 1928, written to Bishop's friend Frani Blough. There are only three letters from the years before the poet entered Vassar, and fewer than a dozen before

Louise Bradley on the beach at Wellfleet and as a college student.
Source: Courtesy Wylie House Museum, a department of the Indiana University
Libraries, Bloomington, Ind.

she graduated from college in 1934, almost all addressed to Frani. The
addition of some sixty early letters, dating back to 1925, gives an intimate view of the teenage Bishop's emotional and imaginative life.

The normal camp term was July and August, but Bishop spent only
a month at Chequesset in 1925, because on August 5 she wrote the letter to Louise from Nova Scotia.

*I am at my grandmothers, having arrived safely after many mis-
haps. . . . A man, passing in the street threw something at our taxi
driver. We immediately stopped dead in the middle of Bostons traf-
fic jam, the driver went tearing down the street after the man, and*

trucks on each side shouted at us to "Move on!" Finaly a police-
man arrived on the scene and peace and order were restored. . . . I
feel imnensly better already for writing does make one feel better,
and I do hope you aren't feeling bored.

The Bishop who emerges from these letters is often bored, unhappy, frustrated with family, with school, with her life. She was a mediocre student who didn't see the point of education, though she could be furiously funny about it. That fall, she attended Saugus High School for ninth grade.

School has commenced and is just terrible! I do hate it so. The
teacher raves at me and says I don't pay attention. . . . I am fairly
well acquainted with several of the girls in school now. They are
awful as far as I know for they argue. I can stand a lot but argueing
never.

With an admirable disdain for school rules, Bishop was already in trouble her first semester:

The Latin teacher sees me through and through, I fear. She sent me
to the office but I lied so convincingly to the principal . . . that I'm
not expelled—for a while anyway. I have a good mind but I will
not use it—I am lazy and indifferent—I look out the window and
dream—etc.

Despite her remark about possessing a good mind, Bishop usually had a low opinion of her intelligence ("I may be very sweet but I certainly am not very brainy"), no doubt made worse because at Saugus she faced, not for the last time, her nemesis, algebra: "Here I am, just a poor freshman and famous for nothing but a terrible dumbness in Algebra. Louise, I got C in deportment, for 'inattention'!" At fourteen, she wrote plaintively, and a touch poetically, "This is a lovely, beautiful world in spite of school and algebra." She even composed a poem titled "To Algebra," on a page ripped from her camp notebook ("And still sometimes I think I see above the board / Where your names are placed in chalky, disordered rows, / The face of all order and all law").

She noted, "This was written when I received the remarkable mark of 37 in an algebra test!"

Things were little better when she transferred the next fall to North Shore Country Day School in Swampscott, about half a dozen miles from her home in Revere. Uncle Jack had attempted to enroll her at Walnut Hill, a boarding school in Natick, midway between Revere and Worcester; but her doctor refused to give her the necessary vaccination until she was in better health. She was forced to repeat the ninth grade.

> You *realize what a weak little thing I am! I'm now going to a private school down on the North Shore. It is a perfect Hades with modern improvements. However, I guess I can struggle along until camp time next year—its my one refuge and even its not so wonderful minus you.*

Bishop might have been held back because of her grades; but some private schools, feeling that public school did not adequately prepare students for a more advanced curriculum, asked new students to repeat a grade. Algebra was again her enemy—and not just algebra: "Today I even forgot how to multiply and my mind hurts—really—when I try to figure it all out." The next day, she wrote again: "So far my marks are—Latin 40—Algebra 20—French 75—English grammar 60—!!! However I head the class in English comp."

If algebra was a horror, there was something perhaps even worse.

> *Have you ever had* logarithms? *And aren't they* terrible! *I have a beautiful, slim brown book and on the inside [of] it are just rows and rows and rows of numbers! I could weep—it looks almost like poetry from the outside.*

Years later, in her poem "Manuelzinho," Bishop wrote of a poor farmer who kept accounts in "old copybooks":

> *Immediate confusion.*
> *You've left out the decimal points.*
> *Your columns stagger,*
> *honeycombed with zeros.*

You whisper conspiratorially;
the numbers mount to millions.
Account books? They are Dream Books.

Bishop couldn't decide whether to buckle down and be miserable or enjoy herself while failing (but writing poetry, she said). "Every bit of my knowledge that makes me interesting or valuable," she exclaimed in despair, "was learned out-side school." As so often later, she was able to turn the most trivial disaster into screwball comedy:

Horrors!! I have just discovered six blots on the wall behind me—
the largest almost an inch across! Pray for me! Auntie just talked to
me yesterday because I got ink on my hair, blouse, rug, furniture—
now the wall!! I shudder.

Bishop made things worse the following fall—and therefore perhaps more bearable—by being cheerfully delinquent when she was at last enrolled at Walnut Hill, where she faced algebra for the third time. She called herself a "dreamer and a useless rebel," considered at school a "sort of intellectual monstrosity." One semester her junior year, she was restricted to the grounds for all but a single weekend because of her behavior. Though she had almost been expelled, as she confided in Louise, most of her shenanigans showed little more than high spirits. Probably in her junior or senior year, she wrote,

I do such crazy things. I dressed up in an awful costume for fire-
drill the other night, and I'm fire assistant, too, so you can imagine
how it upset the drill. And I threw a snow-ball at a girl in study hall
and I swore at another one in class, and oh I was in a disgusting
affair last week. It was so funny—two teachers cried over me!

After a similar escapade Bishop's junior year, the principal of Walnut Hill consulted a psychotherapist, fearing that this intellectual monstrosity might be displaying signs of her mother's insanity. The doctor's opinion was reported to Bishop's uncle: "Elizabeth shows many evidences of the fact that she thinks, for some reason or other, she is different." The therapist believed that the cure would be to make this most unlikely student "feel that she is like other girls."

The Bishops, no doubt with good intentions, had hushed up the scandal of their troubled daughter-in-law, Bishop's mother, unsurprisingly at a time when even doctors believed madness could be inherited. Bishop was aware that some people knew her history, but many must have assumed she was an orphan. In "The Country Mouse," she recalls telling a childhood friend that her mother abandoned her and then died, and at Vassar she noted on her student information card that both her parents were dead. Though she was more forthcoming to close friends, the lie would save many humiliating questions but not avoid the reaction she so resented. As she wrote Louise in 1926,

> I have given up caring what people think about me—at home anyway. That's what I like about camp. They rather expect me to do queer things and everyone is so nice to me—too nice sometimes—I feel as if they were pitying me.

Bishop was an only child, which must also have made her unusual; and she may have been embarrassed that, despite her wealthy relatives, despite summer camp and private school among privileged girls, she lived in a dreary town with her working-class aunt and uncle. Her tendency to rebel might have been in response to the pity (a child who feels different sometimes wants to make that difference felt). Bishop often used the word "crazy" of herself, perhaps with a small twitch of irony—by 1927, it was also slang for "exciting."

Bishop's hijinks were no doubt high crimes at boarding school; but they reveal a girl desperate to relieve her frustrations—and probably anxious to deflect the wrong kind of attention. This girl who was almost always miserable could apparently pour out her unhappiness only to Louise. However low her spirits, her moments of wildness might have been a declaration of self. "I enjoy being *me* so much," she wrote the spring of her junior year.

Bishop had devoted teachers at Walnut Hill, though they may have held her back as much as they pushed her forward. Eleanor Prentiss, her English teacher that junior year, taught writing passionately but apparently developed crushes on her students. ("She would sigh over things, write sentimental notes, that kind of thing," recalled Frani Blough. Prentiss also wore false teeth, which made her a figure of comedy to the girls.) She wrote Bishop a maudlin letter that Christmas:

There are fairy colors in the driftwood blaze in my fire. I picked up the stick down in the rock cave at low tide; and now it is dry it flames a tale in emerald and turquoise and copper-red. I think you would understand it. . . . *Shall I tell you things that can only be told here—ah well, someday when you come!*

Bishop passed the note to Frani with a scribble that called it "too sweet for words." The poet could not have learned much about style, beyond the perfumy sort, from Miss Prentiss. Still, years later, prompted by Frani, Bishop "would groan and say, 'Oh, well, that's right. I guess I do owe her something.'"

Bishop contributed to the literary magazines at her private schools, the *Owl* at North Shore and the *Blue Pencil* at Walnut Hill (where she became editor in chief, preceded by Frani). Later, in college, she appeared in the *Vassar Review*; but, fed up with the conservative editors, she and two friends founded their own avant-garde magazine, *Con Spirito*.

Bishop's prep-school career ended in an inspired denunciation of her final exams.

I am so damned sick of chemical equations and diminished seventh chords—this expresses it somewhat. [An arrow leads toward a staff with three notes and a rest.] Now please harmonize for a string quintet, supplying a melodious tenor with embellishments and enough oxygen at 62°C and 790mm and a second periphrastic. Multiply by 22.4 modulate up a minor third and—the result will be your own age.

Having repeated a grade, Bishop was old for a high-school senior—she turned nineteen the semester she graduated. She was apparently uncertain whether she should even go to college. In an undated letter, probably written just weeks before the start of the Vassar term, she asked Louise, "Am I a social outcast or a Vassar girl? It must be decided. . . . I have to flip a penny about college pretty soon, I suppose."

Among the mysteries the Bradley correspondence solves is what Bishop was doing that summer before Vassar. She wrote Louise from Walnut Hill, probably in February 1930,

I'm going to sell books all summer in a bookstore in Hyannis. Half of its' a toy store but I'm not in that half—I'd much rather be. They sell awfully nice things for dolls' houses—tiny electric toasters and even hair-dryers and vacuum cleaners.

The *Chequesset Log* for that spring mentions that Bishop "is all signed on for whatever is going to happen the week after camp, although she does not know what it is." This was apparently a weeklong cruise along the coast on the *Mouette*; but Bishop's long camp summers were over. Writing Louise from Hyannis that July, though the job goes unmentioned, she noted proudly that she was reading three books a day: "think of most of James Joyce, *Anna Karenina*, the Bible, Norman Douglas,—and so on." She ended, in her usual fashion, "*Please* won't you write to me some more. I am extremely miserable and absolutely alone. I want to have you tell me that you have confidence in me, or something flattering like that."

Vassar proved a terrible disappointment.

College has betrayed me hopelessly and finally. It is a big fraud and I want to get out of it as quickly as I can. I suppose that won't be until my twenty-first birthday next year, though. The work is worthless and I don't think I want to be a student, anyway. . . . I always am a detestable flop at things like this.

The next summer she only reluctantly decided to return.

Whatever the shortcomings of Bishop's many schools, to find a kindred spirit at fourteen—a girl almost in college, a girl who also wanted to be a writer—must have seemed impossibly lucky to that shy ninth grader, living with her somewhat put-upon aunt and uncle. "Auntie just gave me a little 'talk,'" Bishop reported to Louise in 1926. "I am very stuck on myself apparantly. And I have a vastly 'superior' look." Aunt Maude apparently delighted in these lectures (a few months later, Bishop wrote, "Auntie 'talked' to me and said I was becoming as 'cold as a fish'"). The earliest letters to her new friend had begun "Dear Louise," then "Dearest Louise," but within months this became "Dearest of all dear Kindred Spirits," "Louise—*dearest*," and "Dearest, dearest." Later letters were slightly less effusive in address, but not in feeling.

Bishop's Uncle Jack was a shrewder uncle than he was a business-man. When he tried to register Elizabeth at Walnut Hill in 1926, he had written on the application that she was a "lonely little girl." That loneliness drove Bishop to pathetic—or merely droll—fantasies; and in Louise she finally had someone to entertain. In Nova Scotia again for the Christmas holidays of 1925, she invented an imaginary family for herself:

I have made some lovely friends in my new home, a little mussy old library, a dear little brook almost beside my house, a delightful family of eight pine trees and best of all, the cliff. The Cliff is a real one, very high, and just a little beyond the brook. It gives one an awfully farseeing feeling to stand there and look way off at the islands and lighthouses and little ships.

The heartbreaking scene in "Sestina," first published in *The New Yorker* three decades later, seems an echo of that forlorn Nova Scotia holiday:

> *With crayons the child draws a rigid house*
> *and a winding pathway. Then the child*
> *puts in a man with buttons like tears*
> *and shows it proudly to the grandmother.*

The child who felt she was a guest everywhere had to draw her own houses, or make them up. (The poem ends, "The child draws another inscrutable house.") Bishop closed the letter, "Please write to me though as I am so awfully lonely."

Apart from camp, Nova Scotia remained Bishop's only retreat, and even that was not always welcoming. (It's a sign of her alienation from her Massachusetts relatives that in the Vassar yearbook of 1934—of which Bishop was the editor—she listed her home as Great Village, Nova Scotia.) In an undated letter, probably written about 1927, she wrote in her characteristic tone of burlesque misery:

I have been absolutely alone and I have read and walked and played the piano and shaved my grandfather, who is blind, and fixed his rum and hot water, and shivered all night for fear of the ghosts. I feel like a compound of Thomas Hardy, Charlotte Brontë, and the hysterical end of a Russian novel. I'm writing this by the light of an oil lamp in a big cold bedroom with sloping walls. Everyone else has gone to bed, — my grandmother sighs, the puppy whom the housekeeper takes to bed with her, I verily believe, squeals; and I chew spruce gum.

Almost from the start of these letters, however, Bishop had a plan:

Louise — is it right for a young woman to trail off to the ends of the earth — Norway — India — alone? and live in strange places and do strange things — or two young women [—] you come with me. . . . Lets, and then retire to Irland and raise bees — and live by the ocean in a stone cottage — and write poetry for a living. Oh!! will you!

This fantasy of a life together, a life anywhere that was elsewhere (preferably a Romantic elsewhere), became a constant: *"Oh Louise come with me!* And then we'll have the white cottage — don't you think Ireland's a nice place? — *and* — a sailboat and we'll do all sorts of crazy — delightful — things — We live but once *And I'm going* to *live!"*

For years Ireland continued as a potential destination, but Cape Cod and the South Seas also served her dream itinerary: "Let's live on a South Sea island like Stevenson, Louise!" Bishop wrote in 1926. "One can live entirely on cocoanuts." Months later, she elaborated this dream of escape:

But someday — this is true — *I'm going to live in Tahti [Tahiti] or one of those islands — with a piano and stacks of books. . . . So you must come with me and bring the Irish harp and we'll play together — not just music. Wouldn't you like to live on a South Sea Island — and forget calendars, and church, and subways, and doctors, and Logarithms?*

And once more, the year after:

There is an article in this month's Atlantic, *Louise, about a man who lives on a little South Sea Island. We simply* must — *we could*

get a job as traders for some steamship company, I know, and then
we could live in a grass-roofed hut with palm trees and sun on top
and the ocean all around and write and read and dream and write
some more. . . . I'm going to be a quohog fisherman and a truck-
driver and a farmer; and we're going to live in the South Seas.

More than forty years later, in one of her most moving poems, "Cru-
soe in England," Bishop at last found a place for that old dream of the
South Seas. She gave it back to Defoe.

> *Just when I thought I couldn't stand it*
> *another minute longer, Friday came.*
> *(Accounts of that have everything all wrong.)*
> *Friday was nice.*
> *Friday was nice, and we were friends.*
> *If only he had been a woman!*
> *I wanted to propagate my kind,*
> *and so did he, I think, poor boy.*

If only he had been a woman!

It would be tempting to dismiss as mere daydreams Bishop's imagined homes, had she not spent much of her adult life abroad, setting
up house in Brazil with her lover Lota de Macedo Soares—three
houses, really, or four, because apart from the penthouse apartment
they shared in Rio they had an isolated mountain home (where Bishop
built a studio, just the inscrutable house a child without homes might
design); and finally, as their relation grew strained, a house the poet
bought for herself in the mining town of Ouro Prêto. She saw very
early that she had to make a family, not just inherit one. Probably the
spring before she went Vassar, Bishop had written Louise,

You really are my family, you know. I belong to you and I'll do
whatever you tell me—honestly. It's a sort of fairy relationship—I
suspect you will surprise me any minute and turn into a bird or lock
me up in a small brown house until I behave.

"For C.W.B.," one of the poems Bishop published in the Walnut
Hill *Blue Pencil*, closes with the lines:

Let us live where the twilight lives after the dark,
   In the deep, drowsy blue, let us make us a home.
Let us meet in the cool evening grass, with a stork
   And a whistle of willow, played by a gnome.

Half-asleep, half-awake, we shall hear, we shall know
   The soft "Miserere" the wood-swallow tolls.
We will wander away where wild raspberries grow
   And eat them for tea from two lily-white bowls.

Earlier lines have a delightful Carrollian whimsy: "We will live upon wedding-cake frosted with sleet. / We will build us a house from two red tablecloths, / And wear scarlet mittens on both hands and feet" (in the next stanza, they will "dine upon honey and small shiny fish").

Scholars have made various guesses about the identity of C.W.B. In the Library of America edition of Bishop's work, Lloyd Schwartz states that it is Wallace Carmen Bowers, Bishop's first cousin, while Brett Millier, in her biography, believes that it's Bishop's grandfather, William Brown Boomer—but they possess the wrong initials. The poem is so highly romantic and personal, it seems more likely that Bishop addressed it to someone deeply loved, someone with whom she wanted to steal away to a home apart.

Is it possible that the editors of the *Blue Pencil* mistranscribed Bishop's handwriting? Frani Blough was editor in chief that year, however, Bishop an assistant editor—and in any case the capital "L" and "C" in Bishop's eighteen-year-old hand would have been almost impossible to confuse. Perhaps she wanted to conceal from Frani, who probably already knew Louise (Bishop's letter to the older girl the previous fall suggests the possibility), the subject of a poem so intimate. Louise Bradley's middle name was Wylie: L.W.B.

The dream of writing poetry was also part of Bishop's domestic fantasy, for both girls had literary ambitions. Camp Chequesset aspired to be more than a nautical camp, encouraging the girls to write essays or nature notes, skits or plays, poems or whatever they fancied. One of the campers later remembered that Bishop composed a weekly log in verse for her crew. In the summer of 1925, the camp held a poetry contest. Bishop's entry, printed that fall in the *Camp Chequesset Log*, is her first published poem.

The Call

The streets are tramped and muddy
   With the feet of the hurrying crowd,
And over the tall, dark buildings
   The smoke hangs like a cloud.

But the wind, as it blows through the foggy streets,
   Has a taint of the tangy spray;
And the odor, though faint, seems to my heart,
   To come straight from Wellfleet Bay.

I see the seagull dip and swoop,
   Where the fisherman casts his net
And over the calm of the opal sea
   The sun casts a golden fret.

I can hear the wind as it whispers by
   And makes laughter amid the trees,
And the silvery echoes of Taps ring out
   On the fragrant summer breeze.

And so through just a little breeze
   That carried a tang from the sea,
My heart is set all alonging again,
   For that dearest old camp C. C.

The poem is signed "Bishie," as Bishop was known at Chequesset (until she started college, Bishop signed almost all her letters to Louise that way). The humdrum tick of meter and rubbed-over conventional thought, with dulled images straight from the shelf of adolescent verse, show no sign of the poet she would become. The poem received second prize. The first-prize winner had entered a poem about God and the moon and the stars.

   Perhaps the occasion was at fault—Bishop may have tried to appeal to the taste of the judges. In an early letter to Louise (probably from 1926, when the poet was at North Shore—she mentions being placed in an advanced algebra class, but the handwriting and spelling seem more childish than in her Walnut Hill letters), she recorded her thoughts on a subject that roused her:

> One Argument against "Higher Education"
>
> I think I would not be so weak
>   If I knew more of books.
> I would not mind your fingers then,
>   Nor yet your quiet looks.
>
> My heart would quiet be within.
>   All beauty I could name.
> But magic would be lost, I fear;
>   And you—not quite the same.

The fingers are presumably scolding fingers. Bishop had obviously been reading Emily Dickinson, having borrowed her meter, her rhyme scheme, the old-fashioned inversions ("would quiet be within," "All beauty I could name"), and even the elided grammar after one of Dickinson's characteristic dashes. More telling, Bishop has perfected the Amherst poet's timid but slightly flirtatious voice (if there was ever a poet shyer than Dickinson, it was Elizabeth Bishop). In a letter to Anne Stevenson in 1964, the poet remarked, "I never really liked Emily Dickinson much, except a few nature poems, until that complete edition came out a few years ago and I read it all more carefully. I still hate the oh-the-pain-of-it-all poems. . . . This is snobbery—but I don't like the humorless, Martha-Graham kind of person who does like Emily Dickinson." Still, it's hard to imagine where else Bishop could have found this manner. "Some more sophisticated girls" at camp, she recalled in an interview, already knew the poet in white. Dickinson began half a dozen poems with "I think."

Bishop's poem, scrawled in pencil on Vinal-approved camp-notebook paper while her family thought her asleep, is startlingly accomplished for a girl of fourteen or fifteen. At the end, the gain becomes a loss, knowledge estranging the speaker from someone she loves. That sense of cruel transformation, of books destroying the magic of things, is worthy of the modest poet from whom Bishop took inspiration. The thought might have been some comfort to a girl always at odds with school.

This is perhaps the first time in Bishop's poetry where she captures a feeling, not too subtle to be caught, but subtle enough to be interesting when caught. She contributed other poems to the camp log, a 1927 banquet toast to the head skipper ("Where the blue sea slants up to touch the sky, / Held back by a thin finger of purple land, / Her eyes still dream"), and a 1928 Christmas toast to the camp that began:

> *In some still port to-night, the quiet dark,*
> *Where water whispers on taut anchor lines,*
> *Will feel a silent motion, and see signs*
> *Of rigging on the sky, and idlers hark*
> *To voices floating out across the night.*

For a time, Chequesset held a small reunion in Boston after Christmas, which Bishop attended that year (this was another way the owners tried to promote camp spirit and encourage the girls to enroll once more—or, in camp slang, send in their passport for next summer's "cruise"). Written when Bishop was seventeen, two years before she entered Vassar, the toast shows a much stronger command of poetic image. However shopworn the scene and sentiment, those voices drift off hauntingly upon the waters, like tiny ships themselves. The enjambment of the third line is a bit of craft beyond her years.

There are perhaps other adolescent poems in camp logs that have not survived (Bishop may also have written a few of the anonymous poems and songs). The poems dashed off for camp look forward only in scattered lines to her later work; but these were occasional poems meant to serve no more than occasion. At seventeen, writing from Chequesset, she could make fun of her ambitions. "I'm quite drugged and doped and tied up like an ox," she informed Louise, "with not a thought in my head except rage. . . . Just to prove to you that I can write *beautiful* poetry—here is my only brain-child in a month:

> *There was a young woman named Russle*
> *Who wore an enormious bustle.*
> *On a gay buggy ride*

A snake dropped inside—
How Miss Russle's bustle did hustle!"

"Russle" may be Bishop's amused eye-rhyme or simply her bad spelling, which had nevertheless much improved since her first letters a few years before; but "enorm*i*ous" is no mistake—it's a clever way to meet the demands of the meter.

Bishop wanted more than a confidante—she wanted a literary critic. In the spring of 1926, when she was fifteen, she had enclosed two poems to Louise, including "To Algebra." "I do hope you won't mind my laying those *burdens* on you," she wrote, "but remember, almost three years ago you told me I could. No one else knows of my ambitions and if they did would regard it as a huge joke. Please be very critical." (The "almost three years" is confusing. Chequesset awarded Bishop "veteran" status in 1927, earned at the end of a camper's fourth summer—her first year was therefore 1924, less than two years before the letter was written. Math was never her metier.)

That summer, while Bradley was preparing for her freshman year at Indiana University (now Indiana University, Bloomington), she sent Bishop a poem. In the reply addressed "Dear Kindred Spirit," Bishop burst out in despair, "Your poem is lovely. . . . Oh Louise, Louise, *you* are a true poet—I never shall be one." Bishop was still at camp, lodged in the *Mary Louise*. A mist had come in off the harbor one night and she had written a poem, "Mist Song," again on narrow camp-notebook paper (unlined now):

> *Over the austere flats,*
> *Treading—silently inward.*
> *Bending down the eel-grass*
> *Flattening in silken shivers. . . .*
> *Holding old boats with pale fingers*
> *Trailing fragile grey garments.*

The crude personification is all too reminiscent of Carl Sandburg's "Fog," but the barren flats and eel grass show that the younger poet was quietly observing her surroundings. Poetry promised an independence from all she disliked, a private world that could be altered and controlled—it was the more depressing that, to Bishop's critical eye,

Bishop alone on the *Mary Louise*
and with four friends.
Source: Courtesy the Esther Merrell Stockton Papers in the
Archives and Special Collections Library of Vassar College.

she still wrote so poorly. She regretted writing the poem, but only because, she said, "I forgot & left my notebook out. Brownie [a fellow camper] investigated—not the mist one but some others—and when I came in she told me I was crazy—'No rhyme—Bishie what do you write such stuff for?'"

The other campers were not the only ones who lacked a poetic soul:

Last night the moon was just a tiny bow—so delicate. . . . I wished over my right shoulder. You probably can guess my wish. And the sunset—and Cap. Bill talked about—foot habits—clean teeth! If it wasn't for sailing—oh camp could be so beautiful.

You'd hardly know that a year later, at the final camp-banquet in 1927, Bishop would receive, not just a Red Cross Life-Saving certificate and the honor of having her name engraved on the veterans' plaque, but the camp letters for excellence in sailing—or that almost forty years afterward she would recall that at Chequesset she "became passionately fond of sailing." This perhaps made the more mortifying an incident in the summer of 1929, at the annual S.O.S reunion, which took place after the camp's regular season closed. She had taken Louise out in one of the camp sailboats, the *Kut Up*, when a strong wind drove them toward shore. The mainsail caught on a saltwater apple tree and the boat capsized. The girls ended up wet and muddy.

Bishop desperately wanted to know the faults of her poems: "Oh Louise will you tell me what is wrong with them? Little things like rythm & the wrong words and if they are realy poetry after all. You are the only one that ever saw them." (Bishop's self-doubt continued a long while. In 1938, she wrote Marianne Moore, who replaced Louise as Bishop's main critic, about her poems, "I wish sometime you would tell me quite frankly if you think there is any use—any real use—in my continuing with them.") Though Bishop felt she could hardly write a letter with girls like the nosy Brownie around ("I fear I *am* crazy to even think of being a poet"), by the end of the summer of 1926 things had improved: "I did succeed in finding several people who could appreciate the moon without telling me all about it. But no one as perfect as you—you've spoilt me I fear."

That fall, while Bishop was starting her second year of ninth grade, now at North Shore ("I am flunking in every subject but English comp—partly on purpose"), she wrote Louise, looking once more for the consolations of criticism: "Do you mind if I send you another piece of something meant to be poetry? I wish you would tell me all the bad points. I could never show it to any one else and I do want to know if I am *improving*."

When you have a literary friend, at last you can share your enthusiasms—or squabble about them. At fourteen, Bishop was excited by little but her reading: "I have just made a wonderful discovery! Walt Whitman! . . . His poems make one feel like singing and shouting, I think." Some months after, she sneered at a fellow student who thought Tennyson marvelous. "He is all right but a little sugary," Bishop remarked drily. Shelley was different:

> *I am reading everything about him that I can and his ideas on politics etc. just fit mine. I'm going to be a socialist—a Bolshevist perhaps—It seems such a shame to let hair like mine go to waste. . . . But Shelley—oh Louise—I'm sure I'll never be able to write—anything—his poems make me feel half like an angle worm and half like a god.*

Bishop was by then barely sixteen—and loathed her frizzy hair (she'd written the previous year, "I comb it straight back now and look something like a lady Paderewski in a very bad temper"). We get little sense in the letters of Louise's tastes, whether contrary or compatible ("Do you like Edna St. Vincent Millay?" Bishop wrote her. "I *pray* so"); but the poet so rarely confessed pleasure in anything that her solace in reading is the more affecting. As she recalled her childhood, "I lay around wheezing and reading for years." Yet even reading could go from delight to damnation, if the books were required:

> *Do you like George Eliot? I could stand her when I was in a very quiet mood but I have been receiving a lecture on her value every day for a week, now, in English and I fear that I can never stand her again.*

Bishop continued with remarks about Henry James ("He analyzes everything terribly but it makes me think awfully hard and I like to feel my brain work—along that line") and Carlyle ("I like his idea of combining absolute idiocy with the truth—just in the right porportions").

Louise Bradley was having a wretchedly unhappy freshman year at Indiana. She transferred to Radcliffe the following fall, and toward the end of the school year Bishop sent a group of poems from Walnut Hill, where she was then a sophomore.

> *Thank you for saying such nice things about those filthy sonnets. . . . But oh Louise—they're no good. I struggle so hard to get out such terrible things and then they're never what's in me, after all! And I can't do a thing decently except iambic pentameter!. . . . At least you're not "naive"—that's what one of the teachers at school said I was!*

Two of these poems, the more conventional (one begins "I am in need of music that would flow / Over my fretful, feeling finger-tips"), were published that June in Walnut Hill's *Blue Pencil*, of which Bishop and Frani Blough were assistant editors. The unpublished poems, however, are stranger and slightly terrifying.

Day-Dream

And then the great gate softly slipped ajar
And I was safe within, where lilies blow
And where, upon the dim, blue hills afar,
Archangels and the Saints troop to and fro
With wondrous words and silver-folded wings.
Trembling and small, I crept beside the pool
Where God's face lies reflected, and where sings
Forever the white stream of Life. Poor fool!
For I but dipped my fingers in the Light—
Only my finger-tips!—When I heard calls
And followed those who beat upon the walls
And fled from out the Day into the Night.
The fire in my fingers will not cease.
My restless hands will never give me peace.

This suffers from the plaster-cast imagery and period diction, the period being 1850 ("the dim, blue hills afar," the "wondrous words and silver-folded wings"); yet the boldness of beginning five lines with "And," the vision of religion denied (Bishop never fully shared the Baptist faith of her mother's parents, though at Saugus she had joined a church choir), and the disturbing emotion of the final couplet displays her gathering maturity. Bishop had turned seventeen that February.

The untitled second poem, the only one in the group not a sonnet, delights in its showy technical demands.

> The world will creep away and leave me there
>> When I have heard
>> Once more that easily forgotten word
> From olden fields and dim familiar air
>> Moved delicately by a bird,
>> Or where my guardian Angel's wings have lately stirred.
>
> Centuries or more I may turn back the pages
>> That now defeat me
>> To where those wings entreat me.
> Where twilit years unheeded, little ages
>> Half lost, will gently greet me.
>> And in the rain my guardian Angel waits to meet me.

The complicated rhyme scheme and varying line length, as well as the theme, suggest that this uses a bold variation on the stanza in George Herbert's "Affliction (IV)"—the poem that years later provided a phrase for "Wading at Wellfleet."

Whatever Bishop loses in the occasional whiff of the Victorian parlor, she more than gains back in the "dim familiar air" stirred to life by the angel's passing wings, and in the solace, the troubled solace, of death foreshadowed. (The "dim familiar air" is a quiet phrase that bristles.) Drawing out the final line—the alexandrine much longer than the three-beat line preceding—increases the tension of that long-awaited meeting. The poem ends not quite resolved, a high-flown Metaphysical turn drenched in the humid melancholy and feminine rhymes of Edwin Arlington Robinson. Those feminine rhymes on "me" are like tolling bells, the dying fall of "entreat me" and "defeat me" giving way to the notes of hope in "greet me" and "meet me."

This is Bishop's one religiose poem; yet "Affliction (IV)," whose speaker wants to die to reach his beloved (in Herbert's case, the Lord) may have given Bishop more than the stanza. Perhaps the guardian angel was Louise—her intellectual and emotional guardian, the woman she longed to meet in a paradise of books in Ireland, or Cape Cod, or the South Seas. In Metaphysical poems, religious passion and romantic love can be metaphorically identical. In the same 1928 letter, Bishop remarked,

> *I've given up trying to find people who suit me. You were my only success! School is filled with dull fools and I'm considered a big freak there but I have some friends—mostly because I like their looks or the way they talk.*

When Bishop wrote from camp the month after, she was suffering the bane of all writers: "I writhe and nothing comes—not an idea—I have nothing in my head but a sort of battle of the ants. And I have an unpleasant conviction that I never shall write again—not that I ever did in the way I would."

Bishop's final summer at Chequesset, there was a famous poet in camp, the now forgotten Hilda Conkling, who had published three books before she was fifteen, the first with a foreword by Amy Lowell. The child-poet's brief career was over by the time she came to Wellfleet. Bishop limited herself to a single remark: "She is a pudding sort of person who lisps and reads Kathleen Norris all the time." (A popular romance novelist of the day, Norris was married to the brother of Frank Norris.)

There are no letters from Louise Bradley in the Bishop archive at Vassar; but one from February 1934, can be found amid the pile of Bishop's at Indiana, a letter Louise apparently never finished, though she started it twice. Bishop was a senior at Vassar by then; and her letter a month later, scolding Louise for failing to write, suggests that the unfinished letter was also unsent. It reveals more than the sort of criticism Louise offered. Bishop must have enclosed some poems.

> *I like all your sonnets very much. Will you send me more? I am not always sure that I understand these completely; sometimes they seem to flash perfectly clear for an instant, but I think that one needs to read a great deal of anyone's work to appreciate it fully. Your poetry is strangely rich; I suppose that the satisfaction and dissatisfaction*

it leaves me with is one proof of its authenticity. I wish that I were sure enough of myself to say something very discerning about them, but I am perfectly sure of you, which is more important.

Among the letters at Indiana are two loose sheets with typed copies of "Some Dreams They Forgot" and "The Map." These are perhaps the poems Bishop sent—though only the first is a sonnet, the latter, because it is twenty-eight lines, might have seemed a double sonnet. They are of the right date.

Bishop also enclosed a story, apparently unsigned, that has vanished. Louise responded:

The story, which I am sure you wrote, though you didn't say so, is very clever. Darling, I wish that death didn't bother you so much: you're so much alive and have so much to do. Possibly it is better to write about it, work it through, you may know. It is not the value of your writing which concerns me; perhaps I have no right to speak of it, but your happiness matters so much to me.

Bishop may often have felt such morbid thoughts. In 1928, the fall of her junior year at Walnut Hill, she had written Louise, "Death is the rotten core of everything I guess—Oh tell me it's all right—tell me you love me, Louise,—I don't know what to do." And, probably the next fall, she wrote, "You know, Louise, I think I want to die. Perhaps it's an awfully young thought—but I'm all out of time and place in this world and I'm not made to be happy. (Ah me!)"

Was Bishop in love with Louise Bradley? Of course. Partly it was her looks—if we can't see their attraction in the surviving photographs, that doesn't mean they were invisible to Bishop. While others at camp were watching nature, she was watching them:

Happy [another camper]. . . . looks like a myth and a Valentine and a faery tale. . . . Don't you like people's looks? I do—excepting that they frighten me. Why does everything agreeable frighten me so? I'm a fool, I guess—but no one ever knows how terrible lamp light at vespers is—or people in swimming. . . . Things are troubling me here this year. I'm not grown up enough to stop laughing but I am grown up enough to wonder why I do it, and sometimes

I want to kick them all into the bay and let the wind blow things clean and sometimes I want to hold on to someone's finger. Well— this is all very confused and unpleasant.

This was written the summer Bishop was seventeen, bewildered by her response to trivial things like lamplight. However nervous her laughter, her desires were overwhelming: "There is one beautiful girl here—only one, and I look at her. . . . The beautiful girl looks so nice on her knees with a rosary." Bishop had gone to the Catholic church perhaps in part to see her lovely classmate. This is longing without knowing what the longing means. The letter is undated, but was probably written in Bishop's junior year at Walnut Hill.

Chequesset had trained Bishop to look at things intently, almost religiously. However much she stared wistfully (or hungrily) at others, it was Louise whose looks possessed her: "More than any beautiful stranger, I want to watch you and I want to see your rather rippled nose and hear you laugh." Whenever the two of them met—and it was far more rarely than Bishop pined for—the younger girl was tongue-tied. After Louise had given her a ride to Walnut Hill, Bishop admitted seeming "miles and miles away": "This isn't saying anything—anyway I rather doubt if we could ever say anything. I guess I love you too damned much to talk to you." In another letter: "If you were here with me I'd be dumb, though, and just look at you and watch the corners of your mouth—I do like the way they move—like little wings." When Bishop saw her own face in the mirror, however, it was with irritation and disappointment—her hair was so infamous, in the Walnut Hill class poem she was referred to as "Bishop of the barbarous hair."

Bishop was unnerved by feelings she little understood and felt no power to control. There's a poignancy, if also a hint of panic, in her declarations of love to Louise, at first merely in her closings, as if she were kissing the letter shut ("With ever so much love," "With lots and *lots* of love," and, before long, "With love and more love" and "I love you more than anyone in the world"). She ends one letter in the fall of 1926 with what seems like shocked recognition: "I love you so much that my throat aches when I think of it." A couple of years later, she says simply, "Oh I want you."

It's easy to forget how confusing adolescent homosexuality would have been in 1925—it's confusing now, and in ways different from adolescent heterosexuality. Bishop struggled to figure out who she was, but even as an adult she wasn't wholly sure. She often dreamed of Louise, relating the dreams with a sort of detached fascination, as if they were unruly poems her unconscious had called forth (such dreams lost their innocence after Freud, both in the telling and in the having, but Bishop seems happily pre-Freudian).

> I had a very strange dream about you the other night. You and another girl and I were walking about in a very rainy country atmosphere, looking for a Ligget[t] drugstore. We found a beautiful antique inn, all red brick, but with an immense Lig[g]ett sign on front and went in. The front room was very, very small and crowded with bottles and a tan marble soda fountain and a young man in a white jacket and oily black hair. We sat on wire chairs around a little table and ate great dishes of bright orange sherbet. But the funniest thing of all was the way you and the girl were dressed. She had on a gown like those the Wellesley seniors wear, only bright blue, with a net and herringbone collar about the gills and an immense mortar-board on top; and you wore a complete sort of suffraget costume in an awful pea green color—you know, tweed and very "mannish!" with a nice hard collar and striped necktie and a terrible fedora on your yellow hair. . . . I shudder!

Some recipients of such a letter might have been slightly horrified, yet there's no sign Louise was troubled by Bishop's intense feelings.

The poet's curious sensitivity to people's clothes is also evident in a dream she reported from Vassar her freshman year.

> Last night I dreamed about you. . . . It was a very cold, dark blue winter night and I was walking along a country road. It was terribly cold. I was walking fast but I didn't know where I was going. Suddenly you came up from behind me on the right. You were dressed in a long blue coat—very Russian—and a little grey astrakhan cap, with your hair all curling around the edges. You kept pulling my arm and saying "There's the house." I wouldn't look for a long time. Then I did and away off in the sky, it seemed, I could see a little square lighted window pane. You were astonishingly beautiful.

Bishop's yearning for a life apart, a life with Louise, represented somewhere deep in the imagination the rescue the dream embodies within a world of terrifying cold. She kept a picture of Louise on her bureau at home in Revere, but apparently took it with her when traveling—on an overnight visit, such devotion made another girl jealous.

Bishop was not the least shy about her passion for her kindred spirit—perhaps the risk entertained and the pleasure derived were those of a girl who had never felt that sort of love. Her first love was one rarely visited on people, at least people from happy families.

> *I never could like anyone the way you know I like you. And that sounds awful. . . . Why, what else is there besides the fact (what an awful word for it) that I love you? It seems so clear to me when I love a person—but then I'm crazy, I know. . . . Oh Louise—my heart is sick and I need you so.*

Though undated, this letter seems to come from Bishop's later years at Walnut Hill. Since Louise's correspondence has been lost, it's not entirely certain how far she returned these affections. For Bishop to say at fifteen, "Oh I'm so *thankful* I found you—I can stand almost everything because I know that you would feel the same way about it," might seem a girlish crush. To continue to say the same things to the same young woman at eighteen or nineteen, things so easy to desire and so difficult to need, suggests that her love had been reciprocated, not merely tolerated.

The one letter of Louise's we have was meant as a birthday greeting and, more importantly, a Valentine's Day card (Bishop's birthday was February 8):

> *Not being able to decide among the Western Union Valentine sentiments, I shall write you a birthday letter instead. Wouldn't you like to receive (by uniformed messenger) "At miles between us we can laugh, our hearts entwined by telegraph", or "To my Valentine: you've put my heart in such a flutter, I wire the love my lips would utter". The first has a slight flavor of Donne, I think, so you might prefer it. Of course I might compose one myself to go with a letter, as "Like the horse who made this postage glue, I'd gladly give my life for you."*

The casual intimacy here—the leap from Western Union's inadequacies as a Cupid to thought of John Donne as a copy writer—displays the bewitching charm of Louise Bradley. She continued by transcribing an absurd ad for a fruit stand. Her brisk, confident intelligence and the joking familiarity of her valentine doggerel have a thrilling immediacy compared to Bishop's awkwardness in matters of the heart. How could the poet not fall in love with the girl who could write, "I'm making a wonderful collection of Americana for posterity. How, for instance, would you like ice cream moulded into a sitting hen or kissing doves?"

What sort of advice did Louise give? Mostly, it seems, reassurance and encouragement. We can infer something from a few of Bishop's letters, one probably written during her last semester at Walnut Hill:

> You make such beautiful remarks about LIFE, all capitals, that you almost fool me, dear Louise. You are the only person I'd ever take it from, you know—and I enjoy it, too. But nothing can do me any good—I'm evil, hopeless, stupid and mediocre and God knows thats the truth.

And again, when Bishop was about to start her sophomore year at Vassar:

> I wish I could write letters like that. . . . If you will only do it again—keep it up at intervals during the winter months—ah—I'll be a ΦBK [Phi Beta Kappa] in my junior year, a friend to all, and a really delightful character, besides.

Bishop often felt entirely alone. She wrote a few weeks after the Walnut Hill letter, "Did you ever think—no matter how many friends you have—no one can really reach you? I feel sometimes like a person on another planet—watching someone on this world."

Bishop frequently used a receding perspective in her poems, as if turning binoculars the wrong way round, which might be called an economy of scale (sometimes she also turned the binoculars the right way)—observing the conquistadores in "Brazil, January 1, 1502," for instance ("the Christians, hard as nails, / tiny as nails, and glinting") or the palm trees in "Little Exercise" ("all stuck in rows, suddenly revealed / as fistfuls of limp fish-skeletons"). The view from another planet perhaps prefigures her creation of the Kafkaesque figure in "The Man-Moth" (suggested by a newspaper misprint for "mammoth"), who, thinking the moon a silvery hole in the sky, climbs up the buildings to force his head through. Bishop's letter reveals a detachment that might be explained by a childhood so severely unhappy she suffered long periods of emotional numbness, a dissociation from which only her felt connection to Louise could save her.

Louise was never the steady correspondent Bishop begged for, and the poet's letters are full of lover's pleas and mock threats ("I tried to forget you all year—but it was rather impossible when I didn't even have strength of mind enough to take your picture from my bureau"). From the summer after North Shore:

> Won't you send me a postcard with only "Louise" on the back—or perhaps "With, love, Louise," just so I know you haven't forgotten me. I think of you so much.

From Walnut Hill:

> I know if I write to you or think about you for very long I shall begin to get mad—yes, mad, my friend—and want to throw things at you and pull your nice hair.

And from Vassar, a few months before Bishop graduated: "I can never quite decide, in the period of your silences, whether it's just because you're busy or whether my effusiveness has disgusted you."

Their infrequent meetings weren't always satisfactory. When they saw each other in Boston at Christmas 1926, it was the first time since camp the summer a year before. Bishop was taken aback. She recognized, perhaps for the first time, the disparity in their ages:

> You have changed, after all, Louise, but I didn't realize it till I came home and looked at your picture. You have changed and I am still a child, a child who wears woolen stockings and thinks so much that her neck aches.

Despite Bishop's fear that the older girl was merely indulging her ("I sometimes have a horrible feeling that you take a motherly interest in me"), despite the uneasy meetings and laggardly correspondence, Louise Bradley remained Bishop's intimate confidante. Until the poet graduated from college, Louise was perhaps the only person who knew the depths of the poet's misery, or the depths of her love. Only in the poet's last years at Vassar did her feelings grow more measured than those of the fifteen-year-old in the ninth grade, when Louise was having that awful freshman year at Indiana:

> *As if I could ever be disgusted with* you! *Oh* Louise, *what can I do for you? I can just imagine what it all is like. Oh Why, why, why, is the world this way? If it wasn't for you,* one *person who understands—I could jump off the bridge. Don't go back there— ever. I can not write anything comforting—but it breaks my heart to have you unhappy.*

It is possible to read too much into schoolgirl crushes, even when they have long graduated to passion. Easy to read too much, and easier to read too little. What should we make of Bishop's remark, after she had come into possession of Louise's silk tie, left behind at camp ("I will send it to you but I would like to keep it to feel. It feels exactly like you")? Should we infer anything when Bishop writes, "I want to hold on to someone's finger"? There is no convincing sign of physical intimacy—it's not even clear how much sexual experience Bishop enjoyed before graduating from college. Love is hard enough, no matter feelings not just unnamed but unnameable to the adolescent who suffers them or takes solace in them. At Walnut Hill, Bishop was suspected of an abnormal friendship with another girl, Barbara Chesney, though Chesney denied it.

Perhaps her homosexual longings were obscure even to Bishop. She dated at least two men in college, one of whom, Richard Seaver, proposed. The couple made trips alone, spending nights together at inns on Nantucket and Cuttyhunk at a time when that would have been a scandal. Bishop turned him down, or at least made clear her lack of interest. Some months later, he shot himself, but not before sending her a postcard that read, "Go to hell, Elizabeth." In the late sixties, Bishop told Charlee Wilbur, Richard Wilbur's wife, "I did all the wrong things in my life. . . . I should have married. And what I miss more than anything on earth is not having a child." Despite the misdirections of later life, Bishop's feelings for Louise seem the earliest hint of her adult affections. It was certainly a love of uncommon intensity.

What trace remains of Camp Chequesset in Bishop's work? There are poems she could have written had she never gone to camp, though perhaps not in the same way. Bishop had grown up in a Nova Scotia fishing village, and her father's family owned a house in Harwich Port on the lower Cape. She most often lived near the sea—in Great Village, in Revere, in New York, in Key West, and then in Rio, where her apartment with Lota overlooked Copacabana Beach. Bishop's last home was a condo at Lewis Wharf on Boston Harbor. Even her fantasies of keeping house with Louise always kept the sea somewhere near. The summers at Camp Chequesset were part of that long life by the Atlantic—after her camp days were over, Bishop for some years returned to Wellfleet and the Cape.

Even if the idea of the nautical camp had not been her own, it became part of a seaward yearning already established. (She once said cryptically to her friend Barbara Chesney, "If anything ever happens to me, take me to the ocean.") One of Bishop's strongest memories of the Cape was of the night walk she had taken alone after her freshman year at Vassar. She started on the back shore at Nauset Light and walked along the sands the twenty miles or more to Provincetown, stopping to swim now and then. Bishop carried a "little tin lunch box containing a thermos bottle of black tea, a ham sandwich, a tooth brush & comb & a mouthorgan."

"The Map," written that last semester at Vassar or soon after, became the opening poem in her first book, *North and South* (1946).

> The names of seashore towns run out to sea,
> the names of cities cross the neighboring mountains
> —the printer here experiencing the same excitement
> as when emotion too far exceeds its cause.

It's not entirely fanciful to see the lines as unconsciously charting a life for the traveler Bishop longed to be and eventually became. The year after she wrote the poem, she sailed to Europe for the first time, by Nazi freighter.

The sea washes ashore throughout *North and South*: in "The Imaginary Iceberg" ("We'd rather have the iceberg than the ship, / although it meant the end of travel"); in "Casabianca," Bishop's comic turn on Felicia Hemans's old warhorse, once a recitation piece that bedeviled young students; in "Florida," and "Seascape" and "Little Exercise" and "The Unbeliever" and "Large Bad Picture":

> *And high above them, over the tall cliffs'*
> *semi-translucent ranks,*
> *are scribbled hundreds of fine black birds*
> *hanging in n's in banks.*
>
> *One can hear their crying, crying,*
> *the only sound there is*
> *except for the occasional sighing*
> *as a large aquatic animal breathes.*

This was among the earliest poems by Bishop to appear in the *New Yorker*. Before accepting it, Harold Ross, the editor of the magazine, wanted to know which large aquatic animal she had in mind, hoping she would name it. Bishop politely fended off the query (she replied that the animal was imaginary); but the poet might have seen a stray whale on those camp cruises, or perhaps recalled the school of 105 blackfish, as Cape Codders called pilot whales, that had beached down the bay at East Brewster in 1925. The campers had made a special trip to see them.

Bishop's command of sailing gear and nautical slang probably owes something to those months spent on the water. However she railed about them (recall her painful cry, "If it wasn't for sailing—oh camp could be *so* beautiful"), her familiarity must have been acquired somewhere. Bishop's memories of the water rise into her description of ships in "Large Bad Picture" ("square-rigged, sails furled, motionless, / their spars like burnt match-sticks") and the rented boat in "The Fish":

> *the pool of bilge*
> *where oil had spread a rainbow*
> *around the rusted engine*
> *to the bailer rusted orange,*
> *the sun-cracked thwarts,*

> *the oarlocks on their strings,*
> *the gunnels.*

The camp logs revel in the sailor's vernacular, as if it were shared only by the initiated ("The canvass is spread, and you can hear the creak of the windlass as it starts to wind in the cables"). The passage from "The Fish" lacks the sentiment but supplies the poetic conviction missing from the lackluster lines in her 1928 Christmas toast ("the quiet dark, / Where water whispers on taut anchor lines, / Will feel a silent motion, and see signs / Of rigging on the sky").

In Florida, Bishop became a devoted fisherman. Though "The Fish" was written after she caught a sixty-pound amberjack off Key West over the Christmas holidays of 1936, her introduction to fishing probably came at camp. Fishing expeditions, though not always successful ones, are mentioned in the logs from time to time—campers caught perch in one of Wellfleet's freshwater ponds, and one summer the veterans were treated to a deep-sea fishing trip. The last of Bishop's *Camp Chequesset Log* poems was titled "The Fisherman":

> *"The dripping deck beneath him reels,*
> > *The flooded scuppers spout the brine.*
> *He heeds them not, he only feels*
> > *The tugging of a tightened line."*
>
> ———————
>
> *A fisherman without a fish,*
> > *A silent man, and melancholy,—*
> *But he is all that we could wish,*
> > *Let us arise and drink to Jolly.*

Laurence "Jolly" Rogers, who supervised the sailing and swimming at Chequesset, had something of a reputation with hook and line. The mild raillery of this toast precedes "The Fish" by most of a decade; but there already is the language of the sea, and there the fisherman without his fish.

Bishop's whimsical inspection of animals in "The Fish," "The Armadillo," "Roosters," "Sandpiper," "Pink Dog," and others is probably due more to the influence of Marianne Moore than to the didactic methods of William Vinal. Still, the immersion in nature at Chequesset, as well as the requirement that campers write in the natural language of observation, not the fossilated prose of a zoology textbook, perhaps prepared Bishop to be influenced. The habits formed at Chequesset, which may have begun to teach her how to observe animals through the microscope of the poetic, may survive in the letter she wrote Marianne Moore some ten years after that last camp summer,

> *I should just like to let myself go, Marianne, and give you masses and masses of Nature Description. . . . The spring runs into another square hole cut in the rock with a huge stone crock, brown & white, standing in it, to keep our milk and butter, etc., in. In this spring lives a bright pink salamander about 6 inches long, with black freckles. Red brought him up to the house one night and he crawled around on the table under the oil-lamp—he is very clumsy. Then there are skinks that occasionally crawl down my bedroom wall—they are all black except for 4 white stripes down the back, and the tail is a brilliant, irridescent purple-blue—like lightning.*

Like the other senses, the poet's eye must be trained; and even trained it has to find a language of expression. Perhaps more than any serious poet of the last century, Bishop used the pathetic fallacy without succumbing to its sentimental touch. Since this became one of the most sophisticated psychologies of her style, it's surprising to find it in her letters at fourteen. She wrote Louise from Nova Scotia,

> *Great Village is a quaint little town something like Wellfleet. We live in a homely old white house that sticks its little snub nose directly into the middle of the village square. It is an inquisitive house.*

Earlier in the same letter: "Today has a very unsetteled disposition,—hasn't quite made up its mind whether to laugh or cry. I wish it would hurry up and do one or the other." Though it seems to reveal an innocent eye, the later *faux-naïf* manner was not a cynical reversion to childhood, merely a continuation of her writing in the ninth grade. Perhaps this was just the sort of colorful writing Vinal encouraged—it's no great leap to her lines in "Sestina" ("the teakettle's small hard tears / dance like mad on the hot black stove") or "Twelfth Morning;

or What You Will" ("the sandpipers' / heart-broken cries") or "The Bight" ("The frowsy sponge boats keep coming in / with the obliging air of retrievers").

Such stray signs of her camp summers illustrate no more than tendencies, leaving a vague trail through Bishop's poems—like the overgrown King's Highway the Chequesset girls were expected to follow through the dunes of Cape Cod. The traces are as faint as the trail from a phrase in a scolding letter to Louise in 1931 ("I trust . . . you'll tell me what you're doing and where you're going") to the poem where it lodges years after, "Letter to N.Y." dedicated to another Louise, Louise Crane—"nevertheless I'd like to know / what you are doing and where you are going."

Two of Bishop's poems, however, reveal much closer ties to Camp Chequesset. When she returned to Wellfleet in later years, she sometimes rented a cottage near the camp. In the summer of 1933, she pleaded with Louise to visit. "Wading at Wellfleet" was probably begun, if not then, then not long after.

> In one of the Assyrian wars
> a chariot first saw the light
> that bore sharp blades around its wheels.
>
> That chariot from Assyria
> went rolling down mechanically
> to take the warriors by the heels.
>
> A thousand warriors in the sea
> could not consider such a war
> as that the sea itself contrives
>
> but hasn't put in action yet.
> This morning's glitterings reveal
> the sea is "all a case of knives."
>
> Lying so close, they catch the sun,
> the spokes directed at the shin.
> The chariot front is blue and great.

> *The war rests wholly with the waves:*
> *they try revolving, but the wheels*
> *give way; they will not bear the weight.*

This artificial danger, as if the wader might be mown down at the shins by the scythes of the chariot, recalls the real perils of the sea—the summer hurricanes and winter nor'easters, the rocky coasts with their warning lighthouses, the fierce undertow that can drag a casual bather to his death.

The source of an allusion is sometimes less interesting than the context. "All a case of knives" is a quotation from George Herbert, whose poetry Bishop had chanced on in that used bookshop in Provincetown. In "Affliction (IV)," the phrase is embedded in "My thoughts are all a case of knives, / Wounding my heart." The speaker is a "thing forgot, / Once a poor creature, now a wonder, / A wonder tortured in the space / Betwixt this world and that of grace." Of those scalpel-like thoughts, the speaker laments, "Nothing their fury can control, / While they do wound and pink my soul" ("pink" means stab). Though the poem is addressed to the Lord, it is not outlandish to suppose that "Wading at Wellfleet" might have had a different passion in mind, thoughts of a different wound to the heart, thrown up by the sharp glitter of the sea. Might have had, since "Affliction (IV)" was probably the model for Bishop's accomplished high-school poem about her guardian angel.

In the final image, the breaking waves try to revolve, but time after time collapse, crushed by their own weight, as in Exodus 14:25 ("And took off their chariot wheels, that they drave them heavily"). The sea's terrible intention is never fulfilled, overcome by the weight of the water, or is that the weight of such thoughts? This is a more troubling poem than has generally been realized—if the speaker identifies with the sea, the harm is directed toward others, or even toward herself. The violence is a plan the sea "hasn't put in action yet"—but there could come times when the chariot was *not* defeated.

Images that seem fanciful or decorative in Bishop might sometimes be called a subjective correlative, revealing not the object but the shaping form of the viewer's eye, and therefore the emotion concealed by observation. The defeated war machine recalls the legend of King Canute, who ordered the tide to halt, or Xerxes, who had the

Hellespont whipped. Perhaps Bishop had read of the fall of Nineveh and the destruction of the Assyrian empire; but for many summers she had seen the waves at Wellfleet, where after a storm the crashing surf along the back shore would have been worthy of the slashing wheels of the Assyrian chariot. The tone is matter of fact, but beneath lies the threat of the sea, ordinary but dangerous. Though suffused with the free-floating anxiety often present in Bishop's work, the poem never attaches the futility of the waves to failed love or thwarted desire — yet an allusion can be what says nothing while telling everything.

The *Chequesset Log* of fall 1927 mentions that the previous summer Cap'n Bill, then no longer director of the camp, had taken the campers to "see the Hermit." This meeting probably provided the germ of "Chemin de Fer":

> Alone on the railroad track
>> I walked with pounding heart.
> The ties were too close together
>> or maybe too far apart.
>
> The scenery was impoverished:
>> scrub-pine and oak; beyond
> its mingled gray-green foliage
>> I saw the little pond
>
> where the dirty hermit lives,
>> lie like an old tear
> holding onto its injuries
>> lucidly year after year.
>
> The hermit shot off his shot-gun
>> and the tree by his cabin shook.
> Over the pond went a ripple.
>> The pet hen went chook-chook.
>
> "Love should be put into action!"
>> screamed the old hermit.
> Across the pond an echo
>> tried and tried to confirm it.

The typically ambivalent ending, with its large explosion and empty consequence, the high-minded, impractical (or merely desperate) philosophy unconfirmed in its own echo, displays the grace of belief frustrated in the world of practice, like the Christianity Bishop chafed at (she wrote at seventeen, "I've taken quite a Christian trend, lately—except when I go to church"). Part of the comic pleasure of the ending comes from the different ways the feminine rhyme is broken into syllables (FIRM it / HER mit)—even the rhyme is, in a sense, unconfirmed. The ending has an edge of sadness and futility, too, like "Wading at Wellfleet." The saintlike sentiment (the hermit is a desert father—or a lunatic) is as difficult to confirm as a rumor.

A visit to the town hermit, as it happened, was one of Cap'n Bill's favorite excursions, described in the 1921 article for *Nature-Study Review*:

> *Every bailiwick has its hermit. Ours is a grizzly sea-dog who has taken to land some two miles from the coast. He is a Thoreau-like individual reminding one considerably of that famous naturalist who walked the length of the Cape some three-quarters of a century ago. The present recluse has squatted on the site of his great grandsire's claim and his tract reaches unto the shores of the same pond. From the cedar swamp in back he has lugged, dragged, and rolled in turn the logs for the framework of his hut. . . . Of the old days—naught remains to suggest ancestral fortitude or thrift but scraggly apple trees, decrepit, gnarled, and windblown, with a few belichened fence rails.*

Vinal quotes from the field notebook of "Bumps" (Chequesset loved jolly nicknames), then the youngest girl in camp:

> *The lilac bushes and the fruit trees indicate the great age of the place. The Hermit has planted boughs on the north side of his corn to protect it from the cold. He also made a wheelbarrow with much patience and care. He has made a little bird house on the top of a stick driven into an old stump. . . . Back of his house he has made a chicken coop of pine boughs. He has placed boards on either side to weigh the boughs down and keep them together.*

This is a good example of the writing at Chequesset. The "equipment" needed for the social call included a map, drawing paper, crayons, and an "eagerness to hear and understand a backwoods language,—a woodsy speech which has all but disappeared, and a desire to express the experience in writing and in sketch with an understanding heart." The hermit's name was Mr. Dyer. There is the pond and the chicken coop. What of the gun? In Vinal's book *Nature Guiding* (1926), there is a picture of a Chequesset girl shooting the hermit's gun, with the hermit standing alongside. "What greater wealth of material could one wish," Vinal remarked, as if clairvoyant, "for a future school essay . . . or . . . the very joy of writing literature."

The shotgun goes off in anger, or pain, or impotent rage. The hermit possesses the grand idea of love, but apparently is unable to do more than preach it (he's a hermit, after all). One critic has connected the love to Bishop's homosexuality; but it might derive more directly from a love time after time declared, echoed and re-echoed, but never consummated. The suggestions of violence or self-harm make this and "Wading at Wellfleet" much darker poems.

If the setting of "Chemin de Fer" was Cape Cod, the railroad would have been the old Cape Cod Railroad, which ran trains daily from South Station in Boston to Provincetown. Those railroad ties are slyly revealing—it's not just the "pounding heart" that suggests the ties too close together or too far apart might also be ties of love or blood. The ambiguity lies buried just deeply enough to seem telling when you notice it, as if it hovered at the edge of the poet's imagination, to be discovered belatedly, or not at all. *The New Yorker* disliked Bishop's original title, "Fine Examples," which forced irony into the disparity between the grubby hermit and his Christlike philosophy. After some thought, she provided an alternative, the French for "railroad."

Bishop and Louise remained loyal correspondents through Bishop's years at Vassar. There was a flurry of letters in her senior year, after Louise had finally visited her in Wellfleet. The letters petered out months after the poet graduated (by that last year at Vassar, according to her biographer, Bishop had become infatuated with her roommate, Margaret Miller). Then, after a gap of almost a year, Bishop wrote Louise apologetically from a fishing town in Brittany, the "heart and soul of the sardine industry." Eight years passed before a Christmas note in 1943. The last letters were mailed in 1950, after the women had met briefly in New York while Bishop was Consultant in Poetry to the Library of Congress, the ungainly title for what is now called the Poet Laureate.

Louise never married. At Radcliffe she was class historian and editor in chief of the *Radcliffe Daily*, graduating cum laude in English in 1930. She became supervisor of occupational analysis at Raytheon, a manufacturer of rectifiers, electron tubes, and other early electronics, where after the war the microwave was invented. Louise lived in her childhood home in Arlington until she died in December 1979, two months after Bishop. It isn't known if the poet visited during the years, at the end of her life, when she lived on Lewis Wharf in Boston; but there is no entry for Louise Bradley in Bishop's address book.

A Critic's Notebook

My mother's middle name was Belle, a name she loathed all her life. I was surprised that she never tried to change it. It was not, I suspect, a name popular among the young women of Pittsburgh in the twenties and thirties; perhaps it had the magnolia whiff of a bygone age, the age of Southern gentlemen and chivalry and the War of the Secession. I don't see why my mother, who swanned a bit, would not otherwise have enjoyed being confused with one of the extras in *Gone with the Wind*—she was a looker and could have played the part.

Belle was a silent nod by her mother to her own mother, my great-grandmother Isabelle Kelley Drew. Mrs. Drew had descended from an Irish family who owned some tenements in Boston, but her parents and all her siblings had died in an epidemic and she was left penniless. My great-grandmother, whom I knew only as a stooped ancient, must have been a winning young woman because she was more or less adopted by a judge's family. On my mother's death, I found, among other documents squirreled away, a small clipping from a Boston paper about Isabelle's wedding in the judge's home, where Mendelssohn's wedding march had been played. Decades later, the judge's daughter—this must have been in the early thirties—used to come visit my great-grandmother in a limousine.

Nicknames were common in that maternal line. My mother, who also didn't like her given name, Nancy, was called Bonnie. My grandmother Dorothy was known as D. D., and my great-grandmother was called Barbie, pronounced "Bobbie." Indeed, my mother's father, Howard, was known as Tyke and Bobbie's husband, Frank, as Gampie. (Gampie's older brother Philip was called Young Buffalo, but that's another story.) My mother could be vain, refusing to appear in photographs with her glasses on. I caught her in snapshots a few times, but given any chance she would whip off her glasses with a sleight-of-hand flourish. One of her last requests was that "Belle" not be engraved on her tombstone.

In recent years, I have taken to reading while walking. I believe the Romantics were guilty of such behavior; a duodecimo was small enough to fit into a jacket pocket. A close-printed book was just the prop to allow you to ignore fellow passengers in a coach, if your eyes could stand the jostling, but an even better thing to pull out on a country path if you tired of the scenery.

I'm not bored by the local live-oaks and saw-backed palmettos, the shrouds of Spanish moss and violent curlicues of vine that compose the Florida flora; but I've walked the two miles to school so many times I know every weed by heart. It took me years to settle on the route, which winds drunkenly through the griddle of streets in my tiny Southern town. Eventually I found the shadiest path. I know the walk now, every pothole and square of cracked sidewalk, so I read while walking, about ten pages per mile, which at a quarter of an hour per mile is not much worse than reading while sitting. I don't know if the Romantics felt virtuous when they read outdoors, on the hoof; but there's something to be said for it. A paperback book is meant to be portable; early paperbacks were developed around the time of the Crimean War, for the convenience of travelers late in the first era of the train.

I usually walk with the book in one hand and a pen in the other, because in my late age I have taken to marking up books. Reading while walking is only mildly odd; but walking along while making notes is positively eccentric. I wish I had started sooner.

Poetry progresses in part by welcoming the unpoetic and in part by giving up the "poetic"—whatever has been understood as necessary to poetry, whether in diction, meter, the manner of framing an argument (or framing an argument at all), or the fashion and temper of imagery. The amount of real innovation is always much less than the amount of experimentation, even in periods where experiment is felt, not just to be a good thing, but to be the only thing.

What worries me, on days where I agree to be worried, is that young poets frequently know so little about their art—its history, its craft, its traditional manners (as well as its lack of manners), and the long wrestle with style that has produced what we think of as poetry today. You might believe that innovation can't happen when the innovator is trapped by the assumptions of the poetry of last year, or the last decade, or the last century. Eliot and Pound, those two great modernists, knew the poetry of the past thoroughly and would have thought a young poet who refused to learn from it, from both its triumphs and its mistakes, was an idiot. Ideally, innovation ought to be like spontaneous combustion—but then you need oil-soaked rags and a bit of heat.

I have to explain to undergraduates much that would have been taken for granted forty years ago, when I was an undergraduate myself. I don't mean meter—even then, I had to learn that arcane craft alone. When I teach Bishop's "Visits to St. Elizabeths," however, I have to explain Pound's incarceration, give the background of his fascist broadcasts, note that young poets frequently enlivened his visiting hours, and much else. Sometimes I have to explain who Ezra Pound was. Or take Amy Clampitt's "A Cure at Porlock." I was teaching it recently; and one class had no idea, not a single student, who "S. T. C." was. In my other class, two students knew him, though not "Kubla Khan," and hence not the story of the visitor from Porlock. They knew nothing about opium. Of William Bartram, they knew less than nothing, though he walked the Alachua prairie right past the future site of Gainesville and thirty miles north of their classroom found the disappearing river from which S. T. C. drew his inspiration.

These workshops were filled with English majors, many of them seniors, all of them with superlative SAT scores and high grades. I don't blame the students for their sublime ignorance. A minority don't know how to write a complete sentence, though they believe that, if only a "sentence" goes on long enough, it will contain that germ, that mysterious X-factor, that makes it complete. High-school English no longer provides a grounding in grammar or in the classics of English poetry. I'm not sure what high-school English teachers do; but I'm told they spend a lot of time helping students write the "personal essay" they'll need to get into college.

My university matriculates the smartest students in a state that has almost no private universities, a state where such students are paid to go to college. The English department, however, has abandoned the idea that there are classics worth teaching—what students are taught instead is a gallimaufry of "texts," often with fairly overt political messages, and all too often angled toward the teacher's gimlet-eyed interest in race, class, and gender. Some professors were exceptions, of course—but the exceptions tended to be older, which means that in the past ten years most have retired. My best students are readers, pure readers; when they look at the course offerings, they weep in despair, and they get angry. They don't want to be preached at; they want to read good books and learn how to think about them. I feel like a tyrannosaur making this complaint; but tyrannosaurs, at the end, probably had a good deal to complain about.

Viewed historically, what Susan Sontag called the metaphor of illness depends on the evolution of the evolution of disease. Metaphors are not isolate and unaccountable; they vary as the vehicle, the disease itself, varies in the world. What tuberculosis was as a figure to the Romantics—deadly, wasting, consuming (hence, *consumption*), a brilliance-inducing fatal bout of sickness—was not unaffected by the introduction of streptomycin more than a century later. Once the disease was curable, the metaphor lost force. Cancer had more power as a metaphor when the diagnosis was considered a death sentence. This change in metaphor is a natural process and not as tangled in morality as Sontag argues in *Illness as Metaphor*—she wanted to resist the metaphorical use of disease. I long to use it.

Among the arts afflicted by the metaphor of illness, poetry has suffered a good while. We speak of the death or decline of poetry; we pine for readers who will bring it back to health—this frivolous, obscure, all too intellectual art. The evolution of the evolution of this disease, the progress of its progress, suggests that we may be thinking about poetry the wrong way. Perhaps poetry remains just as healthy, just as unhealthy, as it has been for a century or more, a once major art superseded by other arts—by the novel or film. Perhaps poetry has forever lost the attention it commanded in the age before radio, television, the Internet, iPods, smartphones, all those other means of trafficking high art and low (or, as Frost had it, more gloomily, low brow and no brow). That's not such a terrible thing. Let's stop treating poetry as infected or diseased simply because it's no longer the cynosure of arts.

It's surprising how much time characters in nineteenth-century novels spent reading, if they could read, or being read to, if they couldn't. (Think of Mr. Boffin in *Our Mutual Friend*.) We have lost that world, that world of privacy and silence, but we own silences that century could not imagine and have silenced many noises it had to bear—carriages on cobbles, squalling street-vendors, passengers singing on trains. If we cannot hope to see someone like Byron made famous overnight (though didn't Auden come close?), poetry is still present in a way Byron's century would have recognized. It cannot be found, to be sure, in exactly the same places—it has almost vanished from newspapers and from the bookshelves of the modestly educated. No one feels that you have to read Milton or Pope (much less learn to write like them) in order to consider yourself enlightened. Nevertheless, bookstore shelves are jammed with poetry, if you can find a bookstore; and small publishers ever gratify their tastes by bringing out new volumes in stupefying numbers. Magazines proliferate like barn rats, and the Internet has more websites and chat rooms devoted to verse than London once had coffee houses. Though bookstores are disappearing, their carpet and sheetrock toted away in dumpsters, there is the wonder of Amazon, larger than the library of Alexandria by a dozen, or twelve dozen, or a hundred dozen times.

Workmen have been laboring all day to erect a massive blue plastic tent, big as a circus tent, over the house next door. ("Ow!" one man keeps shouting, a masochist of pest control. "Oww! Owwww!") Later they'll pump in poison gas to kill the termites. The owner called me the other evening to warn me, and to suggest that I might do as he discreetly intended to do—that is, leave town.

My house has been tented four times in the past ten years. The infestations were all of dry-wood termites, common to old houses in Florida. (Carpenter bees are less destructive, but they make holes the size of .50 caliber bullets.) There's no way to defend against them. The insects swarm late in summer; if they swarm in your direction, some years later you'll find a miniature version of Grapenuts piled beneath a door or against a molding. That's called frass, the insects' excreta; if they were more sensible they'd hide it, because the frass gives them away—but then termites evolved eating trees, not houses.

We've had the house tented so often because the treatments did not take. I suspect that there are so many books in our attic, packed snugly in boxes stacked in anonymous crowds hard against each another, that the gas never had a chance to poison the deep readers among the termites. That they like books, I know. I once tossed a phone book to the floor. When I picked it up again a few months later, there was a hole drilled neatly through a hundred pages.

I keep articles that catch my attention, each with some odd fact or peculiar idea that one day might turn into a poem. I'll dog-ear a page in the *TLS*, say; then, if I remember, clip it later and throw it upon the desk, where within the month it's buried beneath glass-plate photographs, a bill from the termite-control company, the H–O volume of the *Random House Historical Dictionary of American Slang*. Once a year or so, I sweep the articles into a file, where they decay gratefully in the darkness of a drawer. They almost never emerge again; on the rare occasion that I've gone hunting for some dimly recollected passage, I couldn't find it. Or, if I did find it, it lacked the original spark that made me think there might be a poem within. The fires were cold. One of the few things I've learned about inspiration is that it's more fleeting than love.

Those who don't know the *Random House Historical Dictionary of American Slang* have not lived the right life. The A–G volume was published in 1994 and a second volume, H–O, three years later, both edited by the slightly mysterious J. E. Lighter. Then, in one of the most cowardly acts of American publishing, Random House abandoned the project. A few years ago, determined to revive the dictionary, Oxford University Press announced publication of the third volume in 2006. The year passed, and there is now no mention on the Oxford website of when that new volume will be issued.

The dictionary is my favorite volume of reference. Using the principles of the *OED*, the editor has built a conspectus of American slang, all those words and phrases that lie just beneath the diction of most writing—this makes them hard to trace, as they show up in out-of-the-way publications, slangy novels, attempts to catch in a newspaper the blab of the pave, and sometimes only in the ancient hearing of other slang dictionaries. Lighter and his associates have scoured the shelves and produced a heroic work; any lover of American English who doesn't own these volumes is deaf to the language itself. There, laid bare, are the mysteries of *blue-eyed* (drunk), *blubberhead*, and *blue lightning*, of *candy-ass*, *craphouse luck*, and *cunt-struck* (its first use just after the Civil War), of *dead-bang*, *dead-nuts*, *dead rabbit*, and much, much else.

Why has the project stalled? I once tracked down the editor, who said he had no idea when the next volume would be ready. Why? In a phrase, Google Books. Google now allows the intrepid researcher to browse an ever-expanding library of the past in a way no single reader, no squad of readers, no battalion of readers ever could before. If the *OED* were begun again from scratch, the editors would use Google Books as their prime tool. Indeed, they use it now.

Unfortunately, Google proves an embarrassment of riches. Every word must be crosschecked there, and certain peculiarities of the search engine make some words hard to find. For example, you can delimit a search by date—scanning, say, books published before 1850. Google is vastly more efficient than, say, starting to read every scrap of paper printed in or about America, from the Mayflower Compact forward, noting like a zoologist every word that looks like a strange New World creature.

Slang dictionaries can never be complete. I noticed, just the other day, that those great American words "maverick" and "mixologist" were missing (they're both in the *OED*).

In a recent *TLS*, a literary historian wrote about Kipling's letter to a submarine officer who was planning to write a poem about that branch of the service. "If I were you," wrote Kipling, "I'd go straight ahead with the Song of the Submarine and not bother about who ever else was doing the same thing." The historian commented, "Kipling originally wrote 'not bother whoever else,' which is bad grammar but may well reflect his state of mind."

The phrase may well suggest Kipling's temper, or it may have been a slip of the pen (Kipling then inserted the word "about"); but it's not bad grammar. "Whoever" (or, as Kipling had it, "Who ever") is the subject of the relative clause, and the case of *who* is governed by its function in the clause. We all makes slips — but isn't it embarrassing to whip a dead author for a sin he didn't commit? And isn't it curious that the *TLS* copy editors, whom I think of as ancient and fierce as vultures, didn't notice? Unfortunately, there are still no criminal courts for bad grammar.

An American poet wrote recently that Philip Larkin died

> *at sixty-three,*
> *of gin and loneliness and the stone chill daylight*
> *of Hull.*

My father died at sixty-four; and I suppose, if I were of that temperament, I could write that he died "of martinis and depression and the hard northern evenings / of Long Island." I could write that, but it wouldn't be true. My father, like Larkin, died of cancer after forty years of smoking. Readers might forgive me for making my father's death a romantic gesture; yet I wonder how far we ought to forgive the distortion of literary history that comes from writing that way about Larkin.

In "On First Looking into Chapman's Homer," Keats famously gave credit for the discovery of the Pacific to "stout Cortez" instead of Balboa (metrically it would have made no difference, as the poet pronounced the name COR-tez). Keats had the excuse that he was exhausted when he wrote it, having spent the night before in Clerkenwell, poring over a borrowed folio of Chapman at the lodgings of his friend Charles Cowden Clarke. They had never held a copy of the fabled translation before, and did not have the Greek to read the original. As Keats crossed London Bridge at dawn, returning to his filthy lodgings in the Borough, he must have started to shape the poem as he walked. Likely he had no history book at hand when he dashed the lines down on paper and dispatched them to Clarke by an "early-morning postal messenger," according to Keats's biographer Robert Gittings. His friend read them over the breakfast table at ten the next morning. No one seems to have mentioned the error, then or when the poem was published. (Tennyson was thought to have been the first to notice, but I have discovered otherwise.) It was Keats's first mature poem — he turned twenty-one later that month. One line in Chapman particularly stirred him, "The sea had soak'd his heart through." It's worth remembering that this was not Homer at all—it was Chapman's little invention.

"Ozymandias," one of the few poems I remember reading in high school, is a dream of the ruins of Egypt because no statue matching Shelley's has ever been found. The one that most resembles his description sits not alone in the desert but hard by other monuments (it's a sculpture of Rameses II, whose Greek name was Ozymandias)—by the nineteenth century, its inscription had long been effaced and the legs were gone as well. Shelley was likely working from an account by Diodorus Siculus, who reported the inscription as "King of Kings am I, Osymandias. If anyone would know how great I am and where I lie, let him surpass one of my works." In other words, Shelley invented the poem mostly out of whole cloth. He didn't meet a "traveller from an antique land"—he read a book. He proved better at invention than his friend Horace Smith, who wrote a sonnet on the same subject, probably as a result of some private, festive competition. It began, "In Egypt's sandy silence, all alone, / Stands a gigantic Leg . . ."

We forgive poets their slips of fact and wayward imaginings (Keats says Cortez when he means Balboa); but should we? It's difficult to be killed by gin and loneliness and the daylight of Hull, I expect—you'd have to go about it with a will. After an operation to remove his esophagus, Larkin didn't know he was dying—British doctors, into the eighties and later, frequently didn't advise their patients of a fatal prognosis. My father didn't know, either. As his health declined, he said, "I don't want to die or anything."

I've written that Elizabeth Bishop made such an error when writing of an "eighty-watt bulb" in "Faustina, or Rock Roses." I was mistaken. Google Books points toward a number of uses of "80-watt lamp" ("lamp" was what we now call "bulb") before 1950. A book published by the State Public Utilities Commission of Illinois in 1917 mentions bulbs of twenty, forty, sixty, eighty, and one hundred watts. I will leave to the curator of some Museum of Lighting the task of explaining why the eighty-watt bulb became the seventy-five-watt bulb.

On the other hand, sometimes poets are all too eager to impress others, or impress themselves, with learning lightly worn—which, worn lightly, may not be learning at all. Keats's Cortez is merely a mistake. When Wallace Stevens wrote, "The soldier is poor without the poet's

312 A CRITIC'S NOTEBOOK

lines, // His pretty syllabi, the sounds that stick, / Inevitably modulating, in the blood," he did not mean "syllabi" but "syllables." "Syllabi" might make poetic sense, more or less (a poet's words constitute a sort of syllabus); but the context asks for "syllables," the "sounds that stick." It tells us something about Stevens that his manner contained a little flimflam.

However strange the past, there are times when some minor discovery—like the letter from the Roman legionary in Britain asking his mother for some warm underwear or the six-hundred-year-old bras found under the floor of a castle in Austria—reminds us of certain givens in human nature. It has long been part of modern war to chalk on bombs or cannon shells some rude graffito meant for the enemy, the more vulgar the message the better. Outside Perugia, archeologists over a century ago dug up some eighty lead sling-balls, hurled during Octavian's siege of the legions of Lucius Antonius, Mark Antony's younger brother. (Antonius survived the wars of the triumvirate, as his brother did not, and was appointed governor of Spain.)

The sling is an ancient weapon, widely distributed, with two or three different techniques of delivering a missile. When David fought Goliath, he was probably using what is called a shepherd's sling, which employs a vertical release either underhand or overhand. The sling had a range greater than a long bow and could be devastating when used in a massed attack. Molding the lead balls was relatively simple (you could shove your thumb into sand and pour molten lead into the depression), and apparently slingers had the spare time to decorate their shot with messages for the enemy—think of it as hate mail, hate airmail. Perhaps a possessive magic was thereby created—the enemy might have felt it unlucky to reuse a missile so inscribed, though I doubt it. Roman *pilum* tips were made to bend when they hit something, so they couldn't be hurled back. They would have been difficult to pull out of a shield or a wounded soldier.

What graffiti ornamented these ancient bullets? "I want Octavian's ass." "Octavian's got a limp cock." "Hey, Octavius, you suck dick." Both sides indulged in this raillery. The troops knew their politics—one ball says, "I'm looking for Fulvia's clit" (Fulvia was Antony's wife). And there was that most devastating insult, "Lucius is bald." Perhaps the slinger had run out of better things to say. I've based the translations on those in Anthony Everitt's *The First Emperor*, where he has the relevant citation to the early publication of these inscriptions in *Corpus Inscriptionum Latinarum*.

It makes you wonder why swords, down through history, have been engraved with noble sentiments and uplifting military platitudes, while sling balls and bombs have been marked with vulgar insults. Perhaps it's merely the difference between a weapon you keep by your side, part of your identity, and one you mean to throw away.

I also learned from Everitt that, when Octavian had defeated Antony and Cleopatra, he asked to see the corpse of Alexander, whose tomb stood at Alexandria's main crossroads. The great conqueror had died some three centuries before. Shown the mummified body, Octavian placed a gold diadem upon its head. Unfortunately, in leaning over he accidentally broke off a piece of Alexander's nose.

A Forgotten Movie

I have a small thing for Miriam Hopkins. It's not the big thing I have for Barbara Stanwyck, but it's a thing. Hopkins was not the most gifted actress of her generation — she was too shrill, too Southern, too blonde; and in many of her roles she chewed the curtains, the sofa, the pillows, and everything else in sight, including the other actors. Still, before the Hays Code spread its fireproof blanket over the movies, her roles had the raw edge and atmosphere that, for a time, suggested that Hollywood welcomed the realism of Zola. The Code silenced the clamor of Christians upset by the movies' "immorality." In 1934, however, when it was first strictly enforced, this Code (also called the Production Code) crushed the artistic independence of the studios; for decades thereafter, movies were no more sinful than a Sunday afternoon prayer-meeting.

In repressive societies, the artist often finds a way to escape — censorship is the mother of ingenuity. If one kind of movie was blocked, another flourished — the screwball comedy. In the screwball, the sophistication of Noel Coward met the tomfoolery of the Keystone Cops. Its origins lay in the prohibitions of the Code; and it matured through the Depression and into the war in Frank Capra's *It Happened One Night* (1934), Leo McCarey's *The Awful Truth* (1937), Howard Hawks's *Bringing Up Baby* (1938) and *His Girl Friday* (1940), George Cukor's

The Philadelphia Story (1940), Billy Wilder's *The Major and the Minor* (1942), and in all the genius of Preston Sturges's *The Lady Eve* (1941), *Sullivan's Travels* (1941), *The Palm Beach Story* (1942), *Hail the Conquering Hero* (1944), and *The Miracle of Morgan's Creek* (1944). Without the Code and the gloom of the Depression, the screwball comedy might never have existed. As for Sturges, no Hollywood director ever produced such a row of masterpieces in so short a time—how he lost his talent thereafter is one of the great mysteries of film.

The Mating Season (1951) is a late addition to the genre, so late it seems to have escaped notice by film historians who date the screwball comedy's end during the war. By the fifties, Hollywood was already turning toward the message movies that make films of that decade so dreary to watch (where there's a message, you might say, there isn't much movie). Directed by the now forgotten Mitchell Leisen, the movie stars Gene Tierney, whose cheekbones were to the forties what Angelina Jolie's are to us. The set-up is simple. Thelma Ritter owns a Jersey City hamburger joint that's on the skids. There's too much competition from the soda fountains at nearby drugstores, and she owes her bankers money she can't pay.

"They give you a three-course dinner if you buy a box of aspirin tablets," she says morosely. A pleasant young man from the bank asks if she can't at least put a hundred bucks toward her loan. "To raise a hundred dollars," she replies in exasperation, "I would have to sell 13,000 hamburgers between now and six o'clock tonight. Do you know anybody that's that hungry?"

She takes off her apron, tells her customers to buy their hamburgers from the Jersey City National Bank, and hitchhikes off to live in Ohio with her son, John Lund, a rising executive with the Kalinger Machine Tools Company. While she's en route, we see the son in his office in the middle of the night, trying to revise an important report for the umpteenth time. He's exhausted. His bottle-blonde secretary, whom he's obviously dating, is fed up. There's a phone call on his boss's private line. A boy says the boss's car is stuck on Summit Ridge, with a girl in it. The boss, Junior Kalinger, is lying drunk on his office sofa.

Lund loyally goes off to straighten things out and finds Gene Tierney perched in a swanky convertible teetering halfway over a cliff. "If you must talk," he says, "use small syllables." He rescues her just before the car goes crashing to its destruction, and they fall in love—the man and the woman, that is. Tierney is the daughter of a former U.S. ambassador whose death has left his family impoverished. She has been dispatched to friends in Ohio by her mother, Miriam Hopkins, in hopes that she might find a rich beau among the social set. Tierney turns down the reptilian Junior Kalinger, however, in favor of her rescuer. The young couple are quickly betrothed and Tierney is left trying to explain by telephone this precipitous engagement. Her mother is living in a hotel in Venice—you can tell it's Venice, a cardboard Venice, by the silhouette of the Campanile seen through the French doors behind her.

Hopkins, all Southern high temper, flustered and domineering at once, is completely nonplused. "You just can't suddenly marry somebody named McNulty you met on a cliff," she exclaims—then she adds, more winningly, "If your father were alive, he'd turn over in his grave." Tierney, for her own part, is having none of it. "She's a fine one to talk," she says of her mother. "When she met Father in Shanghai, he just stuck out his hand to say hello and never got it back."

The day of the marriage, Thelma Ritter shows up in town at the bus station. Her son, though genuinely fond of her, is ill at ease with her manners. Told it will be a wedding "small, but fancy," she offers to help out. "Maybe they could use some of my hamburgers to go with the beer," she says. Instead, her son gives her money for a new hair-do and a new dress. She pushes it back, though we know she has less than five dollars in her pocket. She doesn't show up at the ceremony—actually she's skulking behind a bush, emerging only to throw one of her shoes, for luck, at the couple's departing car.

Ritter secretly goes to work in town, saving up her salary so she can present herself properly to her daughter-in-law. On the day she does so, in an eighteen-dollar hat, there's a huge mix-up. Tierney is trying to prepare for a party in the couple's new apartment; the turkey is on fire and the kitchen a wild mess. At the door, she mistakes Ritter for a maid. After failing to make matters clear, Ritter accepts her fate, pitches in, and the party is a success. (There's some lively overlapping dialogue, showing that the device far predated Robert Altman—it was used in other screwball comedies like *His Girl Friday*.)

Ritter is a rough gem who, despite her son's objections, goes to work for the couple as their cook, without revealing her identity even to his wife. Ritter knows that she doesn't fit in her son's new milieu. "Listen," she argues, "if you're a chicken, you can fool people about your feathers; but, when you start laying eggs all over the place, they know you're a chicken." She has all too many reasons why her son should stay silent, but one is a capper. "Look" she says, " I started out living with my mother-in-law, and you know how it ended? I hit her once . . . with a banana."

The complications come even faster when Hopkins peacocks in for a visit. She's the classic mother-in-law as well as the classic mother. Meeting her daughter at the airport, she says cheerily, "Why, you look fine . . . except around the eyes. Oh, you're still wearing that trashy little hat." In short order, she has sneered at the décor in the couple's tiny apartment ("How soon can you break *that?*" she asks, pointing to an ugly lamp), commandeered the single bedroom, and installed herself for an endless stay. There are further screwy turns of plot, involving a visiting businessman and his snobby wife ("My wife was born with rigor mortis," he observes sadly), as well as the owner of the Kalinger firm, Junior's father, for whom Hopkins sets her cap. Worse, when Hopkins raids the refrigerator one night ("The spirit is willing, but the flesh is increasing," she says about her diet), she wildly misinterprets a conversation between Ritter and her son—she thinks they're having an affair. (It's hilarious merely watching Hopkins caught in the light of the refrigerator, holding a chicken leg.) Her daughter doesn't believe her—it's too absurd that her husband would be kissing a woman twenty years older.

"Why I myself," Hopkins says defensively, "once knew a brigadier general who couldn't be left alone with a French telephone."

Eventually Tierney discovers that her cook is her mother-in-law; she dumps her husband in a fit of pique; the senior Mr. Kalinger plays deus ex machina; Lund stands up for his mother; and all ends happily. I watched the movie because I wanted to see Hopkins, whose career was in steep decline by the fifties. In the thirties, though, she'd starred in three Lubitsch films, most importantly the screwball comedy *Design for Living* (with Gary Cooper and Fredric March), as well as in Rouben Mamoulian's *Dr. Jekyll and Mr. Hyde* (again with March), King Vidor's *The Stranger's Return* (with Lionel Barrymore), Howard Hawks's *The Barbary Coast* (with Edward G. Robinson and Joel McCrea), and William Wyler's *These Three* (with Merle Oberon). She also starred in *Becky Sharp*, for which she received an Oscar nomination. In the forties, her career slackened, but she still managed to star in Michael Curtiz's *Virginia City* (with Errol Flynn) and William Wyler's *The Heiress* (with Montgomery Cliff, Olivia de Havilland, and Ralph Richardson). It was a fine career, to which *The Mating Season* was a minor coda—fine but unlucky, because she did not appear in the finest works by any of these directors.

The Mating Game did not receive sterling reviews (the *New York Times* called it a "bad mix of artificial nonsense and peculiarly genuine warmth"), though Thelma Ritter received an Oscar nomination for her seemingly artless performance. (Ritter was one of those Hollywood gems, a great character actress who over and over played, always winningly, the same heart-of-gold, rough-around-the-edges character—a real dame. She was nominated for six Oscars.) I started watching to see Hopkins, but before the first scene was over I was listening to the dialogue. I had to wait to find out who was responsible; and it was, perhaps not surprisingly, Charles Brackett. This remarkable writer has been half forgotten. Once *The New Yorker*'s drama critic, he wrote Lubitsch's extraordinary *Ninotchka* (with Greta Garbo), as well as *Ball of Fire* (a screwball gem with Barbara Stanwyck and Gary Cooper), *The Bishop's Wife* (with Cary Grant), *Niagara* (with Joseph Cotten and Marilyn Monroe), and six Billy Wilder films, *The Major and the Minor, Five Graves to Cairo, The Lost Weekend, The Emperor Waltz, A Foreign Affair*, and *Sunset Blvd.* Brackett was nominated eight times for the Oscar and won three, for *The Lost Weekend, Sunset Blvd.*, and *Titanic.* Even in *The Mating Season*, the writing shone. I have gone on at length out of a critic's enthusiasm. It's rare, as you age into movies—or into poetry, for that matter—to find something that has been a little overlooked.

A List of Don'ts

Don't do what all the other little buggers are doing.
Don't try to make the poem look pretty. You're not decorating cupcakes, Cupcake.

Don't think you're the only bastard who ever suffered—just write as if you were.

Don't eat someone else's lunch. For *eat* read *steal*. For *lunch* read *wife*. For *wife* read *style*.

Don't be any form's bitch.

Don't be the fashion. Murder fashion.

Don't think if you cheat on form or slip the meter, no one will notice. They'll know and think you a fool. Don't think it impossible to cheat on form. If you do it well, they'll think you a genius.

Don't think if you declare yourself avant-garde, your sins will be forgiven.

Don't blubber if you never receive prizes. Look at the poets who won the Pulitzer fifty years ago. See who's there. See who's not.

Don't think you're special. Stand in a library amid all those poets who thought they were every inch the genius you think you are.

Don't double-space your lines and think the poem better. It just takes up more room.

Don't think regret is 20/20. Regret is myopic. Hope is astigmatic. Trust is blind.

Don't tell yourself lies. Tell yourself truths until they become lies.

Don't think what you have to say is important. The way you say it is what's important. What you have to say is rubbish.

Don't think you don't have to read. You read in order to steal. Read more, steal better.

Don't read, read harder.

Don't think your poems are good because they sound good read aloud. Get your hearing checked.

Never write poems about poetry.

Don't plead the Fifth. Write the Ninth.

Don't play to the audience. Your audience is full of dopes, cheese-balls, and Johnny-come-latelies—besides, they're laughing at you all the way home.

Don't think you've been anointed by early success. Look at the critical darlings of a hundred years ago. Look at the darlings of twenty years ago.

Don't pay interest on loans you don't owe.

Never wish you were there. Wish you were here.

Don't think you can ignore grammar. You need grammar more than grammar needs you.

Never eat the pie if you can own the fork.

Don't think new is better. Don't think new is not better. Don't think, read. Don't think, ink.

Poetry is the nude that stays nude.

Never write the first line if you already know the last. The best poem is the unwritten poem.

Don't break the window before you look at the view.

Don't think that if you have two manuscripts, you have two manuscripts. You have one manuscript.

Don't eat jargon, because you'll shit jargon.

Don't think poetry is a religion. It's more important than religion.

Permissions

"Against Aesthetics," *New Criterion*, September 2013.

"The Unbearable Rightness of Criticism," *New Criterion*, April 2012.

"Verse Chronicle: Shock and Awe," *New Criterion*, December 2008.

"Verse Chronicle: You Betcha!," *New Criterion*, June 2009.

"The Sovereign Ghost of Wallace Stevens," *New Criterion*, October 2009.

"Eliot in Ink," *New York Times Book Review*, October 2, 2011. Copyright 2011 by the New York Times Company. Reprinted by permission.

"Larkin's Toads," *Poetry*, September 2012.

"Verse Chronicle: From Stinko to Devo," *New Criterion*, December 2009.

"Verse Chronicle: Trampling Out the Vintage," *New Criterion*, June 2010.

"Frost's Notebooks: A Disaster Revisited," *New Criterion*, February 2010.

"Heaney's Chain," *New York Times Book Review*, September 26, 2010. Copyright 2010 by the New York Times Company. Reprinted by permission.

"Heaney's Ghosts," *New Criterion*, April 2009.

"Verse Chronicle: Weird Science," *New Criterion*, December 2010.

"Verse Chronicle: Blah Blah Blah," *New Criterion*, June 2011.

"World War II Poetry, Reloaded," *Southwest Review* 98, no. 4 (2013).

"Frank O'Hara's Shopping Bag," *New York Times Book Review*, June 28, 2008. Copyright 2008 by the New York Times Company. Reprinted by permission.

"The Village of Louise Glück," *New York Times Book Review*, August 30, 2009. Copyright 2009 by the New York Times Company. Reprinted by permission.

"Verse Chronicle: Civil Wars," *New Criterion*, December 2011.

"Verse Chronicle: Guys and Dove," *New Criterion*, June 2012.

"Nobody's Perfect: The Letters of Elizabeth Bishop and Robert Lowell," *New York Times Book Review*, November 2, 2008. Copyright 2008 by the New York Times Company. Reprinted by permission.

"Elizabeth Bishop at the *New Yorker*," *New York Times Book Review*, February 20, 2011. Copyright 2011 by the New York Times Company. Reprinted by permission.

"Elizabeth Bishop at Summer Camp," *Virginia Quarterly Review*, Spring 2012.

"A Critic's Notebook," unpublished.

"A List of Don'ts" (under the title "The Nude That Stays Nude"), *Poetry*, April 2013.

Books Under Review

Verse Chronicle: Shock and Awe

Mary Oliver. *Red Bird*. Beacon Press, 2008.
Cole Swensen. *Ours*. University of California Press, 2008.
Thomas James. *Letters to a Stranger*. Graywolf Press, 2008.
Yusef Komunyakaa. *Warhorses*. Farrar, Straus and Giroux, 2008.
Claudia Emerson. *Figure Studies*. Louisiana State University Press, 2008.
Sharon Olds. *One Secret Thing*. Alfred A. Knopf, 2008.

Verse Chronicle: You Betcha!

Billy Collins. *Ballistics*. Random House, 2008.
Thom Gunn. *Selected Poems*. Ed. August Kleinzahler. Farrar, Straus and Giroux, 2009.
Jim Powell. *Substrate*. Pantheon, 2009.
Katha Pollitt. *The Mind-Body Problem*. Random House, 2009.
Rita Dove. *Sonata Mulattica*. Norton, 2009.
Arda Collins. *It Is Daylight*. Yale University Press, 2009.

The Sovereign Ghost of Wallace Stevens

Wallace Stevens. *Selected Poems*. Ed. John N. Serio. Alfred A. Knopf, 2009.

Eliot in Ink

The Letters of T. S. Eliot. Ed. Valerie Eliot and Hugh Haughton. Volume 1: 1898–1922. Rev. ed. Yale University Press, 2011.
———. Volume 2: 1923–1925. Yale University Press, 2011.

Larkin's Toads

Philip Larkin. *The Complete Poems*. Ed. Archie Burnett. Farrar, Straus and Giroux, 2012.
——. *Poems*. Ed. Martin Amis. Faber and Faber, 2011.

Verse Chronicle: From Stinko to Devo

Charles Bukowski. *The Continual Condition*. Ed. John Martin. Ecco, 2009.
Franz Wright. *Wheeling Motel*. Alfred A. Knopf, 2009.
Beth Ann Fennelly. *Unmentionables*. W. W. Norton, 2008.
Marie Ponsot. *Easy*. Alfred A. Knopf, 2009.
Joanna Rawson. *Unrest*. Graywolf Press, 2009.
John Ashbery. *Planisphere*. Ecco, 2009.

Verse Chronicle: Trampling Out the Vintage

C. K. Williams. *Wait*. Farrar, Straus and Giroux, 2010.
Tony Hoagland. *Unincorporated Persons in the Late Honda Dynasty*. Graywolf Press, 2010.
Keith Douglas. *Simplify Me When I'm Dead*. Selected by Ted Hughes. Faber and Faber, 2010.
Don Paterson. *Rain*. Farrar, Straus and Giroux, 2009.
Derek Walcott. *White Egrets*. Farrar, Straus and Giroux, 2010.
Anne Carson. *Nox*. New Directions, 2010.

Frost's Notebooks: A Disaster Revisited

Robert Frost. *The Notebooks of Robert Frost*. Ed. Robert Faggen. Harvard University Press, 2009.

Heaney's Chain

Seamus Heaney. *Human Chain*. Farrar, Straus and Giroux, 2010.

Heaney's Ghosts

Dennis O'Driscoll. *Stepping Stones: Interviews with Seamus Heaney*. Farrar, Straus and Giroux, 2008.

Verse Chronicle: Weird Science

Maxine Hong Kingston. *I Love a Broad Margin to My Life*. Alfred A. Knopf, 2011.
Thomas Lynch. *Walking Papers: Poems 1999–2009*. Norton, 2010.
Eiléan Ní Chuilleanáin. *The Sun-Fish*. Wake Forest University, 2010.
Kimiko Hahn. *Toxic Flora*. Norton, 2010.
Paul Muldoon. *Maggot*. Farrar, Straus and Giroux, 2010.
Gjertrud Schnackenberg. *Heavenly Questions*. Farrar, Straus and Giroux, 2010.

Verse Chronicle: Blah Blah Blah

Richard Wilbur. *Anterooms*. Houghton Mifflin Harcourt, 2010.
Yusef Komunyakaa. *The Chameleon Couch*. Farrar, Straus and Giroux, 2011.
Carl Phillips. *Double Shadow*. Farrar, Straus and Giroux, 2011.
Rae Armantrout. *Money Shot*. Wesleyan University Press, 2011.
Les Murray. *Taller When Prone*. Farrar, Straus and Giroux, 2011.
———. *Killing the Black Dog*. Farrar, Straus and Giroux, 2011.
Geoffrey Hill. *Oraclau | Oracles*. Clutag Press, 2010.

Frank O'Hara's Shopping Bag

Frank O'Hara. *Selected Poems*. Ed. Mark Ford. Alfred A. Knopf, 2008.

The Village of Louise Glück

Louise Glück. *A Village Life*. Farrar, Straus & Giroux, 2009.

Verse Chronicle: Civil Wars

Michael Dickman. *Flies*. Copper Canyon, 2011.
Henri Cole. *Touch*. Farrar, Straus and Giroux, 2011.
Katherine Larson. *Radial Symmetry*. Yale University Press, 2011.
Billy Collins. *Horoscopes for the Dead*. Random House, 2011.

Michael Longley. *A Hundred Doors*. Wake Forest University Press, 2011.
Geoffrey Hill. *Clavics*. Enitharmon, 2011.

Verse Chronicle: Guys and Dove

Mark Strand. *Almost Invisible*. Alfred A. Knopf, 2012.
Geoffrey Hill. *Odi Barbare*. Clutag Press, 2012.
Vladimir Nabokov. *Selected Poems*. Ed. Thomas Karshan. Alfred A. Knopf, 2012.
The Penguin Anthology of Twentieth-Century American Poetry. Ed. Rita Dove.
    Penguin, 2011

Nobody's Perfect: The Letters of Elizabeth Bishop and Robert Lowell

*Words in Air: The Complete Correspondence Between Elizabeth Bishop and Rob-
    ert Lowell*. Ed. Thomas Travisano and Saskia Hamilton. Farrar, Straus and
    Giroux, 2008.

Elizabeth Bishop at the *New Yorker*

Elizabeth Bishop and The New Yorker. Ed. Joelle Biele. Farrar, Straus and Gir-
    oux, 2011.
Elizabeth Bishop. *Prose*. Ed. Lloyd Schwartz. Farrar, Straus and Giroux, 2011.
——. *Poems*. Farrar, Straus and Giroux, 2011.

Index of Authors Reviewed